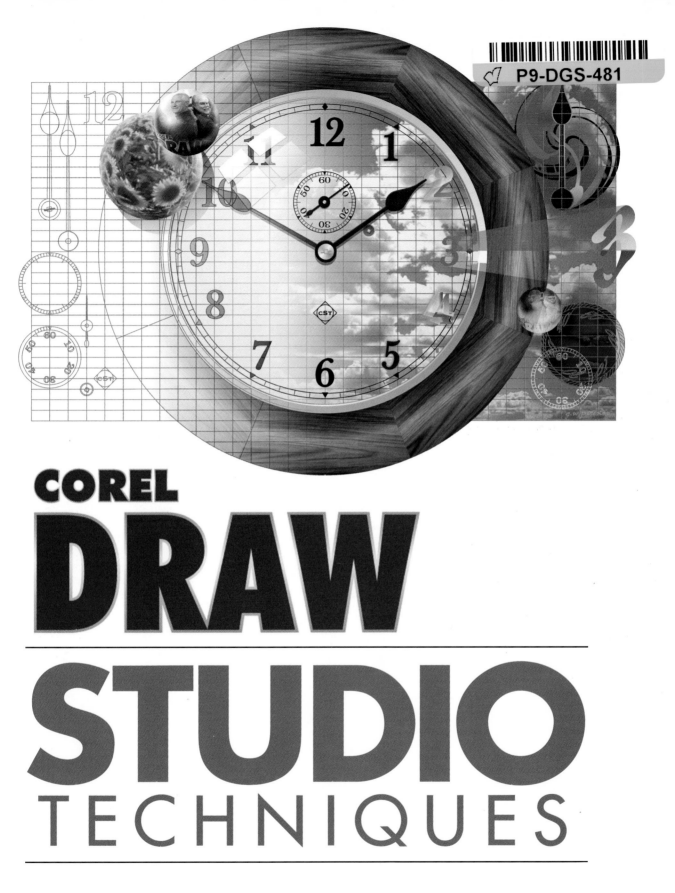

COREL
DRAW
STUDIO
TECHNIQUES

DAVID HUSS & GARY PRIESTER

Osborne/McGraw-Hill

Berkeley New York St. Louis San Francisco Auckland Bogotá Hamburg
London Madrid Mexico City Milan Montreal New Delhi Panama City
Paris São Paulo Singapore Sydney Tokyo Toronto

Osborne/**McGraw-Hill**
2600 Tenth Street
Berkeley, California 94710
U.S.A.

For information on translations or book distributors outside the U.S.A., or to arrange bulk purchase discounts for sales promotions, premiums, or fund-raisers, please contact Osborne/**McGraw-Hill** at the above address.

CorelDRAW Studio Techniques

1234567890 2WEB 901987654321098

ISBN 0-07-882450-8

Publisher	Brandon A. Nordin
Editor-in-Chief	Scott Rogers
Acquisitions Editor	Megg Bonar
Project Editor	Jennifer Wenzel
Editorial Assistant	Stephane Thomas
Technical Editor	Jennifer Campbell
Copy Editor	Kathy Hashimoto
Proofreader	Sally Engelfried
Designer	Jil Weil
Computer Designer	Jean Butterfield
Cover Illustration	Gary Priester
Cover Design	Regan Honda

CONTENTS

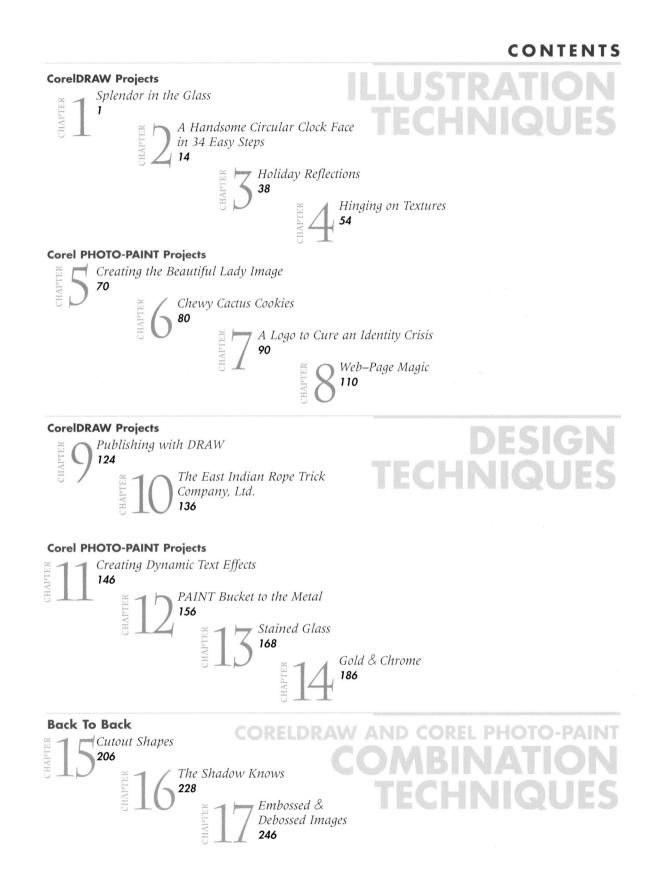

DEDICATION

This book is lovingly dedicated to my two wonderful children Jonathan and Grace because they have been the delight of my life and also because they said if I didn't dedicate one to them soon, they were going to kidnap my stuffed Pooh bear.

DAVE HUSS

This book is dedicated to Mario, wherever he may be, and to Mrs. Maigret, otherwise known as The Chicken Lady, who administered to my needs and put up with my extreme grumpiness, not only while I hunted and pecked my way through this book, but for the last 24 years of our life together.

GARY PRIESTER

DEDICATION

FOREWORD

CorelDRAW™ Studio Techniques is an exciting addition to the CorelPRESS™ library of books, and represents the latest in this series of important collaborations between Corel Corporation and Osborne/McGraw-Hill.

The framework of this book goes one step beyond the existing CorelPRESS titles as it highlights the strengths of two products—CorelDRAW and Corel PHOTO-PAINT™—together in one book. Two of the industry's best authors bring their knowledge and expertise to this new approach, and you the reader get the benefit. Follow along with Gary Priester and Dave Huss as they walk you through a selection of impressive projects designed to show off the power of CorelDRAW and Corel PHOTO-PAINT.

New CorelDRAW users, and those already familiar with the program, will find significant value in the beautiful use of four-color work in this book, and all will benefit from the in-depth knowledge these authors have developed from their experience with the software.

The CorelPRESS series represents an important step in the ability of Corel to disseminate information to users with the help of Osborne/McGraw-Hill, the authors, tech reviewers, editors and designers involved in the series. Congratulations to the entire CorelPRESS team at Osborne on the creation of this exciting new book in the series!

Dr. Michael J. Cowpland
President and CEO
Corel Corporation

ACKNOWLEDGMENTS

There are many individuals involved in getting a book like this into print. We should acknowledge the trees that were dragged kicking and screaming into the pulp mills to produce the paper and the baby seashells that were snatched from their little seabeds to produce pigment for the inks, but we won't.

In truth, the one deserving the most recognition is our acquisitions editor, Megg Bonar, who convinced the powers to be at Osborne/McGraw-Hill to boldly go where they had not gone before. We must also commend all of the staff and others at Osborne for their seemingly tireless effort in producing this book. Included in this tip of the acknowledgement hat is project editor, Jennifer Wenzel, who had the discouraging and seemingly never-ending job of trying to make sense out of what both the old man (Gary) and I had written and lay it out in such a way as to be comprehensive and stylish. Sincere thanks to the other Jennifer, Jennifer Campbell, our technical editor, who painstakingly recreated every project in the book and made sure that you the reader will be able to do the same. We must also commend another at Osborne, Stephane Thomas, who was almost on a clock face —a very timely inside joke, which for $50.00 cash we will confess all.

It goes without saying (but we're going to say it anyway) our heartfelt thanks goes to our associates and friends at Corel in Ottawa. Thanks start at the top of the corporate food chain with Dr. Cowpland who is ultimately responsible for DRAW and PHOTO-PAINT. Thanks also to Michael Bellefeuille who continues to be a good friend and strong supporter of these books,and to our favorite leprechaun at Corel, Michelle Murphy-Croteau, who, we are becoming convinced can do almost anything. On the technical side, we commend Doug Chomyn, PHOTO-PAINT product manager, for his assistance and input over the past few years and David Garett, in PHOTO-PAINT QA, who has now answered over 1,000,000 questions from Dave. Dave has also listed pretty near everybody in the Ottawa phonebook, however, we wish to thank the Corel Development team, Denise Zutrauen, Joe Donelly, Warren Tomlin, Ellis Lindsay, and the rest of the folks at Corel who work in the pressure cooker at 1600 Carling Avenue, cooking up a new product, year after year. And I, Gary, would be ungrateful not to acknowledge young Dave himself for proving that Austin, San Francisco and Berkeley aren't really that far apart.

Lastly, I, Dave, want to acknowledge a name unknown to almost everyone, Alex Link. Many people email me looking for answers to questions they have about things I have written about, either in my books or in my magazine articles. Alex, takes the techniques I demonstrate in magazine articles and creates some pretty incredible images. I have never met this man, but I stand amazed at what he does with PHOTO-PAINT.

ABOUT THE AUTHORS

GARY

Gary W. Priester lives in Black Point, California with his wife Mary, their eight hens, five cats, four doves, two finches, and one extremely talented canary. Priester is a partner in The Black Point Group Design, a graphic design firm. He is the author of Looking Good in Color, Ventana Press, and contributing editor to *Corel Magazine* and the *CorelDRAW Journal*. His articles have appeared in *HOW*, *Publish*, and *Dynamic Graphics* to name a few. Priester hosts the Trompe L'Oeil Room at http://trompe.i-us.com and can be contacted via e-mail at themook@slip.net.

DAVE

I hate biographies where you speak of yourself in the third person so here is my biographical information. I was born (that was for the Dickens fans). I began writing PHOTO-PAINT™ books back with PHOTO-PAINT 5. I also wrote the PHOTO-PAINT 5 Plus manual, but that's another story. Since that time I have written 4 more books on PHOTO-PAINT, not counting this one. My big thrill last year was winning the Grand Prize in the 1997 Corel World Design Contest. I enjoy speaking and teaching scanning and PHOTO-PAINT at conferences all over the world. I write articles in monthly Corel publications such as *Corel Magazine* (US and Germany), *CorelDRAW Journal*, and *Corel User* (UK). In my spare time, whom am I kidding...what spare time?

FROM DAVE

This book began as a result of an article by the old man, (as I refer to Gary Priester, five years my senior) in an issue of *CorelDRAW Journal*. I was looking at the article and thinking that, while it was very good, I could do it better in PHOTO-PAINT— and I did. Motivated by this brief flush of success, I began to look through back issues of the journal for more articles by this author. His writing was cynical and he clearly was very opinionated (these are positive points) and his techniques and studies of shadows and reflections were excellent. So I sent an email message to Gary Priester and soon we were trading technique recipes. Figuring that there must be similar books about DRAW techniques, I began going through the book-shelves only to discover that many of the books on DRAW seemed to be amplified retellings of the DRAW help files with color inserts of winning art from the Corel World Design Contest. I have never been a fan of this style of book. While it is nice to see what actually can be done with the product, I know many of the artists that created these masterpieces. They have discussed the hundreds, if not thousands, of hours necessary to produce the art that adorns the color inserts in these books and 99 percent of the readers cannot recreate the art. Frustrated by this lack of intermediate to advanced books (there are a few but they date back to DRAW 5 and 6) I discussed the idea of writing a full-color book that would be a "cookbook" of techniques with the old man. What you have in your hands is the result. The original title was "Grumpy Old Men Do CorelDRAW" but we couldn't agree who gets Sophia Loren and who gets Ann Margaret.

Our intention with this book is to demonstrate techniques that help you, the reader, get the most out of your Corel product—the whole product, not just CorelDRAW or Corel PHOTO-PAINT. The power of the product comes in learning to use the products together. Our other goal in creating this book is to make money. We figure the only way we could make tons and tons of money (OK, maybe pounds and pounds) is to make a book that is so compelling that you feel you have to buy it.

INTRODUCTION

FROM GARY

Dave and I saw the composition of the book slightly differently. The book I had in mind had 20 chapters devoted to CorelDRAW and an obligatory two or three chapters about Corel PHOTO-PAINT. Funnily enough, Huss saw it pretty much the same, except the weight was slanted in favor of PAINT. What we did agree upon was that the time was right for a book that went beyond the basics and showed examples with full-blown step-by-steps of how such fantastic art could be created using DRAW and PAINT.

In spite of our best efforts to create a book that was completely free form and unstructured, the editorial department insisted on a modicum of continuity and conformity to which we reluctantly agreed. As a result, the book is now divided into three sections. The first section features illustration projects and step-by-step instructions for how to create them.

The second section covers desktop publishing and Web-graphics projects. The final section features three back-to-back chapters where Huss and I create similar effects using our respective applications while taking affectionate pot shots at one another.

Each chapter begins with an Overview providing background about the project along with much metaphorical throat-clearing that less indulgent editors would have eliminated right off the bat. Huss and I then attempt to make the hard projects look easy with a series of short, recipe-like steps that you readers can follow along to recreate the art. Each chapter concludes with a section entitled Variations on a Theme in which Dave and I provide additional applications of the techniques covered in the chapters. The variations suggest additional uses for the techniques covered, not unlike the "Serving Suggestions" you might see in cookbooks.

We tried to make the material covered in this book simple enough that even a beginner could work through the projects. In reality the book assumes that the reader be familiar with the basics in DRAW and/or PAINT. The images presented in each chapter have been reverse-engineered into a series of short but well-documented steps to ensure you can follow along and use the techniques we present here on projects of your own. Remember, if Priester and Huss, given their arrested attention spans and slightly-below-average intelligence, can create these things then surely you the reader (who was intelligent enough to buy this book) should have no trouble at all.

So, enjoy the book, and have fun. Who knows. you might just be the next Dave Huss or Gary Priester.

Splendor in the Glass

Living on the edge of the California wine country, 15 minutes south of Sonoma, I have developed an appreciation for fine wine. I love all kinds of wine, but my favorite is Cabernet Sauvignon. Over the years, I've had the opportunity to work on many winery accounts. Part of my work included working with photographers and often photographing elegant bubble glasses of Cabernet. In this chapter, we'll re-create a classic photograph of a glass of Cabernet. The final illustration may appear daunting, but remember, the most complex illustration is nothing more than a series of small steps. So pop the cork and let's get started.

Because this illustration is going to be printed in CMYK color, I have enabled Color Correction. This is done by selecting Color Correction, then Accurate in the View menu in DRAW 7. In DRAW 8, open the Application Settings dialog box (in the Options menu) and go to the Color Options tab. This makes the screen colors simulate four-color process printing. The colors in this chapter will not appear correct unless you enable Color Correction.

N O T E

The illustration in this chapter was done in DRAW 7; the same steps apply in DRAW 8.

Most of the colors used in this chapter are part of DRAW's default palette. I have created two pale blue colors and added them to the palette. You can create these two colors and add them to your palette for this illustration. The pale blue is 30 Cyan, 10 Magenta, and 10 Yellow. The second color, very pale blue, is 15 Cyan, 5 Magenta. I also use a pale version of Faded Pink and Ice Blue. To lighten Faded Pink, open the Fill Color dialog box (the Rainbow icon) in the Fill Tool fly-out and drag the slider to the left to create a lighter version. Use this technique whenever you want a lighter version of a default color. In DRAW 8, simply click and hold on the color, and in a few seconds a menu will pop up with shades and tints for you to choose from.

1

We'll begin by creating the bowl of the wineglass. Draw a big circle, approximately four inches across. Add two ellipses, as shown in Figure 1-1. The top ellipse is not as deep because it is closer to the horizon line.

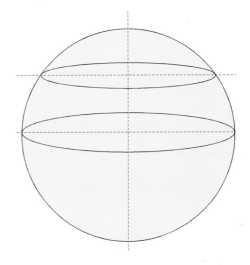

Figure 1-1: Draw a large circle and two ellipses

2

We need to break the large circle into three parts. To do this, draw a horizontal line through the middle of each of the two ellipses. Both lines should extend beyond the width of the ellipses. Select both lines and Combine them (press CTRL+L, or click on the Combine button on the Property Bar). Select the lines and then the big circle and click on the Trim button on the Property Bar. Select the circle, and from the Arrange menu select Break Apart. This breaks the large circle into three separate shapes. Delete the combined lines. Figure1-2 shows the results.

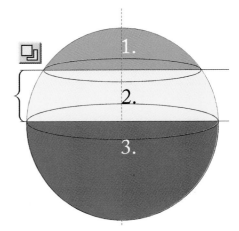

Figure 1-2: Use two combined horizontal lines to Trim the circle into three parts

STEP

3

Make a Duplicate (+ key on the numeric keyboard) of the top ellipse and set it to the side. Select the middle section (yellow) and the top ellipse and click on the Weld button on the Property Bar. This produces one continuous shape, as shown in Figure 1-3.

Figure 1-3: Weld the top ellipse to the center section of the circle

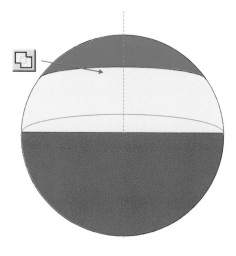

STEP

4

Delete the top portion (blue) of the circle. Make a duplicate of the larger ellipse using the + key on the numeric keyboard and set it aside. Select the larger ellipse and the top portion of the glass (pale yellow), and from the Property Bar click on the Trim button. Your image should resemble Figure 1-4.

Figure 1-4: Use the larger ellipse to Trim out a section of the top of the glass

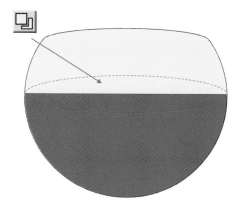

STEP

5

We now have the three essential elements for the top portion of the glass, as you can see in Figure 1-5.

Figure 1-5: The three main elements for the bowl of the glass

6 Fill the larger ellipse with a solid color (I've used pink for the moment). Align the smaller ellipse Top and Center over the glass top (yellow), as shown in Figure 1-6. We'll use these two ellipses to create the rim of the glass.

Figure 1-6: The elements for the top portion of the glass

7 Select colors to temporarily rough in the top of the glass and wine (I've filled the top of the glass pale blue and the top of the wine light pink). Cabernet Sauvignon (pronounced Ca-bear-nay So-veen-yone) is very dense in color and appears dark and opaque in a large glass. A photographer would place a small section of mirror directly behind the bowl and reflect a bright light through the wine, producing a red-orange glow. To achieve this effect, select the bottom portion of the glass and apply a three-color Radial fill, beginning with Blue on the outside, Red in between, and ending with Orange. Select the fill with the Interactive Fill tool (on the main Toolbox) and drag the center of the fill to the top, as shown in Figure 1-7.

Figure 1-7: A three-color fill produces a radiant, glowing effect

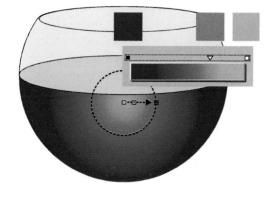

8 For this image, we'll say that the photographer has placed a soft light over and slightly behind the glass, backlighting the surface of the wine and giving it a pale pinkish color. Select the pink ellipse and apply a three-color Linear Fountain Fill, beginning with Deep Pink (top), going to Faded Pink, and ending on a very pale version of Faded Pink. Figure 1-8 shows the results.

Figure 1-8: The surface of the wine

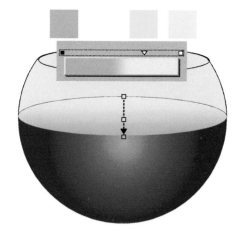

STEP

9

Add a complex Interactive Fountain Fill to the top part of the glass, as shown in Figure 1-9, using a combination of the pale blue and very pale blue that we created in the beginning of this chapter. Add white at about 75 percent to create a highlight. Now select the pink surface of the wine (the ellipse), make a Duplicate (+ key), and drag the duplicate up about three points. Select the original (directly under the duplicate) and apply a three-color Linear Fill, using Purple, Light Violet, and Purple. This adds the appearance of a slight thickness to the wine's surface.

Figure 1-9: The glass is colored and a duplicate ellipse created and colored, to add depth to the surface

STEP

10

Select the small ellipse (the rim of the glass). Make a duplicate and drag the front and side in about two points. The top edge of the duplicate should be closer to the top of the original and more space should be between the two in front. Select both shapes and Combine them (CTRL+L). Apply an Interactive Conical Fountain Fill, beginning with White, then light blue (the custom color we created earlier), Mint Green, light blue, and ending with White. Rotate the direction of the Conical Fill so that the white area creates a highlight on the front left portion of the edge, as seen in Figure 1-10. Remove the outline.

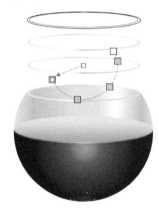

Figure 1-10: The top edge of the glass with highlight front left

STEP

11

The photographer would probably add a few bubbles in front, using a mixture of glycerin and water, to give the wine a "just poured" look. These bubbles are painstakingly created and placed. Glycerin bubbles will last a long time, as opposed to real bubbles, which will pop almost immediately. Create a series of small bubbles (circles) of various sizes, as seen in Figure 1-11. Apply a Radial Fountain Fill of Pale Violet, Faded Pink, and White to each one. Position the white portion of the Fountain Fill slightly up and left of center to create a highlight. Position the bubbles halfway between the surface of the wine. Apply a Uniform, Normal Transparency, 50 percent to the bubbles.

Figure 1-11: A few well-placed bubbles give the wine a "just poured" appearance

12 Wine has viscosity, which causes it to slightly creep up the back of the glass. To replicate this effect, make a Duplicate of the wine surface. Create another duplicate and drag the top down about 1/16 inch, as shown in Figure 1-12. Select both ellipses (shown here with red outlines and no fill) and click on the Trim button on the Property Bar. Select the bottom portion and delete it. Align the new crescent-shaped section so it lines up with the top of the wine surface. Apply a two-color Radial Fountain Fill using light blue and pale blue. Draw a freehand shape for a reflection on the wine's surface. Apply a two-color Linear Fountain Fill, using Blue and Purple.

Figure 1-12: A reflection is added to the wine's surface, and a dark blue crescent shape is added to create the impression of viscosity

13 The photographer would probably add a rectangular highlight to the glass by bouncing light off a white foamcore rectangle. The white card is placed just out of the frame to create a highlight that is brighter on the side closest to the white card. This highlight adds roundness to the glass bowl.

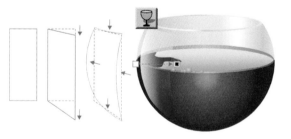

Figure 1-13: A white highlight gives the glass roundness

To create this effect, begin with a white rectangle and Convert To Curves (CTRL+Q). Use the Shape tool to distort the rectangle, as shown in Figure 1-13. Still using the Shape tool, select all the nodes and then click on To Curve on the Property Bar. Use the Shape tool to drag the sides of the white shape to conform to the shape of the glass. The left side should closely follow the side of the glass; the right side should be less round. Select the shape and apply an Interactive Transparency, Linear Fountain beginning at 0 percent (opaque) and ending at 100 percent (transparent).

This completes the bowl of the glass. Now might be a good time to take a break and pour yourself a small medicinal glass of red wine for inspiration.

GET A HOLD OF THIS

STEP

1

The stem of our wineglass is slightly concave. We'll create this by applying an Envelope to a rectangle. Draw a slim rectangle. Select the rectangle and select Envelope from the Effects menu. Click on the second Envelope button, which to the best of my knowledge has no name. Click Add New to initiate the Envelope function. Drag the nodes, as shown in Figure 1-14. When you're happy with the shape of the envelope as indicated by the red dotted line, click Apply. In DRAW 8, the Envelope function is now Interactive and the shape changes in real time.

Create a base using an ellipse not quite as wide as the bowl. The ellipse should be wider (top to bottom) than the wine's surface, as it is lower in relation to our eye level. Make a duplicate ellipse and move the bottom center control handle up about 1/16 inch. Create a smaller ellipse centered on the base ellipse for the base of the stem. Move the stem over the small ellipse and position it about 1/2 inch over the ellipse. Use the Freehand tool to draw a parallelogram, with the top and bottom sides dissecting the base of the stem and the small ellipse. This is the shape that joins the stem to the base. For lack of the correct term, we'll call this shape the stem connector.

STEP

2

Select the stem connector and use the Shape tool to select all the nodes; click on To Curves from the Property Bar. Use the Shape tool to drag on the sides, as shown in Figure 1-15.

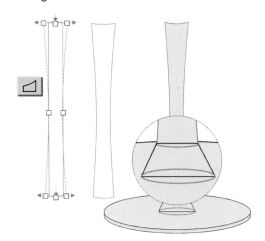

Figure 1-14: The stem and base of the glass

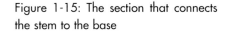
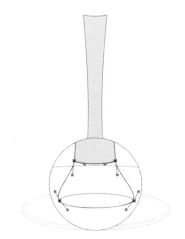

Figure 1-15: The section that connects the stem to the base

3

a. Select the top ellipse for the base and place a Copy in the clipboard (CTRL+C)

b. Select both base ellipses and click on the Weld button on the Property bar.

c. Select the welded shape with the Shape tool. Remove the center node from each side (see inset of Figure 1-16c).

d. Paste (CTRL+V) a copy of the ellipse on top of the welded shape. Select the copy of the ellipse and the welded object and click on the Trim button on the Property Bar. This trims everything directly underneath the ellipse.

e. Select the top ellipse and apply a simple Linear Fountain Fill from pale blue to White. Select the edge of the base and apply a three-color Radial Fountain Fill, beginning with White to Mint Green to Sea Green. Figure 1-16 details all the steps.

The next step gets a tad involved, so this might be a good time to take a break—and by all means, save your work.

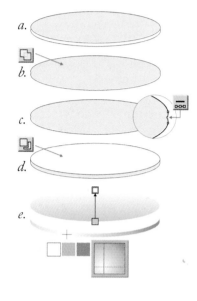

Figure 1-16: The base of the glass is created by welding two ellipses and pasting a duplicate on top

4

The stem is transparent glass, but this does not mean it's invisible. There's a lot going on in there.

a. Select the stem and make a Duplicate. With the duplicate selected, press and hold the SHIFT key (to constrain resizing from the center) and drag the top middle-bounding box handle toward the center. Select one of the middle side bounding box handles and repeat the process. Make a duplicate of the center section and set it aside for a moment. Apply a Linear Fountain Fill to the biggest stem object, using Light Green to Ghost Green (no outline). Fill the inside duplicated section with a Linear Fountain Fill, using pale blue to White (no outline).

b. Select both shapes and create a 20-Step Blend.

c. Select the duplicate of the center section (which we just made), make a duplicate of it, and reduce it as shown in Figure 1-17c. Pull the bottom of the duplicate down to about 1/8 inch from the bottom.

d. Draw a rectangle as shown in Figure 1-17d. Select the rectangle and the back section and click on the Trim button on the Property Bar. Repeat this process on the smaller section. Make sure when you do this that the rectangle is in front, since the front object does the trimming.

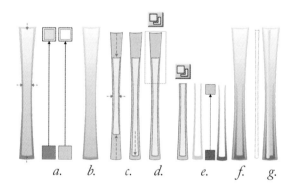

Figure 1-17: The steps required to produce the stem

e. Select both shapes and click on the Trim button on the Property bar. This will produce a U-shaped object. Apply a Linear Fountain Fill, using Grass Green and pale blue (no outline).

f. Position the U-shaped piece over the stem.

g. Create a long, slender rectangle just about the height of the stem, Linear Fountain Fill it blue and White (no outline), and position it left of center on the stem. Figure 1-17 details all the steps.

STEP

5

Hang in there, it's almost happy hour! Because that last step was so complicated, we'll throw in an easy step. Select the connector (the part that goes between the stem and the base), and apply a three-color Linear Fountain Fill, beginning with Grass Green to Mint to White, as shown in Figure 1-18.

Figure 1-18: The connector (the thing that goes between the stem and the base)

STEP

6

Because of its shape, the connector thingy creates some complex reflections. Basically these shapes are elliptical, so we'll create a series of elliptical shapes.

a. Create two sets of two ellipses, as shown in Figure 1-19a. Select each group individually and click on the Trim button on the Property Bar. Delete the smaller sections, leaving two crescent shapes. Fill them Grass Green with no outline. Create a 1-Step Blend. Click on the blend with the right mouse button and select Separate. Select the center shape and select Ungroup from the Property Bar.

b. Use the Freehand tool to create an L shape (kind of like the Nike swoosh). Use the Shape tool to smooth the shape. Make a Duplicate and flop it horizontally.

c. Use the two swooshes to bracket the crescent shapes. Select the swooshes and the crescents and click on Weld on the Property Bar.

d. Position the welded shapes over the connector thingy. Figure 1-19 details all the steps.

Figure 1-19: Reflected shapes add depth to the connector thingy

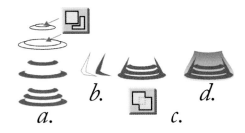

7 Create a reflection shape for the connector, as shown in Figure 1-20. Apply a Radial Fountain Fill, beginning in the center with White, then pale blue, and ending on Grass Green.

Figure 1-20: A reflection of the connector thingy

8 Assemble and position all the stem and base elements. Looks pretty darn convincing, don't you think? We'll add three little highlights that are really going to make the stem and base sing. Construct two very small circles and an ellipse, as shown in Figure 1-21, and position them over the stem and connector. Apply a simple two-color Linear Fountain Fill, White to Ghost Green, to each.

Figure 1-21: A reflection of the connector thingy

9 We have but one task left before we break out the Cabernet Sauvignon and toast the finished image. Position the wine and bowl over the stem. That wasn't so hard, was it? To give the surface of the wine a more realistic effect, we'll apply a modified Texture Fill. Select the wine surface (the ellipse) and apply a Sky 3 Colors Texture Fill (Styles Texture Library). Alter the colors so that the sky is Purple, the atmosphere is Hot Pink, and the clouds are Light Violet, as indicated in Figure 1-22.

Figure 1-22: A modified Texture Fill adds realism to the surface of the wine

A VOTRE SANTÈ—TO YOUR HEALTH!

That's it. As I promised in the beginning, even the most complex illustration is merely a series of short steps. Figure 1-23 reveals the final illustration. I couldn't resist adding a single, elegant Cabernet grape and reflection. I also created a 16-point Polygon star for a small starburst highlight, which I added to the lip, stem, and base. Your homework for this chapter is to reproduce these elements on your own. Salud!

Figure 1-23: The finished wineglass sporting a single elegant Cabernet grape and three starburst highlights

W ell, we sure gave Draw a workout on this exercise. Let's pause while we savor our glass of Cabernet and reflect on what we learned. First, we learned how to pronounce Ca-bear-nay So-veen-yone, which is worth the price of admission in and of itself. We learned how to use Corel's default palette, plus a couple of custom pale blue colors, to re-create the appearance of glass and red wine. We considered the image from a photographer's point of view to learn how to light a glass of red wine and did our very best to incorporate those professional lighting techniques into our illustration. Finally, we learned that glass, although clear and colorless, is very, very complex. The basics of this technique can be used to create a variety of glass objects, which can be used as illustrations on a menu, wine list, or sales sheet or just as an attractive addition to your portfolio.

IN A PERFECT WORLD:

Many of these Fountain Fills are very complex and can be problematic when printing. I converted the more complex fills to bitmap, including several of the elements in the stem.

Variations on a Theme

Here we show how the wineglass illustration can be used in a poster design. Other uses for the wineglass could be as an illustration for the cover of a wine list, as part of an invitation to a wine-tasting party, or just as an attractive image to print out, frame, and hang over your bar.

When I created this image, it was kind of a what-if thing. I had no use or purpose in mind—I just did it to see what it would look like. I modified a Texture Fill called Exhaust Fumes, which is very ugly and smoggy looking, by changing the brownish color to Sky Blue. I filled a square with the new fill and added a window pane highlight. Then I converted the shapes to bitmap and, using the 3D Effect, Map to Object, and Spherical, I created a crystal ball. I created a rectangle and modified it with perspective and applied the same fill. I added part of an ellipse with a darker version of the fill and applied linear transparency to make it fade out. I created a beveled edge and, with the colors used for the stem of the wineglass, applied the fill to the bevels.

I used the same fill with a modified ball from the wineglass for this figure. Could be the perfect drink for airheads. What you think? Waiter, the water looks a little cloudy!

I used the same colors from the stem and base of the wineglass to create the pub mirror shown here. I altered the fill to a Square Fill and applied it to the beveled edges. Refer to Chapter 14 for more tips on creating goldlike fills. The figures with the hoops are from the Sports Symbols Library.

I set Laurel Avenue Glass Works in a font called Anna (seen here). I created a base using a rounded rectangle with the bottom lopped off and two triangles trimmed out. I applied a similar fill to that in the image in the "Bottoms Up" section above, and added a bevel from the Extrude-Bevel menu, using the Use Object Fill option to give the beveled edge a transparent glass look.

A HANDSOME
Circular Clock Face
IN 34 EASY STEPS!

I have to confess (well, I don't really have to confess, I mean, nobody's making me) that I have a fondness for old windup clocks. There, I said it! I have several vintage Seth Thomas clocks, including the one that is the basis for the illustration in this chapter. Not only is the clock rewarding to look at, but the tick-tock sound is very soothing to listen to as well. I had intended to do this entire project in **DRAW 7**, which is theoretically possible; however, I ran into several snags and had to do part of the illustration in **PAINT**. On the positive side, this chapter will be a good chance for us DRAW devotees to poke around in Dave Huss territory and play with some of the toys therein.

The clock on the cover illustration is almost identical to the one we'll create in this chapter

IMPORTANT

This image is fairly complex, and there are dozens of items to keep track of. If you work with the Layers roll-up and create different elements on different layers, your life will be a lot easier. Layers can be locked to keep you from accidentally deleting something important and made invisible when the drawing gets too cluttered or you just need to concentrate on a particular area. I always forget to do this until it's too late. But since I have the benefit of hindsight, I can save you from having the same problem. I've added suggestions for using a new layer when it is appropriate.

THE PROBLEM—THE SOLUTION

DRAW 7 cannot rotate a texture or bitmap fill. DRAW 8 can, and DRAW 8 users should be able to produce this illustration entirely in DRAW, although this is a good opportunity to work with PAINT. To get around DRAW 7's rotation limitation, I created bitmap images of the wood fill, rotated them, and PowerClipped the rotated bitmaps in the appropriate clock parts. Then I created grayscale shading objects and applied transparency. Onscreen, this looked terrific. But when I tried to print the image, convert the image to bitmap, or export the image as a TIFF file, the wood-filled areas had large dropped-out sections. Ug-ly! I spent the better part of a day trying every possible scheme I could think of, but alas I came up with the same results each time. So, rather than have all of you frustrated readers wanting to lynch me, I found a workaround in PAINT, which will be revealed shortly. Let's get started.

TIP

This project can create some fairly hefty files, so make sure that you have a lot of disk space available. This is also a pretty long project, so please take eye breaks frequently and SAVE your files often.

ON THE FACE OF IT

Figure 2-1, seen on the next page, is the basic drawing of the clock. I've added a few dimensions for the major pieces. We'll just construct the face of the clock in this chapter. If you feel daring, you can recreate the rest of the clock using the final illustration as a guide.

Figure 2-1: The clock drawing and major dimensions

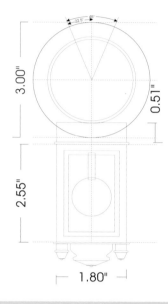

We're going to create eight separate 45-degree sections for the round portion of the clock face. In DRAW 8, you can create and fill one section and then rotate the section in 45-degree increments, and the wood grain fill will rotate accordingly. We're going to do it the hard way, however, in DRAW 7, like real men and real women.

S T E P

1

Select the Ellipse tool and construct two concentric circles, 3 inches and 2 1/2 inches in diameter. Combine the two circles (CTRL+L) and apply a yellow fill, as shown in Figure 2-2. Enable Snap To Objects, found in the Layout menu. Drag horizontal and vertical guidelines that intersect the circles. Turn off Snap To Objects and turn on Snap To Guidelines. With the Freehand tool, draw a vertical line from the center of the circles, extending about 1 inch over the top. Double-click on the line to toggle into Rotate/Skew mode, and drag the rotation bull's-eye to the intersection of the two guidelines. In the Angle of Rotation text box on the Property Bar, type 22.5 degrees and press ENTER. Duplicate the line (+ key) and enter -45 degrees and press ENTER. You should have two lines forming a V. Select the two lines and Combine them (CTRL+L). Select the Freehand tool and draw a line connecting the top nodes of the two lines. With the wedge selected, use the Shape tool to marquee-select the bottom two nodes and click on the Join Two Nodes icon on the Property Bar. With the Pick tool, select the yellow combined circle and the triangular shape and click on the Intersect icon on the Property Bar. Fill the intersected shape red.

Figure 2-2: Two circles combined with a 45-degree intersection shown in red

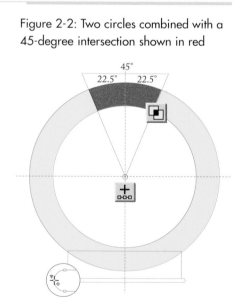

With the Rectangle tool, draw a rectangle under the combined circles about 2 inches wide by about 1/2 inch high. Draw a wide, slim rectangle directly underneath and use the Shape tool to round the corners (see inset).

STEP

2

Move the large combined yellow circle to the side—we'll need it for the next step. Click twice on the 45-degree intersected shape to toggle into Rotation mode and drag the rotation bull's-eye to the intersection of the two guidelines. Snap To Guidelines will ensure the Rotation bull's-eye is in the exact center. Use the Rotation roll-up (in the Arrange menu, choose Transform-Rotate) to rotate seven Duplicates, 45 degrees each, clicking on the Apply to Duplicate button (see Figure 2-3). Select every other section and change the fill to yellow.

Divide the rectangle (under the eight segments) into two rectangles by dragging one side control handle to the center guideline, then flopping a duplicate to the opposite side. To do this, press and hold the CTRL key while dragging the control handle across the guideline, then click the right mouse button to drop a duplicate before you release the left mouse button. Fill one rectangle blue and the other green.

STEP

3

Draw a rectangle slightly larger than the top segment (the red one) and apply a wood-grain fill, as shown in the center inset in Figure 2-3. Here's how: open the Fill tool and click on the checkered icon to open the Pattern Fill dialog box, as illustrated in Figure 2-4. Click on the Bitmap radio button and click Load. (You will need to have CD-ROM #2 in your CD-ROM drive.) Use the browser to find the CD-ROM drive and locate the Tiles folder. From the Tiles folder, select the Wood folder and the Large subfolder. Click on WOOD21L.CPT and click Open, as shown in Figure 2-5, to select the fill, and then click OK to close the Pattern Fill dialog box.

Figure 2-3: Eight 45-degree sections make up the clock face

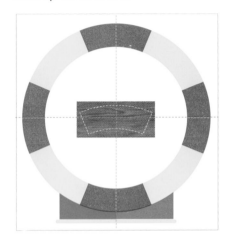

Figure 2-4: The Pattern Fill dialog box with the default fill displayed

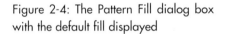
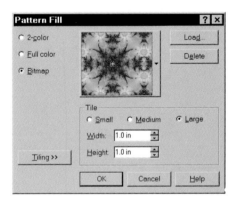

Figure 2-5: The Pattern Fill dialog box with Wood21l.cpt selected

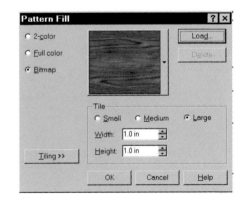

S T E P

4 Select the combined yellow circle, and from the Arrange menu select Break Apart. Set the fill to none for both shapes. Select the outside circle and open the Contour roll-up by selecting Contour in the Effects menu. We're going to apply a Contour because we want to create two slim circles with the inside and outside dimensions exactly the same as the inside and outside dimensions of the eight face segments. Apply a 1-Step Contour, Inside, offset .02 inches as shown in Figure 2-6. Click on the Contour group with the right mouse button and select Separate from the fly-out. Click on the Group of one objects again with the right mouse button and select Ungroup. Select both lines and Combine (CTRL+L). Fill the slim circle black with no outline.

> **N O T E**
>
> DRAW 8 simplifies the Separate-Ungroup process by automatically Ungrouping a Separated Contour effect.

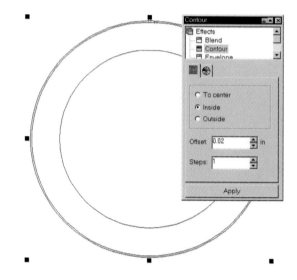

Figure 2-6: A 1-Step Contour to Inside maintains the exact outside dimension

S T E P

5 Select the smaller circle and apply the same Contour, but this time apply it to the Outside, as shown in Figure 2-7. Repeat the process of Separate, Ungroup, Combine, and fill black with no line stroke.

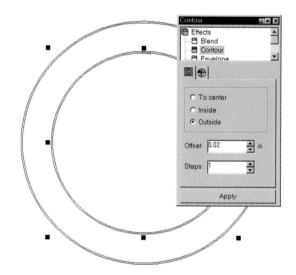

Figure 2-7: A 1-Step Contour to Outside maintains the exact inside dimension

6 Select the two thin circles and apply a 1-Step Blend, as shown in Figure 2-8. Click on the Blend with the right mouse button and select Separate. Click again with the right mouse button and select Ungroup. Fill the center thin circle white and move it up about four points.

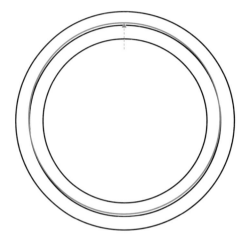

Figure 2-8: A 1-Step Blend of the two thin circles is filled with white (shown in blue for detail) and moved up four points

7 Working in Simple Wireframe view, select the white curve and the outside black curve and apply a 50-Step Blend, as shown in Figure 2-9. Select the white curve again (check the status bar to make sure it reads Control Curve) and then select the inside thin black circle and apply another 50-Step Blend.

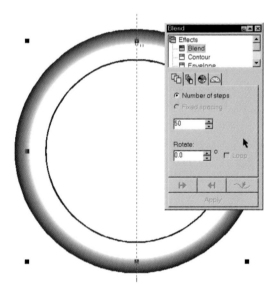

Figure 2-9: A 50-Step Blend of the center and outside thin circles

TIP

Selecting the beginning and ending Control Curve of a Blend can be difficult, especially if your eyes are shot (like mine). Repeated pressing of the TAB key will cycle through all the elements on your page, which you can do until you select the desired control curve. Pressing SHIFT+TAB cycles backward.

S T E P

8

Construct a square slightly larger than the blended circle, fill it yellow, and send it to the back, as shown in Figure 2-10.

Figure 2-10: The two-part blend is placed over a solid yellow square

S T E P

9

We need to prepare the elements to bring into PHOTO-PAINT. We'll save the eight curved shapes, the wood-filled rectangle, and the two base rectangles as one file and the blended circles as a second file. Draw a rectangle around the eight segments, two bottom rectangles, and wood fill. Fill the rectangle white with no line stroke. Select this group, and from the File menu select Save As. Check the Selected Only option to save the selected group only, name your file, and click Save. Repeat the process with the blended circle with the yellow background. You can create your own file names.

PAINTING OURSELVES OUT OF THE CORNER

We're going to use PAINT to rotate the wood grain, fill the various wooden clock parts, and apply transparency. We'll use the blended circles to impart a rounded shape to the wood. Trust me, this will work! Click on the red Corel C logo button on the Property Bar and select PHOTO-PAINT from the drop-down menu to open PHOTO-PAINT.

1

Open the first CDR file (the eight sections, wood fill, and rectangles). PAINT will convert the image to bitmap CPT (Corel PHOTO-PAINT) file format. The Import Into Bitmap dialog box will open, as shown in Figure 2-11. Select 16 Million Colors and Super Sampling. The resolution setting will depend on what you plan to do with the final image. If you do not plan to print the object, select 100 dpi for screen resolution. I plan to print the image in high resolution, so I have typed in 266 dpi, which translates into 133 line screen. Click OK.

Figure 2-11: The Import Into Bitmap dialog box converts the vector CDR image into a bitmap image

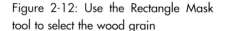

2

Select the Rectangle Mask tool (the default mask tool), drag a rectangle inside the wood-filled rectangle, then click on Grow on the Property Bar. Figure 2-12 shows the selection. Select Copy from the Edit menu. Open the Mask Tool flyout and select the Magic Wand Mask tool. Click inside the top red rectangle to select it. From the Edit menu, select Paste Into Selection. This pastes the selection inside the mask, as you can see in Figure 2-13. From the Mask menu, select Remove (CTRL+D) to turn off the mask. Use the Magic Wand to select the bottom rectangle and repeat the process.

Figure 2-12: Use the Rectangle Mask tool to select the wood grain

Figure 2-13: The wood grain is pasted into the selected masked segment

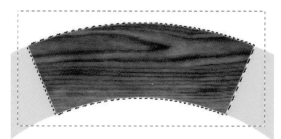

STEP

3 Select Paste As New Object from the Edit menu. From the Object menu, select Rotate and Free and type 45 in the Angle text box. Click on Transform, then Apply, as shown in the Tool Settings dialong illustrated in Figure 2-14. This rotates a copy of the object 45 degrees. From the Edit menu, select Copy. Use the Magic Wand to select the segment at 11 o'clock and paste the fill into it, using the Paste Into Selection option. Select the opposite panel at 4 o'clock and fill it, using the Paste Into Selection option.

Figure 2-14: The Tool Setting dialog box is used to rotate the selected object

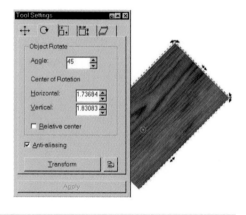

STEP

4 Continue filling the eight circle segments by using Paste As New Object, rotating the wood rectangle the appropriate amount, copying it, then using Paste Into Selection into a Magic Wand-selected segment. Select the original horizontal rectangle and Copy it. Use the Magic Wand to select the left rectangle (under the circle segments) and Paste Into Selection. Paste As New Object the rectangle, and from the Object menu select Flip and Horizontally. Copy and Paste Into Selection to the other half of the rectangle. Figure 2-15 shows the final results with all the wood fills in place.

Figure 2-15: All of the shapes have been filled with the wood grain fill

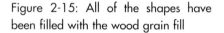

IN A PERFECT WORLD

I would have repeated the previous process by selecting the slim, rounded rectangle on the bottom with the Magic Wand Mask and Paste Into with the wood fill. However, a bug in PAINT 7 refuses to perform as expected. So, I used the Magic Wand Mask to select the slim rectangle. Next I clicked on the Fill icon on the bottom of the screen, selected the checkerboard icon to open the Select Fill dialog box, and clicked on Edit, then Load from the Bitmap Fill dialog box. From here I located the same wood fill in the TILES\WOOD folder and clicked OK. When all the dialogs were closed, I clicked on the Fill Tool icon, then clicked inside the slim rectangle to apply the fill.

5 Open the second CDR file (the blended circles) and enter the same settings in the Import Into Bitmap dialog box as you used on the first CDR file (step 1 of this section). From the Mask menu, select Mode, then Additive. This enables you to make multiple mask selections. Click on the outside yellow area with the Magic Wand and then, while pressing and holding the SHIFT key, click on the inside yellow area. Both areas are now masked, as indicated by the "marching ants," as they're affectionately referred to (see Figure 2-16). From the Mask menu, select Invert to make the blended shape the selection. Copy (CTRL+C) the selection to the clipboard.

Figure 2-16: The blended circles are masked and copied

6 We will use the blended circles as a transparency lens to add a rounded appearance to the wood circle. Minimize or close the window with the blended circles, and restore the window with the wood fills. Paste As New Object the blended circles and center them top and sides over the wood-filled circle. Select Add from the Property Bar Merge Mode options with an amount of 25 percent, as shown in Figure 2-17. This adds a curved appearance to the shape, but it looks washed out. No problem—we can fix that. Copy the current selection to the clipboard.

Figure 2-17: An Add Merge Mode of 25 percent is applied to the blended circles

MERGE MODE	
Type:	Add
Object Opacity:	25%

TIP

PAINT opens without rulers, which are necessary if you want to use guidelines. Select Show Rulers from the View menu. You can drag guidelines to help you position the transparency mask over the wood face.

S T E P

7 Paste As New Object the lens, change the Merge Mode to Multiply, and change the amount to 60 percent, as shown in Figure 2-18. That's more like it. Save your file, close or minimize PHOTO-PAINT, and restore DRAW.

Figure 2-18: The copied transparency lens (the blended circles) are copied and pasted on top, and the Merge Mode is changed to Multiply 60 percent

ABOUT FACE

PAINT was amusing, bugs and all, but now it's time to return to familiar territory as we construct a face for our clock. This section gets a bit involved, but if you work with me we'll get it done and you'll be a happy camper. Fortunately, much of the repetitive tasks can be automated. Ready?

S T E P

1 Here's the easy part. Draw three concentric circles, 2.5 inches, 2.4 inches, and 2.875 inches in diameter, as shown in Figure 2-19. Give each a line weight of .5 points.

Figure 2-19: Draw three concentric circles

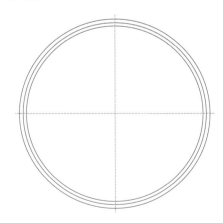

2

This is very important. Enable Snap To Objects in the Layout menu and drag a horizontal and a vertical guideline through the center of the circles (it helps if you zoom in tight). The guidelines will snap to the center of the circles. Disable Snap To Objects and enable Snap To Guidelines. Zoom in on the upper half of the circles. With the Freehand tool, draw a line at 12 o'clock inside the two inner circles and set the line weight to .5 points. Click twice on the line with the Pick tool and drag the Rotation bull's-eye to the center of the circles. It should snap to the two guidelines. From the Arrange menu, select Transform then Rotate and enter a Rotation Angle of -6 degrees (negative numbers go clockwise; positive number go counterclockwise). Click on Apply to Duplicate. Repeat this three more times. The face should now look like Figure 2-20.

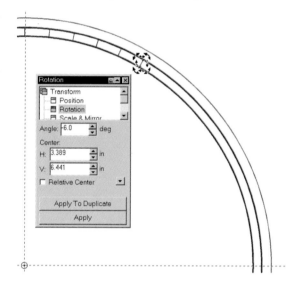

Figure 2-20: A minute tick mark is rotated/duplicated in -6-degree increments

3

Open the Symbols roll-up, go to the Zapf Dingbats library, and select an upward-pointing triangle (#115). Scale it down to the height of the minute tick marks and position it at 12 o'clock. Click twice to toggle on Rotate/Skew mode and rotate it -30 degrees. Select and group (CTRL+G) the four tick marks and the triangle (but not the line at 12 o'clock). Drag the rotation bull's-eye to the center and enter a rotation angle of 30 degrees. Click on Apply To Duplicate 11 times. Replace the tick mark at 12 o'clock with a small square, stretched vertically a tad and rotated 45 degrees, as shown in Figure 2-21.

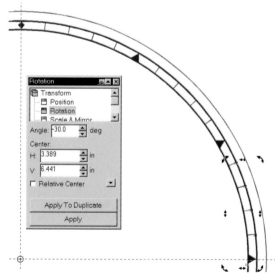

Figure 2-21: A triangle is added at the five-minute mark and grouped with the previous four tick marks, then rotated 30 degrees to add all of the minute and hour tick marks

STEP

4

Place a Roman numeral XII at 12 o'clock. I've used the font Onyx, which is perfect because it's very condensed. Select the XII with the Text tool and click on the center align button on the Property Bar. Center the XII on the guideline and click twice to enter Rotate/Skew mode. Drag the Rotation bull's-eye to the intersection of the center guidelines. Use the Transform Rotate menu and rotate the XII in 30-degree increments until you have 12 numbers. Individually select each with the Text tool and change to the appropriate Roman numeral, shown in Figure 2-22.

NOTE

The Roman numeral used for 4 on clocks is IIII instead of IV.

Figure 2-22: A Roman numeral XII is set at 12 o'clock and rotated eleven times. The individual numerals are selected with the Text tool and edited to the correct numbers

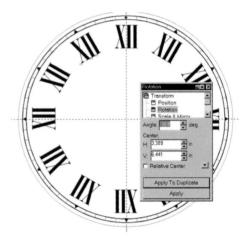

STEP

5

Next we'll draw a dial for the second hand. Return to Layer and draw two smaller circles under the XII (about one-third the diameter of the top half of the dial), as shown in Figure 2-23. Enable Snap To Objects and drag a guideline through the horizontal center of the circles. Turn Snap To Objects off. Add ten tick marks at six-degree intervals using the technique we used for the minute and hour tick marks. Make the tick mark at five longer toward the center of the circle. Replace the tick mark at ten with a small downward-facing triangle. Group these elements and rotate/duplicate at 60-degree increments. Add a small 60 at 12 o'clock, center align it and rotate duplicate at 60-degree increments. Use the Text tool to edit the numbers to 10, 20, 30, 40, and 50. Group all of the minute and second circles and tick marks and move to a locked layer.

Figure 2-23: The dial for the second hand

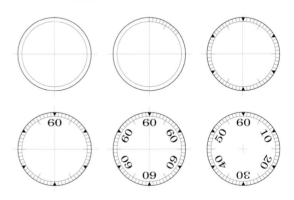

Our clock face will not do us much good without a method of depicting the time. We'll use a combination of rectangles and ellipses and a small amount of node-editing to create the gracefully shaped hour, minute, and second hands.

S T E P

1

Figure 2-24 details the steps needed to make the minute hand. Return to Layer 1 and draw a small circle in the center of the dial and a thin rectangle that extends to the top of the XII. Convert the rectangle to curves (CTRL+Q). Select the top-left node with the Shape tool and use the arrow keys to nudge it toward the center.

Nudge the top-right node in by the same amount. We are after a tapered effect, not a sharp point. Select the lower-left node and nudge it outward a couple of clicks and repeat the process for the lower-right node. Construct an ellipse toward the top of the rectangle as shown. Convert it to curves and drag the center node upward with the Shape tool. Zoom in real tight, and add two nodes at the top of the ellipse where it intersects the rectangle. Select the two new nodes and then click on the Cusp button on the Property Bar. Use the Shape tool to pull the sides inward a little, then click on the nodes and drag the Bezier handles downward, as indicated in the inset (magnified circle) in Figure 2-24. When you're happy with your handiwork, select all three elements and click on the Weld button on the Property Bar.

Figure 2-24: Steps for creating the minute hand

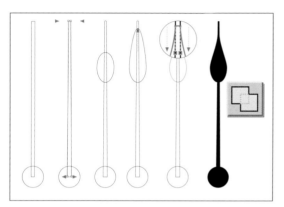

N O T E

I like to set the Nudge units to .1 or .5 points and the Super Nudge to 2 points (in the Options menu). By default, the setting is about 1 point, which to me is more of a shove than a nudge!

STEP

2

We'll modify a duplicate of the minute hand to make the hour hand. Duplicate the minute hand and scrunch the top down by dragging on the top center bounding box handle. Press and hold the SHIFT key and drag one of the middle side bounding box handles outward a bit. Draw a circle, slightly larger than the one at the bottom of the minute hand, at the bottom of the hour hand, select it, and Weld it, as shown in Figure 2-25.

Figure 2-25: The steps for modifying the minute hand into the hour hand

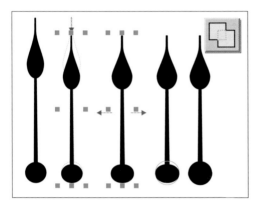

STEP

3

Next we'll construct the second hand. Draw a slim rectangle and circle, as shown in Figure 2-26. Make the Layer containing the second dial visible and use the dial to determine the height. Convert the rectangle to curves, add a node in the middle, and use the Shape tool to nudge the top nodes inward to taper the point. Add an ellipse to the other end and convert the ellipse to curves. Use the Shape tool to modify the ellipse to create a shape similar to the tip of a paint brush, as shown. Select the three units and click on the Weld button on the Property bar.

Figure 2-26: Constructing the second hand

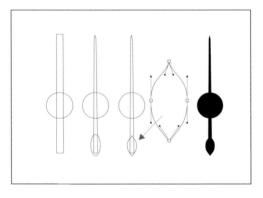

STEP

4

A small circular brass unit fits over the hands and is held in place with a small metal wire. This brass unit secures the hour and minute hands. Create a circle that is slightly smaller than the round part at the bottom of the hour hand. With the circle selected, click on the Interactive Fill tool. Select Fountain Fill from the Fill Type drop-down menu on the Property Bar, then click on the Conical Fountain Fill icon. Drag the following colors onto the fill path, as shown in Figure 2-27, beginning with Gold to Chalk to Brown.

Figure 2-27: The brass connector unit that holds the hands in place

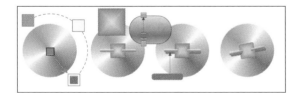

Draw a small square in the middle to represent the unit to which the hands attach. This unit has a pyramid-type taper on the end, which we can simulate using a simple Square Fountain Fill, from 40 percent Black to white (I always knew there was a use for the square fill!). Draw a very small rectangle (zoom in close) and use the Shape tool to round the ends. Convert the rectangle to curves and apply a three-color Linear Fountain Fill, beginning on top with 30 percent Black to 60 percent Black to 40 percent Black. Place a duplicate on the other side of the square unit. Make two more duplicates, fill them Brown, and position them under the slim rectangles to create a tiny drop shadow. Details like this are important and add realism to the illustration; even if they are too small to see, we still know they're there!

STEP

5

Just a few more little details and we can begin assembling the face. Draw a circle about the size of the center circle on the second hand. Make a duplicate circle about 1/16 inch smaller. Draw a small square in the center. This is the keyhole and unit that the key fits over to wind the clock, as detailed in Figure 2-28. Apply the same gray square fill to the small square that we used in step 4, and rotate the square a touch. Select the smaller circle and apply a simple linear fill from 70 percent Black to 50 percent Black. Select the outer circle (bring the smaller circle and square to the front by pressing SHIFT+PAGEUP) and apply a simple Conical Fountain Fill from white to 40 percent Black. Make sure that the white portion is toward the bottom right. This will add a small amount of edge to the keyhole.

Figure 2-28: The keyhole assembly

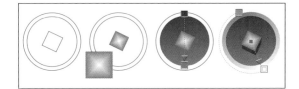

STEP

6

We're almost finished, so hang in there. This particular Seth Thomas clock sports a small ST logo, which is a piece of cake to create. Draw a square about as wide as the circle on the bottom of the minute hand. Make a duplicate (+ key) of the square and use the Shape tool to round the corners to a perfect circle. Rotate the original square 45 degrees. Type **ST** and add it in the center. I've used Copper Plate Gothic Bold BT. Group the three units, as shown in Figure 2-29. See, I said it would be easy. While you're in text mode, type **SETH THOMAS** in Copper Plate Gothic Bold BT the same size as the ST.

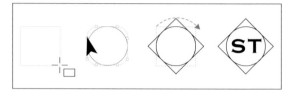

Figure 2-29: The Seth Thomas ST logo

STEP

7

If they're not there already, drag a horizontal and vertical guideline to the exact center of the dial. Position the minute hand and then the hour hand so that the circular bottoms are centered over the center of the dial. Click on the minute hand twice to enable Rotate mode and drag the Rotation bull's-eye to the center of the dial. Rotate the minute hand to about 50 minutes. Repeat this process with the hour hand, rotating it to just short of 10 o'clock, as the timely illustration, Figure 2-30, shows.

If you look at photographs of watches and clocks in advertisements and brochures, you'll notice that most timepieces have the hands in this same position (I suppose some marketing person decided that this is the most pleasing arrangement of the hands). Rotate the second hand to 9 seconds.

Figure 2-30: The hands are positioned on the dial

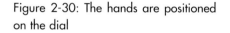

STEP

8

If you have not already positioned the other elements on the dial, by all means do so, as detailed in Figure 2-31. Select the largest circle of the dial and apply a very subtle Linear Fountain Fill from 10 percent Black (at about 11 o'clock) to white (at 5 o'clock). Make duplicates of the hour, minute, and second hands, weld them into one unit, position them under the originals, move them down about three or four points, and apply a Uniform Transparency, Normal, 50 percent, to create a realistic drop shadow.

Figure 2-31: The dial shaded and drop shadows are added under the hands

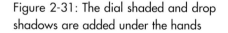

TRANSPARENCY	
Type:	Uniform
Transp. Operation:	Normal
Amount:	50%

9

The brass bezel that covers the glass has two parts: a wide, flat part and a thinner, beveled edge. On a new Layer, draw three circles: the smallest the same size as the dial, the next biggest about 1/16 inch larger, and the largest about 1/8 inch larger still. Make a duplicate of the center circle and Combine it with the largest circle. Apply an Interactive Linear Fountain Fill, as shown in Figure 2-32a, beginning at the top with Gold to Chalk to Pale Yellow to 10 percent yellow to Gold, ending with Chalk.

Select the two smaller circles and Combine them. Apply an Interactive Conical Fill, as shown if Figure 2-32b. This fill begins on top with Gold to Pale Yellow to Gold to Walnut to Gold to Pale Yellow to Gold.

Figure 2-32(b): The brass bezel

(a)

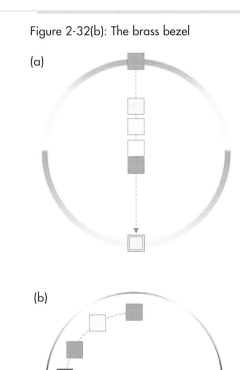

(b)

TIP

To add 10 percent yellow to the screen palette, open the Uniform Fill dialog box and enter 10 in the Yellow text box (make sure your palette is CMYK and not RGB or one of the other palettes). Click on the small arrow in the upper right (the Color Options flyout) and click on Add Color to Palette.

10

Position the bezel over the dial, as shown in Figure 2-33. Have you been saving your drawing regularly and taking eye breaks?

Figure 2-33: The brass bezel and dial

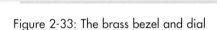

STEP

11

To create the appearance of glass over the face of the clock, we'll create a large circular fountain fill, apply transparency, and add my patented window pane highlight. Draw a circle the exact size of the dial and apply a Black to White Radial Fountain Fill. Offset the center of the fill up and left, as shown in Figure 2-34.

Figure 2-34: The glass covering the face begins as a Radial Fountain Fill

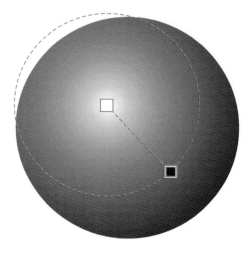

STEP

12

Draw four squares, as shown in Figure 2-35. Fill them pale gray for the time being (we'll eventually fill them white). Combine the four squares and scrunch them horizontally. Apply a straight-sided envelope (select Envelope in the Effects menu) and Convert to Curves (CTRL+Q). Apply a simple curved-sided envelope. The right side should conform to the curve of the edge of the glass, the inside less so.

Figure 2-35: Constructing a window pane highlight

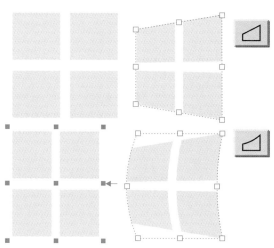

13

With the Radial Filled circle placed over the dial and selected, apply a Uniform Transparency, Multiply, 70 percent. Change the fill for the window pane highlight to white, then rotate and position it, as shown in Figure 2-36, and apply a Linear Fountain Transparency, Normal, beginning top left at 10 percent transparency and ending toward the center of the dial at 90 percent.

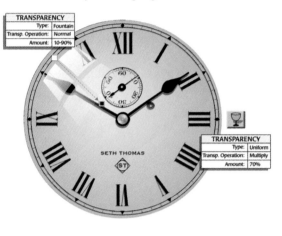

Figure 2-36: The glass dial cover and transparent highlight

Boy, that was some accomplishment. Take a short break, check your e-mail, go to the bathroom if necessary, and treat yourself to a snack. When we come back, we'll add the dial to the clock face.

14

There are a lot of transparencies applied over transparencies in this illustration. If we tried to export this file as an EPS (Encapsulated PostScript) file, our service bureau would probably put a contract out on us, so discretion being the better part of broken thumbs, we'll go to plan B. Save the drawing under a new name and open it in PHOTO-PAINT, being careful to use the same settings as when we did the octagonal face (step 1 of "Painting Ourselves out of the Corner"). Select the face with the Magic Wand Mask tool, with the Additive mode enabled to allow us to make multiple selections. Press and hold the SHIFT key, select the four white corners, and click on the Invert Mode icon on the Property Bar. Copy and then Paste As New Selection, then position it over the octagonal wood portion, as handsomely illustrated in Figure 2-37. Pretty slick-looking, eh?

Figure 2-37: The completed clock face

OUT OF TIME AND OUT OF SPACE

I originally intended this chapter to cover the entire clock, as seen in Figure 2-39. Unfortunately, by the time I finished, there was enough material for an entire book. After arm wrestling with the editorial department, we decided to include the final illustration and a few brief notes. The case and the scrollwork base of the clock were created using the same metholds used to create the face—solid wood-grain-filled shapes, using grayscale-shaping masks and transparency to achieve the three-dimensional look. The elements were assembled in PHOTO-PAINT.

STEP

1   I assembled the final sections of the clock and placed them inside a rectangle a bit larger than the clock. I selected the clock and Cut it to the clipboard. I filled the rectangle with a Bitmap fill, MIDLAGEL.CPT, from the Paper folder in the Tiles folder on the CD-ROM, a handsome background for the clock. I pasted a copy of the clock with Paste As New Object, filled it solid Dark Brown, and moved it down and right about 1/4 inch in each direction. I expanded the mask by selecting Shape in the Mask menu, then Expand and Width: 25. Next, I applied a Gaussian Blur of 20 (by selecting Blur in the Effects menu) to soften the edges. Finally, I selected Merge Mode and Multiply, amount 70, as shown in Figure 2-38.

Figure 2-38: A copy of the clock is filled with dark brown, blurred, and used to cast a shadow on a marbleized paper background

I then pasted the clock on top with Paste As New Object. The final results are shown in Figure 2-39.

Figure 2-39: The finished illustration

What did we learn? I don't know about you, but I learned a lot. I discovered that bugs in DRAW 7 prevented me from doing the entire illustration in DRAW.

On the positive side, I got to learn how to do what I needed to do in Dave Huss territory, PHOTO-PAINT. Together, we learned how to create transparency masks and apply them in PAINT to give shape and depth to the flat wood finish. We used a Blend of three circular shapes to make a transparency mask to give the rounded wood clock face a curved appearance. We made extensive use of the Rotate function in the Transform menu to rotate a bunch of stuff around the clock dial. We found a practical uses for the Square Fountain Fill. Finally, we learned that even a very complex image, such as the clock face, is no more than a whole bunch of short steps—34, in this case. But who's counting?

Variations on a Theme

Here are a few additional applications of the techniques we learned in this chapter (as if this chapter weren't long enough already!). This figure places the clock over a sky background, with the shadow falling onto the clouds. I set Seth Thomas in Flemish Script and applied a gold-type fountain fill. I added the lens flare and composed the elements in PAINT. This makes an elegant poster.

This figure uses various wood-grain fills. I converted the image to bitmap and applied a 3D Effects-Emboss, Direction 320, and Depth 2, which added an interesting dimension. This technique, minus the Emboss step, is good for creating the appearance of inlaid wood or marble.

ONCE UPON A PEDESTAL

Here we see a variety of fills and blends to create a transparency bitmap/mask, which when applied over the solid wood-filled shape creates a credible pedestal and sphere. Notice how I adapted the shadow to go across the floor, up the floor molding, across the top, and up the wall.

IT'S ALMOST SURREAL

This figure uses a variety of transparent texture-filled shapes to create a surrealistic image.

Holiday Reflections

We'll use some of DRAW 7's powerful new tools—Interactive Fill, Interactive Transparency, Convert To Bitmap, Natural Pen Tool, and more—to create a Christmas card illustration featuring a Christmas tree, a shiny red glass ornament reflecting a child with a teddy bear, a colorful gold garland, and a bright green light.

We'll employ a magical square-to-sphere technique to inflate our ornament.

IMPORTANT

Because this image will be output to four-color printing, change your color correction to Accurate (in the View menu, choose Color Correction, then Accurate in DRAW 7. In DRAW 8, go to the Tools Menu, then Options, then Global, then Color Management). This alters the appearance of your screen colors to approximate CMYK colors.

CREATING THE CHRISTMAS CARD

'Tis the season to put DRAW's tools to good use as we create a festive Christmas holiday scene. We'll create the illustration in three parts: the ornament shape, light and garland; the branches and pine needles; and finally the ornament and reflection. We'll use the Layer Manager to keep everything tidy. We'll finish the card by adding a seasonal greeting.

SETTING UP THE LIGHT, ORNAMENT, AND GARLAND

STEP

1

Draw a 4 1/4-inch × 2 3/4-inch rectangle, a large 2 3/4-inch circle, and other elements as seen in Figure 3-1. (Don't worry about the bulb shape in the upper-left for now—I've just roughed it in place. We'll create the actual bulb in step 7.) Group all the elements. We'll use this as a working drawing for the illustration (see Figure 3-1). If you use Layers, put this working drawing on a separate layer. Place the guidelines on a separate layer as well, so you can turn them on and off when needed. Layers are a good way to organize complex drawings. My problem is I always think to use them after the drawing is completed.

Figure 3-1: The working drawing is roughed in

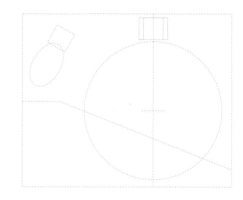

STEP

2

Draw a two-part straight line over the lines we roughed in in the previous step. Select the nodes with the Shape tool and, from the Toolbar, click on To Curve. Use the Shape tool to drag the line segments into two graceful curves, as shown in Figure 3-2.

Figure 3-2: A two-part line converted to curves is shaped with the Shape tool

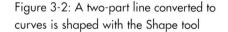

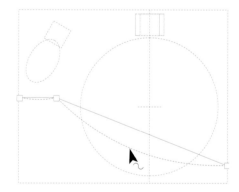

S T E P

3

Draw a small circle at each end of the curved line. Apply a Custom Radial Fountain Fill on the left circle, using the colors in Figure 3-3: Chalk, Gold, Green, Moon Green, and Chartreuse. In the Fountain Fill dialog box, change the Offset Center values to 10 Horizontal and 10 Vertical. Change the Edge Pad setting to 10. This moves the center of the fill up and to the right. Duplicate and drag this circle to the end of the curved line. Change the colors as displayed in Figure 3-3: Gold, Red, Pink, and Red. Change the Horizontal offset to -10. The first golden circle in what will become a garland is reflecting the green light, and so the upper portion is green. The second circle is reflecting the red glass ornament and as such reflects more red.

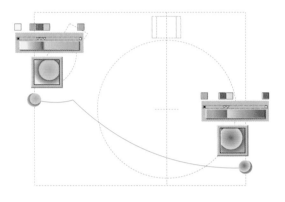

Figure 3-3: Two circles will be used as the beginning and end of a garland

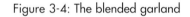

S T E P

4

We want the circles to touch but not overlap, as shown in Figure 3-4. Select both circles and apply a Blend with just enough steps (approximately 16 to 20) so the circles do not overlap.

Figure 3-4: The blended garland

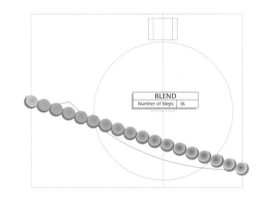

S T E P

5

With the Blend selected, click on the To Path button shown in Figure 3-5. Select New Path from the flyout menu, use the arrow cursor to designate the path (the curved line), and click Apply. When you're happy with the blend, click on the path and set the line color to None by clicking on the X at the top of the onscreen palette with the right mouse button.

Figure 3-5: The garland blend is blended to the curved-line path

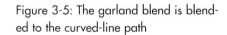

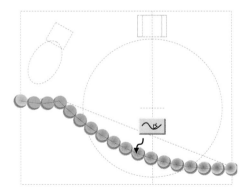

6

Next, we'll construct the metal part at the top of the glass ornament. Begin by constructing a rectangle and converting the rectangle To Curve (Figure 3-6a). Use the Shape tool to select the rectangle. Click on the bottom of the outline and add two nodes (Figure 3-6b). To add a node, click on the line where you want to add the node, then click on the Add Node(s) button (the one with the + shown here) on the Property Bar. Drag the bottom left and bottom right nodes up about four points, or until it matches Figure 3-6c. Marquee-select the entire shape and click on the To Curve button. Use the Shape tool to round the top and bottom three line segments (Figure 3-6d). To add a bright green reflection of the green light, apply an Interactive Linear Fountain Fill (Figure 3-6e), beginning on the left with Brown, to Gold, to Moon Green, to Chartreuse, to Brown, to Pale Yellow, to Gold.

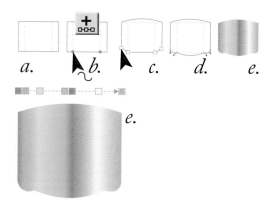

Figure 3-6: The steps used to create the metal top

7

Construct the three elements are used to create the glass bulb of the Christmas tree light: a circle, an ellipse, and a parallelogram whose sides are tangent to the circle and ellipse (Figure 3-7a). Select the three shapes and click on the Weld button on the Property Bar, shown in Figure 3-7b. Make a duplicate with the + key and reduce it by holding down the SHIFT key and dragging one of the corner bounding box handles. Repeat to make a smaller duplicate in the center, as shown in Figure 3-7c. Fill the largest shape Green, the middle shape Chartreuse, and the smallest shape Moon Green. Remove all outlines from the three bulb shapes. Reposition the two smaller shapes down toward the bottom of the largest shape, as partially shown in Figure 3-7d. Select the largest and middle-sized shape and apply a 30-Step Blend. Select the center shape (make sure the status bar displays Control Curve and not Blend) and the smallest shape, and apply another 30-Step Blend. Figure 3-7e shows the results of the double blend. This creates the impression that the green light is brightly glowing.

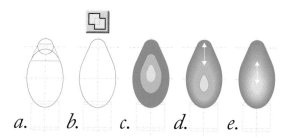

Figure 3-7: The steps used to create the light

STEP

8

The socket for the light consists of a square and two oval edges, shown in Figure 3-8a. Draw a wide, shallow rectangle (for the top edge) and use the Shape tool to round the edges by dragging one of the corner nodes until the edge is round, or setting the slider on the Property Bar to 100 percent. Place a duplicate rounded rectangle to the bottom, as shown in Figure 3-8b. Draw a square that intersects the horizontal center of both rounded rectangles. Convert all shapes To Curve (CTRL+Q). Fill the square with a Custom Fountain Fill, beginning with Forest Green to Spring Green to Forest Green, as indicated in Figure 3-8c. Select the top rounded rectangle and apply a Radial Fountain Fill, using Chartreuse for the center and Spring Green for the outside to reflect the bright green light, as you can see in Figure 3-8d. Apply a Radial Fountain Fill to the bottom rectangle, using Forest Green on the outside to Spring Green, shown in Figure 3-8e. Add the light bulb to the socket and group all the elements shown in Figure 3-8f. Rotate the bulb into position (about 150 degrees).

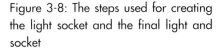

Figure 3-8: The steps used for creating the light socket and the final light and socket

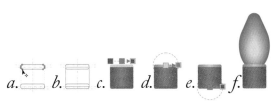

STEP

9

A blend of two lines will create the effect of electrical wires. Draw a three-part line as shown in Figure 3-9a. Marquee-select the line with the Shape tool, convert the line To Curve, and use the Shape tool to drag a loop and gentle curve, as shown in Figure 3-9b. Select the line and change the line weight to four points and the line color to Forest Green. Create a duplicate (+) and change the line weight to one point and the line color to Spring Green. Select both lines and apply a 5-Step Blend (Figure 3-9c). Group the light and the wires, making sure that the light is in front.

Figure 3-9: A line is modified, duplicated, and blended to create electrical wire

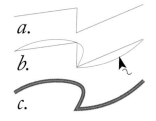

Figure 3-10 shows the completed light, ornament top, and garland of gold-colored balls. This is a fine time to name and save your drawing and to take a short break. I have a craving for Christmas cookies.

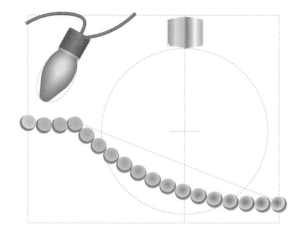

Figure 3-10: The light group, garland, and metal top are finished

CREATING A TREE—IN MINUTES

We'll use the new Natural Pen tool (inside the Freehand Tool flyout) to create branches and pine needles. The Natural Pen tool is the successor to the Power Lines effect, which disappeared around version 6. I've placed red and blue guidelines, indicating two separate branches.

S T E P

1 With the Natural Pen tool selected, select the fourth button (Preset Natural Pen Type) from the Toolbar. From the drop-down menu of preset pen shapes, choose the right-facing bullet shape and set the Natural Pen Width setting to .13 inches. Drag three Natural Pen tool lines over the red guidelines, as shown in Figure 3-11. Then draw five lines over the blue guidelines.

Figure 3-11: The Natural Media Pen tool is used to draw tapered shapes for a branch

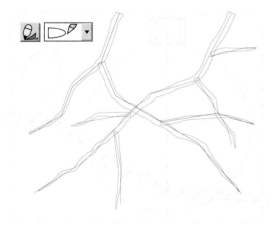

N O T E

When you drag the pen line, it looks like a black blob; however, when you release the mouse button, the line turns into a gracefully tapered shape.

2 Select all the Media Pen lines that are over the red lines, and from the Property Bar, click on the Weld button. Select all the Media Pen lines over the blue lines and repeat the Weld process. Your image should bear a passing resemblance to Figure 3-12. You can delete the red and blue lines.

Figure 3-12: The Media Pen lines are welded, making two branch shapes

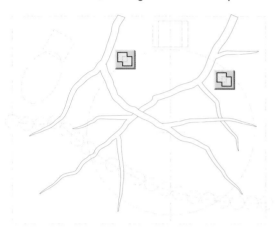

3 Select the three-part branch and open the Texture Fill dialog box (Fill Tool flyout). From the Styles library, select Mineral Speckled 2-Colors and click OK. This gives the branch a mottled, more realistic appearance, as you can see in Figure 3-13. Select the second branch and apply the same fill, only this time change the Brightness setting to -20 and click OK. With a little creativity and imagination, Texture Fills can be modified to duplicate a variety of textures and surfaces. Draw a background rectangle and apply the same Mineral Speckled 2-Colors fill, but this time change the colors to Forest Green and Spring Green and change the Softness setting to 50. This provides a soft, out-of-focus background for the branches and other elements.

Figure 3-13: A Texture Fill is applied with three variations, creating the branch surfaces and background

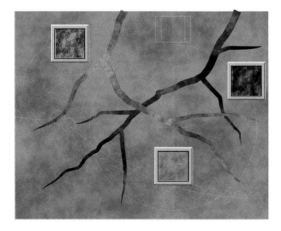

4 You can set defaults for the line and fill attributes other than the current settings. You've probably done this by accident at least once. (Remember when everything you created had an eight-point red dotted outline? You probably inadvertently changed the defaults and had to spend 30 minutes waiting for Corel tech support to set you straight.) Changing the default fill and line attributes will save steps when we create the pine needles, because the pine needles will automatically fill with the appropriate fill. With nothing selected, click on the Forest Green swatch on the onscreen palette. A warning box appears, as shown in Figure 3-14, advising you that you're about to alter the default settings. Make sure that only Graphic is checked and click OK.

Next, click on the X at the top of the onscreen palette (if your palette is vertically placed on your screen) or to the left of the palette (if your palette runs across the bottom of your screen) with the right mouse button. The same warning for Outline Color will appear. Make sure that only Graphic is selected and click OK. The new default for new graphic objects is solid Forest Green fill and no line weight. We will alter these default settings as we progress.

Figure 3-14: Creating a fill or line attribute when no object is selected brings up this warning dialog box, which allows you to create new line and fill default attributes

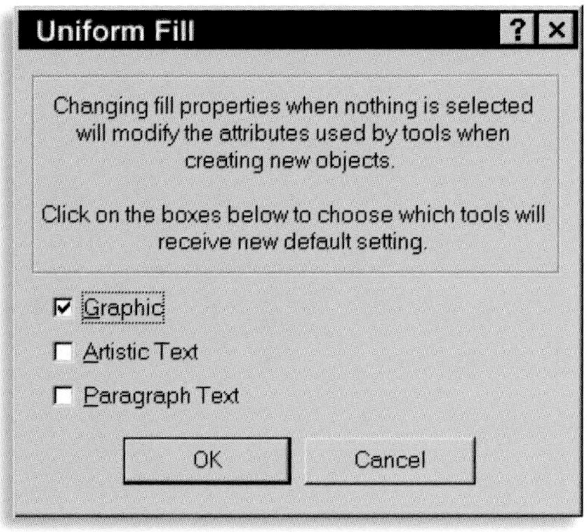

Uniform Fill   ? ✕

Changing fill properties when nothing is selected will modify the attributes used by tools when creating new objects.

Click on the boxes below to choose which tools will receive new default setting.

☑ Graphic
☐ Artistic Text
☐ Paragraph Text

[OK]   [Cancel]

5 Change the Natural Pen tool Width setting to .03 inches. On a new layer, draw a series of freehand pine needles, as shown in Figure 3-15. Select the needles, group them (CTRL+G) and bring the branch (minus the needles) to the front. With nothing selected, open the Linear Fountain Fill dialog box and set the default fill colors from Forest Green to Spring Green. Draw more needles of varying lengths for the forward pine needles.

Figure 3-15: Using the Natural Pen tool to draw pine needles

STEP

6 Continue this process until you've filled the visible areas of the branches with pine needles. Select an assortment of needles closest to where the green light is going to be, and from the Property Bar, click on the Weld button. Apply a Linear Fountain Fill from Chartreuse to Spring Green. This adds the illusion that the needles are being illuminated by the light, as seen in Figure 3-16. Save your drawing and take an eye break.

Figure 3-16: Pine needles closest to the light are filled with brighter greens to create the illusion of the needles being illuminated by the light

CREATING THE ORNAMENT (THE WORLD IS SQUARE)

Next, we'll create the red glass ornament reflecting a happy young lad with his Christmas present, a friendly teddy bear. We'll create a tableau for the reflection inside a square shape and then use a Bitmaps-3D Effect to create the illusion of a spherical ornament.

STEP

1 The tiny toddler with his teddy bear is Chldtddy.cmx from the People B&W clip art folder on CD-ROM #3. Flop, resize, and place the image in your drawing, as shown in Figure 3-17. If you're using Layers, begin a new layer. Draw a square the same size as the circle representing the ornament on our working drawing. Make a duplicate of the square and resize each square so you have a top rectangle about three-fourths the height of the bottom rectangle. Center Align the toddler over the bottom rectangle, select the toddler and the rectangle, and from the Property Bar, click on the Weld button to make one continuous shape.

NOTE

I've moved the rectangles apart for clarity. They should, in fact, be centered.

Because dark red is a very hard color to mix onscreen and equally difficult to predict when printed in CMYK, I've used three TRUMATCH CMYK colors for deep red, medium deep red, and lighter deep red. All of these colors are darker than the Red on the onscreen palette. I selected the colors from my TRUMATCH ColorFinder swatchbook and then keyed in the color codes in the TRUMATCH palette. The TRUMATCH palette is in the Fill Tool dialog box. Click on the Palettes button (the four small squares), then from the drop-down list, select TRUMATCH colors. The three colors are 4-a6 (deep red), 4-d3 (medium deep red), and 4-e3 (lighter deep red).

Select the top rectangle and apply a Linear Fountain Fill from Light Violet (bottom) to Red. Select the bottom section (with the toddler) and apply a Linear Fountain Fill from Red (bottom) to TRUMATCH 4-a6 (deep red).

S T E P

2

Make a duplicate of the green light and wire and scale it down to about 75 percent. Draw a branch and needles, using the technique from the prevous chapter, to cover the green light's wires. Fill the branch and needles with TRUMATCH 4-a6. Select and duplicate a bunch of needles nearest the light, Weld, and apply a Radial Fountain Fill with Chartreuse in the center to 4-a6 on the outside, as shown in the center of Figure 3-18.

S T E P

3

Position the light and pine needles as shown in Figure 3-19. Create a duplicate of the branch and needles and apply a solid deep-red fill. Make another, smaller duplicate. Position these on the bottom of the composition and flop the branches horizontally.

Create a circle centered over the brightest part of the green light and fill it Moon Green. Apply an Interactive Radial Fountain Transparency. Click on the center node and change the setting on the Property Bar slider to 20 percent. Click on the outside node and change the slider setting to 100 percent. Drag the outside node toward the center until the hard edge is replaced by a soft edge, as seen in Figure 3-19a. Make a

Figure 3-17: Two rectangles, one with a clip art toddler welded to it, make one square shape, which will be used to compose the elements in the glass ornament

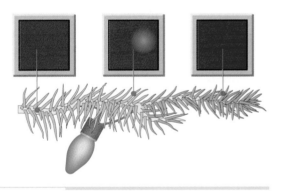

Figure 3-18: A branch is added to a smaller duplicate of the light to cover the wires

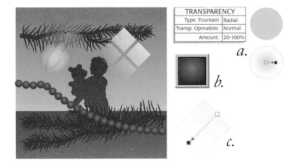

Figure 3-19: The light, branches, duplicate garland, and window highlight are arranged in the square

duplicate of the garland, resize it to fit the width of the rec-tangles containing the child, and change the fill to a simple Radial Fountain Fill of TRUMATCH 4-e3 (lighter deep red) and 4-a6 (deep red), illustrated in Figure 3-19b. This adds a reflection of the big garland. Since we're only seeing the back of the garland in the reflection, it should be darker and have less contrast.

Draw four squares to make a window shape. Select all four squares and combine them (CTRL+L). Rotate the shape 45 degrees, fill it with 10 percent Magenta and 5 percent Yellow, and apply a Linear Transparency from 10 percent to 100 per-cent, as shown in Figure 3-19c. Move all of the elements toward the center, as indicated in Figure 3-19.

S T E P

4

Select all of the elements shown in Figure 3-20 and choose Convert To Bitmap in the Bitmaps menu, with the following options selected: 24-Bit 16 Million Colors, Use Color Profile, Super Sampling (anti-aliasing). Select a dpi setting for your final output. I've used 266 dpi for commercial printing.

Figure 3-20: The elements are converted to bitmap

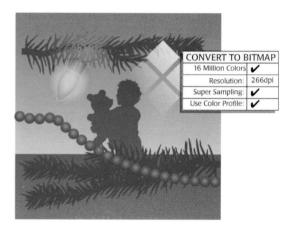

CONVERT TO BITMAP	
16 Million Colors	✔
Resolution:	266dpi
Super Sampling:	✔
Use Color Profile:	✔

N O T E

Whenever you are using Accurate Color Correction (in the View menu, choose Color Correction in DRAW 7; in the Options menu, choose Global settings in DRAW 8) to simulate printing colors onscreen, select the Use Color Profile option when exporting an image to bitmap or converting an image to bitmap. This is very important if you have any transparent objects in your drawing.

5

Here's the cool part, where we make the square image appear spherical. Select the bitmap, and from the Bitmaps menu, select 3D Effect, then Map To Object, Spherical, Amount 25 percent, and click OK. Figure 3-21 shows the results. Kind of pops right out, doesn't it?

Figure 3-21: A 3D Effect, Map To Object-Spherical Bitmap effect makes the image appear round

6

Draw a circle just inside the square bitmap and position it over the bitmap. Select the bitmap, and from the Effects menu, select PowerClip then Place Inside Container, then click on the circle with the arrow cursor. Position the metal top. Drag a duplicate of the metal top down and use SHIFT+PAGEDOWN to position it beneath the top. Apply a Linear Transparency to create a reflection of the top in the ornament, as seen in Figure 3-22.

Figure 3-22: The spherical bitmap is PowerClipped into a circle, and the top and its reflection are added

TRIMMING THE TREE

We're almost through. I hope you've been saving your changes.

STEP

1
Select the background with the branches and Convert To Bitmap, using the same settings as those used in step 4 of the preceding section (creating the ornament). From the Bitmaps menu, choose Noise, Colored, Level: 25, Density: 25. Now from Bitmaps, select Blur-Gaussian, amount 5. This softens the image a little bit, creating a photographic appearance with narrow depth of field, as shown in Figure 3-23.

Figure 3-23: The branches and background are Converted to Bitmap, and Noise is added

STEP

2
To make our composition more dramatic, as shown in Figure 3-24, we'll darken the background (except the area with the green light). Draw a rectangle the same size as the background, fill it Black and apply a Radial Interactive Fountain Fill, making the center White. Drag the circle's center over the area where the light is going to be. Apply an Interactive Transparency with these settings: Uniform, Subtract, amount 50.

Figure 3-24: A rectangle with a black-and-white radial fill and transparency applied adds drama to the background

Type **Merry Christmas** in a nice script font big enough to fit the area (I've used Flemish Script, 54 points). Apply a shiny gold-type Fountain Fill, beginning at the bottom with Chalk to Gold to deep red (TRUMATCH 4-a6) to Pale Yellow to Gold, shown in Figure 3-25. Copy the type to the clipboard (CTRL+C). Select the type, fill it Black, and add a four-point Black outline. Paste (CTRL+P) the original type on top.

Figure 3-25: The text is filled with a Fountain Fill to produce a shiny gold look, and a duplicate of the text with a four-point black outline is placed behind

Position the ornament first, then the light over the background. Create another circle filled with Moon Green, like the one we created in step 3 of the preceding section (creating the ornament), and apply the same Radial Transparency to add a diffused glow to the light. Position the garland in front, and finally, add the type in front of everything, as you see in Figure 3-26. Save the image and open it in PHOTO-PAINT as a CPT file and crop.

Figure 3-26: All of the elements are arranged over the background

T hat's it! Not that hard, don't you think? If you have a color ink-jet printer, you can use the image to make your own Christmas cards. While I was in PAINT, I applied an Effects, 2D, Whirlpool filter. You can see the results in the illustration at the beginning of this chapter.

Variations on a Theme

Here you see my fastball. Strike! I created two red stitches, using lines with Round Caps, and Blended the lines on an s-curved path. I filled a square with a texture fill to add a subtle raised grain to the horsehide skin. I applied a Radial Fountain Fill to the text with the center over the letter o. I placed a same-sized square on top with a black-and-white Radial Fountain Fill and applied a minimal Interactive Transparency to add subtle shading. I converted the elements to Bitmap, then applied a Bitmap 3D Effect, Map To Object-Spherical effect. The bitmap was PowerClipped inside a circle.

DOOR TO NOWHERE

This image began as a gold dome atop a flag pole. Well, so much for simplicity. I created the sphere in a square in the same manner as the Christmas ornament. I added an overlay using a cloudy Texture Fill, altering the colors to Brown and Pale Yellow. I applied a Linear Interactive Transparency, keeping the top transparent but adding a faint cloud pattern to the gold fill. I converted the elements to Bitmap and repeated the 3D Spherical effect. I PowerClipped the gold dome inside a circle combined with a door-shaped rectangle. The PowerClip left the rectangle open. I couldn't resist adding the door and doorknob. Ditto the flare.

GRASS-EYE VIEW

I revisited the Natural Pen tool to create the blades of grass shown here. I used the Calligraphic fixed width Pen to draw free-mouse some blades of grass. I filled one grouping dark green. I placed a second group of grass blades on top and applied a Linear Fountain Fill, using the dark green at the bottom and Green on top. I made a third set of blades and lightened the top of the fill, substituting Chartreuse for Green. I placed a linear-filled sky in the background. I added a butterfly from the Animals 1 Symbols Library with a Radial Fountain Fill consisting of Pale Yellow and Pale Orange. I created a largish white circle and applied a Radial Transparency. I converted everything to bitmap.

POP UP

This image is a bit of fluff. I created a 5-Revolution Spiral. I selected the spiral with the Shape tool and clicked on the Auto-Close button on the Property Bar. Filling the shape created the cool effect seen in the image. I made an overall repeating pattern of the spirals, selecting all the resulting pattern and Combining the spirals into one path, to which I applied a gold-colored Linear Fountain Fill. I placed a black-filled square behind the spiral pattern and changed the fill to Linear Fountain Fill, matching the horizon lines. I added a starburst (seen in the lower-left horizon). The bitmap image looked so swell after I applied the 3D Map To Object-Spherical effect, that I left it that way. I added a gold beveled edge.

POLITICALLY CORRECT SNOWPERSON

This figure was a pleasant surprise. I spent about an hour creating a palm tree effect against a bright blue sky. I added "Aloha You All!" to the final image. It was dumb, and it looked dumb too. Sigh. Then the thought struck (or maybe it was that I hadn't eaten all day)—why not do one of those cute snowpersons inside a snow-filled glass sphere? I did it, and here it is. See if you can figure out how to re-create it, using the techniques covered in this chapter.

Hinging on Textures

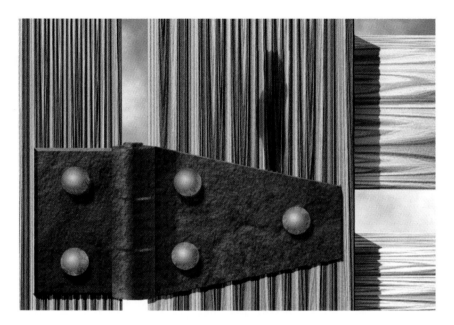

I've always been a big fan of Corel's Texture Libraries. Well, sort of. What I mean is that I've always been a big fan of the potential of Corel's Texture Fills as opposed to the actual fills themselves. In this chapter, I'll show you what I mean, as we modify textures with unlikely names such as Exhaust Fumes, Curtains, Rock-Speckled-Eroded 2C, and Rock-Swirled-Eroded to create a photographically realistic image of a rusty hinge clinging to a weathered wood gate against a brilliant blue sky, as you can see for yourself in the final illustration shown above.

CAUTION

DRAW's Texture Fills are capable of producing files of humongous size. Apply Transparency on top of these Texture Fills, and the files become astronomical. This does not even address the fact that most of these files can never be printed on your printer or output by your service bureau. However, there is a very simple solution: convert your image to a bitmap. A pixel is a pixel is a pixel and will print every time.

We're about to create weathered wood and rusty metal out of thin air. But, before we start, we need to rough in the elements of our drawing. Follow the steps below and before you know it, you'll have created the aging effects only many seasons of exposure to the harsh elements of nature could have wrought.

STEP

1

Draw a rectangle 4 inches tall by 5 1/2 inches wide and fill it pale blue. Add four additional rectangles, as shown in Figure 4-1, and fill them 10 percent Black. The red outline represents the position and size of the hinge we'll be creating in the second half of this chapter. The two gray rectangles on the right side represent a small portion of the horizontal slats; their height is not critical. The white rectangles are the tops of the slats.

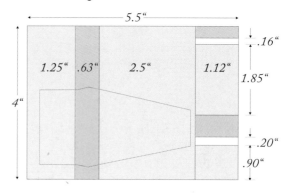

Figure 4-1: The working drawing is roughed in

STEP

2

Select the two left gray vertical rectangles and open the Texture Fill dialog box. From the Samples library, select Curtains. Although the name of the fill is Curtains, I think it looks more like weathered wood, with the grain etched deep by the wind and rain. With a few modifications, I think you'll agree, as you look at Figure 4-2.

Change the Texture # to 20108. Click on the first Color button and change the color to 60 percent Black and click OK. See, doesn't that look like raised-wood grain? By default, DRAW's Texture Fills are set to screen resolution, which is swell if you just plan to view the textures onscreen. If you intend to print your final image or output it to film, you'll

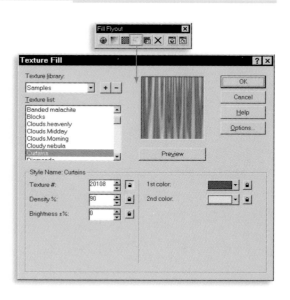

need to change the bitmap resolution, otherwise your image will be noticeably pixilated. Click on the Options button and change the Bitmap Resolution option to 266 dpi.

Figure 4-2: The posts and slats filled with a Texture Fill that resembles old weathered wood

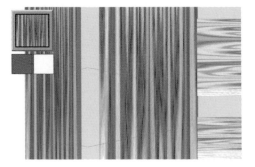

S T E P

3   Next, we need to fill the two slats on the right side of our composition. DRAW 8 users can apply the same Curtains Texture Fill, rotate the fill 90 degrees, as shown here, and go to the kitchen for a Coke and a short break. DRAW 7 users, skip to step 4.

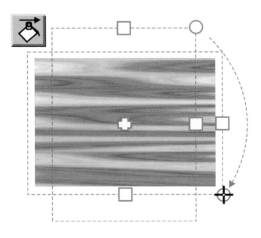

4

DRAW 7 cannot rotate Texture Fills. The outline rotates, but the fills remain stubbornly the same. No problem—we have other resources available. Select the two slat rectangles, rotate them 90 degrees, and apply the Curtains Texture Fill. Individually select each slat, and from the Bitmaps menu select Convert to Bitmap. Set the options to 256 Shades of Gray and Super Sampling. If you just plan to view the image onscreen, set the Resolution to 100 dpi. If you plan to print or output your image to film, increase the Resolution to 266 dpi. With the Texture Fills converted to bitmap, rotate them 90 degrees (see Figure 4-3).

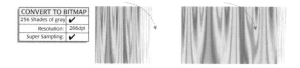

Figure 4-3: In DRAW 7, the Texture Fills can be rotated when they're converted to bitmaps

5

We'll create a small amount of decay to add to the post. Draw a freehand shape similar to the one in Figure 4-4. You can use the Freehand tool and draw a continuous shape, or you can click a series of short, connected line segments, using the Shape tool to change the lines to Curves, and dragging the lines to smooth curves. Fill the shape 50 percent Black. Apply a Contour To Center (select Contour in the Effects menu), with the Offset amount .005 inches. The Fill color should be Black. Select the Contoured Group, and from the Bitmaps menu select Convert to Bitmap. Choose the same options as selected for the previous bitmap, but select Transparent Background.

Individually select each piece of wood and convert to bitmaps using the previous settings, but this time without the Transparent Background option. Draw a rectangle over the top of each slat and fill them using the CMYK values shown in Figure 4-5. This will add a warm, orangish color and create a top edge. Draw two more rectangles for shadows and fill them with the CMYK values shown. This will add a purplish shadow. Select the decayed wood shape and position it as shown. Apply an Interactive Transparency, Uniform, Multiply, with the slider set to 20 percent.

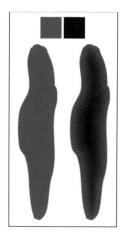

Figure 4-4: A decayed wood section is created using a Contour effect

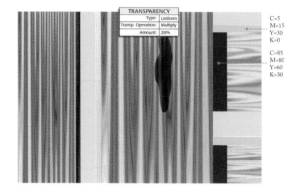

Figure 4-5: Highlight and shadow edges are added and transparency is added to the decayed wood shape

STEP

6

Select the shadows and apply an Interactive Transparency, Fountain, Linear. Drag the directional arrow, as shown in Figure 4-6. Click on the beginning node (left side) and change the slider value to 30 percent. Click to select the end node and make sure the setting shows 100 percent.

Select the pale orange rectangles and apply an Interactive Transparency, Uniform, Subtract, amount 60 percent. This imparts a warm, sunlit glow to the top of the wood.

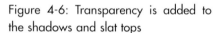

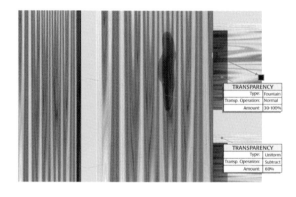

Figure 4-6: Transparency is added to the shadows and slat tops

STEP

7

The wood is looking pretty good, but we'll administer a three-step process to bring out the grain and make it look better still. Place the shadow and slat-top sections aside for a moment. Individually select each of the four wood elements and do the following three actions to each, as detailed in Figure 4-7. First, Convert to Bitmap (located in the Bitmaps menu), 24-bit, 16 Million Colors, and Super Sampling. Use the same resolution setting from the previous Convert to Bitmap settings. Second, select 3D Effects, then Emboss from the Bitmaps menu. Choose the Original Color option and change the Depth setting to 8 and the Direction to 135 degrees. Third, in the Bitmaps menu, select 3D Effects, Noise, then Add Noise. Choose Gaussian and set the Level and Density values to 20 percent. Now that looks like wood. Almost.

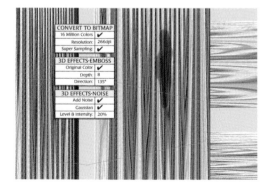

Figure 4-7: Three bitmap operations bring out the grain and impart texture to the wood

8

The wood looks a little too gray. It should—after all, it is gray! A little tint of color will remedy that. Before we apply the remedy, replace the slat tops and shadows. Draw rectangles over each section of wood, except the slat tops and shadows, as shown in Figure 4-8. On the slats, the rectangle should meet, not overlap, the shadows. Apply a plain Brown fill to each rectangle and set the line width to none. Apply an Interactive Transparency to each of the brown rectangles, Uniform, Subtract, amount 80 percent.

Select the background rectangle (the one we filled pale blue in the first step.) You can resize it so that it only covers the three openings in the wood. Open the Texture Fill dialog box, and from the Samples 6 library select Exhaust Fumes. (Yuk! Reminds me of Los Angeles.) Click on the Background color button and change the values to 85% Cyan and 50% Magenta. Change the Texture # to 24002. From the Options section, set your desired resolution. Click OK. (Now it looks like L.A. after a big rainstorm.) Select the beautiful blue sky and apply an Interactive Linear Fountain Transparency, beginning at the top of the image at 0 percent (no transparency) and ending at the bottom of the image at 100 percent. Finally, select the entire composition and Convert to Bitmap, 24-Bit, 16 Million Colors, Super Sampling, and your choice of resolution. Do not select Transparent Background.

We've done in a brief period of time what Mother Nature took years to accomplish. That deserves an eye break and a quick trip to the kitchen for a compensatory snack.

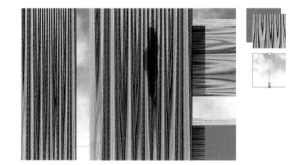

Figure 4-8: The final touches are added and the entire composition converted to a single bitmap

HINGING ON THE POSSIBLE

Next, we'll create a metal hinge and add about 20 years' worth of rust to match the weathered appearance of the wood.

1

Construct the basic shapes shown in Figure 4-9. The green part of the hinge is really a rectangle converted to curves (CTRL+Q) and the end nodes dragged toward the middle. Place these shapes over the wood and sky bitmap (which we just completed in the previous section) to ensure the correct size. The red rectangle is just a placeholder until we complete the cylindrical portion of the hinge. Make duplicates (+ key) of the blue and green hinge shapes—we'll need them in a few steps.

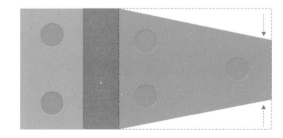

Figure 4-9: The basic shapes for the hinge

2

Select the left rectangle and apply a simple two-color Linear Interactive Fountain Fill, as shown in Figure 4-10. The two colors used are 10% Black and 50% Black. Drag the directional arrow as shown. Select the right side of the hinge and apply a four-part Interactive Linear Fountain Fill, beginning with 80% Black to 70% Black to 20% Black to 40% Black. Simply drag your colors from the onscreen palette onto the directional path. Slide the center two colors close together, as shown, to create a shadow for the cylinder. Remove all outlines.

Figure 4-10: A shading overlay is created for the flat sections of the hinge

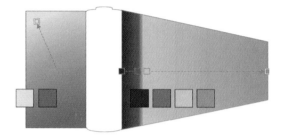

3

Individually select each of the two fountain-filled sections and Convert to Bitmap, 256 Shades of Gray, Super Sampling, and your choice of resolution. For the tapered section, select the Transparent Background option. Select the tapered section, and in the Bitmaps menu choose Blur, then Gaussian, Radius 5. Click OK. Next, from the Bitmaps menu select and apply Noise (by selecting Noise, then Add Noise) to each flat section. Choose Gaussian as the type, set the Level and Density values to 20, and make sure that Color Noise is unchecked (see Figure 4-11).

Rock-Swirled-Cracked 2C, shown here, does not at first glance remind one of rust. However, with a few modifications, the transformation is astonishing. Well, maybe I exaggerate a bit, but it does create a convincing appearance of rusty metal.

Figure 4-11: A shading overlay is created for the flat sections of the hinge

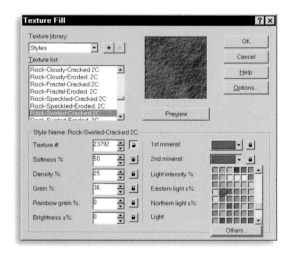

4 Select the two duplicate shapes for the flat sections of the hinge and open the Texture Fill dialog box. Change the first Mineral and second Mineral colors to Walnut. In the Options section, change the Resolution setting to your desired resolution. Click the Preview button until you find a combination that looks like rusty metal, then click OK. Make a duplicate of the rectangle shape and a smaller duplicate, as shown on the left of Figure 4-12. The top, bottom, and left sides should be equally spaced. Enable Snap To Objects (either from the Layout menu or the Property Bar) and use the Freehand tool to click a series of line segments to create a top, left, and bottom beveled edge. With Snap To Objects enabled and using the corners of the two rectangles as a template, your line segments will automatically snap to the appropriate corners. Position the bevels over the rust-filled rectangle and apply the same Texture Fill to all three edges (you can use Copy Properties From in the Edit menu, or you can drag the Texture Fill from the rectangle to the bevel, click the right mouse button, and select Copy Fill Here from the pop-up menu). Individually select the bevels, and in the Texture Fill dialog box change the Brightness setting as follows: +20 for the top, -10 for the left side, and -20 for the bottom. Position the two bitmaps from step 3 (Figure 4-11) over the rusty shapes and apply an Interactive Transparency, Uniform, Multiply, 20. The shading we created adds depth and realism to the shapes, and the noise adds a bit of gritty texture.

Figure 4-12: A rusty-looking Texture Fill is applied to the hinge shapes, and transparency is applied to the bitmaps

5 There's a nifty way to make the bolts look like partially rusted metal, and it goes like this. Make five same-sized circles, about 3/8 inch in diameter. Select all five and apply a Rock-Swirled-Cracked 2C Texture Fill from the Styles Texture Library. Change the first Mineral color to Light Orange and the second Mineral color to Ruby Red. From the Options section, set your desired resolution. Select each of the five circles individually and click on the Preview button to change the fill so that you wind up with five different fills. The fills that show a lot of a golden-ochre color will work the best, as shown in Figure 4-13. Select all five circles and create duplicates (+ key). Apply a simple black-and-white Radial Fountain Fill with these settings: Horizontal Offset -10 percent, Vertical Offset 10 percent, and Edge Pad 10 percent. Click OK. Select all the radial-filled circles, center them over the texture-filled circles, and apply an Interactive Transparency, Uniform, If Lighter, 20. Isn't that awesome? I discovered it quite by accident (Huss will probably claim that he's known it all along!).

Figure 4-13: A Texture Fill and a Radial Fountain Fill overlay with transparency applied creates a convincing slightly rusted bolt appearance

STEP

6

We're getting close to closing the gate. In my zeal, however, I've forgotten to add a bevel to the tapered shape. Use the same process from step 4 to create and fill the bevels. Bring the transparent bitmap to the top (see Figure 4-14). We'll make some soft shadows to give depth to the bolts. Make a circle the same size as one of the bolts. Drag the bottom middle bounding box handle down to elongate it and click the right mouse button (while still pressing the left mouse button) to drop a duplicate, as shown in Figure 4-14a. Select the new ellipse and double-click to toggle into Rotate mode. Drag the rotation bull's-eye to the center of the circle, then rotate the ellipse to the right, as shown in Figure 4-14b. Select both shapes, and from the Property Bar click on the Trim button to remove a circular section from the shadow, as shown in Figure 4-14c. Delete the circle. Fill the shadow shape Black and draw a slightly larger white rectangle, as shown in Figure 4-14d. Set the line width for the white rectangle to none. Select the shadow shape and the white rectangle and Convert to Bitmap, 256 Shades of Gray, and Super Sampling. Do not select Transparent Background. Select the resulting bitmap and apply a Gaussian Blur, Radius 10 (by selecting Blur in the Bitmaps menu), as shown in Figure 4-14e. Position the bolt group over the shadow, as shown in Figure 4-14f. Select the shadow and apply an Interactive Transparency, Multiply, 30, as shown in Figure 4-14g.

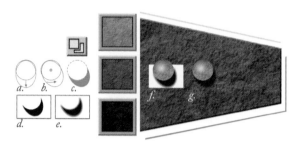

Figure 4-14: Bevels are added and a transparent soft shadow is created for the bolts

NOTE

A Multiply Transparency makes white totally transparent but retains all of the dark values. Lower settings (50 to 0) increase the amount of darkness.

The final step looks harder than it is. Honest. I wouldn't ask you to do anything I couldn't! This is probably a good time to take a break before we start, so save your file and admire your handiwork so far.

The final section of the hinge is the cylindrical center. We'll take it in a series of short steps.

S T E P

1

This seems odd, but it works. The top of the cylinder is a tight ellipse, whereas the bottom—because it's further below our eye level—is more open. So, on a new layer draw two 1/2-inch-diameter ellipses, as shown in Figure 4-15a.

Figure 4-15: The necessary steps to create the cylinder

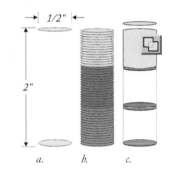

S T E P

2

Position the ellipses two inches apart. Select both ellipses and apply a 45-Step Blend, as shown in Figure 4-15b.

Figure 4-15 (cont'd)

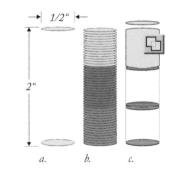

S T E P

3

Select the blend and Separate it (by selecting Separate in the Arrange menu), then select the center part of the blend and Ungroup it (CTRL+U). I've colored the ellipses to make this next instruction easier. Count down from the top and remove the sixteenth ellipse (shown in blue). Count up from the bottom and remove the sixteenth ellipse (shown in blue). Remove all but the first and fifteenth in each group. Make a copy of the top ellipse in each of the three groups (CTRL+C). Drag a rectangle the width of the ellipses that intersects the top and bottom ellipse in the first group (shown in yellow). Select all three elements, and from the Property Bar click the Weld button. Repeat this process for the green and red groups. Paste the copies of the top ellipses (CTRL+V) back on top, as shown in Figure 4-15c.

Figure 4-15 (cont'd)

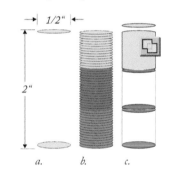

STEP

4

Create two small ellipses centered over the yellow cylindrical shape and a rectangle the same width that intersects the two small ellipses. Copy the top ellipse and Weld the three elements. Paste the copy of the small ellipse back on top, as shown in Figure 4-15d.

Figure 4-15 (cont'd)

d.   e.   f.

STEP

5

Select all the shapes of the cylinder except the duplicate tops, make a duplicate, and Weld the shapes into one continuous outline (shown behind the originals in yellow). Select the cylinders and apply a four-part Interactive Linear Fountain Fill. Begin with 60% Black to 10% Black to Black to 70% Black. Select the four top ellipses and apply the same fill, but change the fill type to Conical, as shown in Figure 4-15e.

Figure 4-15 (cont'd)

d.   e.   f.

STEP

6

Select all of the cylinder shapes (except the solid yellow Welded shape) and Convert to Bitmap, 256 Shades of Gray, Transparent Background, Super Sampling. Select the resolution appropriate for your final output. Select the bitmap and apply Noise, Gaussian, Level and Density 20, as shown in Figure 4-15f.

Figure 4-15 (cont'd)

d.   e.   f.

7 Fill the welded outline of the cylinder with the same Texture Fill that we used on the flat hinge shapes. Bring the solid, texture-filled shape to the top and position it directly over the bitmap cylinder. Apply an Interactive Transparency, Multiply, 0 percent, as shown in Figure 4-15g. Figure 4-15h is the finished cylinder.

Figure 4-15 (cont'd)

g.   *h.*

8 Position the cylinder over the other hinge elements and put the bolts in place, as shown in Figure 4-16. I added a shadow under and to the right of the hinge to visually adhere the hinge to the wood. The shadow (shown under the image) was filled 85 percent Cyan, 80 percent Magenta, 60 percent Yellow, and 30 percent Black. I applied an Interactive Transparency, Subtract, amount 55.

Figure 4-16: Transparent shadows below the hinge add a final touch of realism

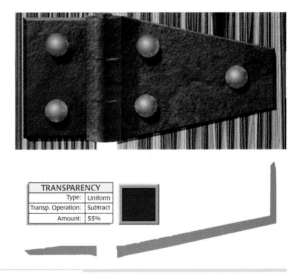

9 Now that looks convincing. The wood looks old and weathered, the sky looks blue, and the hinge looks rusty. And all of this was done in DRAW. But, you know, it all looks too crisp. So if you don't tell Huss (he'd never let me live it down), we'll just sneak into PAINT and add a few tiny embellishments!

10

The edge of the shadows are too even. If the wood were weathered, as we took such pains to replicate, the shadows would reflect the embossed nature of the surface. I dragged a slim rectangular Mask encompassing about 1/8 inch of the wood and 1/8 inch of the shadow and applied a 2D Effects, Ripple, Horizontal, Period 9, Amplitude 1, Direction Angle 90 degrees effect. Look at Figure 4-8 and then the final illustration and you will see what a difference this filter makes. For the shadows under the hinge, I altered the Ripple to Vertical. I added two small transparent triangles to the top of the slats to add direction to the shadows. Figure 4-17 shows off the final illustration. That's it, honest! I know that Huss spends more time in DRAW than he'll admit to, so I don't feel too guilty.

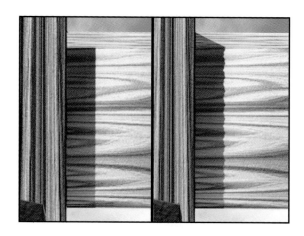

Figure 4-17: A few embellishments are added in PHOTO-PAINT to complete the image

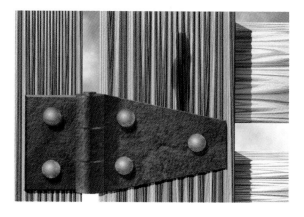

Before I shut down the computer and head upstairs for dinner, let's recap what we've done. First of all, give yourself a big round of applause. This was a tough exercise, and if you've read this far, it's a safe bet you've completed the image. Or it could be that you were captivated by my amusing writing style. Not!

The most important thing we learned is that if there's a texture you want and it doesn't exist in the Texture Library, you can find a similar texture and modify it for excellent results. We created rust from rock and wood from curtains. And we cleaned up the smoggy exhaust sky and made it look like Montana.

We made good use of DRAW's new bitmap features to tame the unwieldy Texture Fills and their attendant lenses effects. We created grayscale shading masks and applied transparency to create dimension and depth. And we weren't too proud to admit that there are a few features in PAINT that DRAW doesn't possess that could make our illustration swing, or creak, as the case might be.

Variations on a Theme

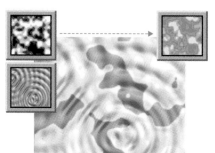

Not to be redundant, but DRAW's Texture Fills cry out to be modified and liberated from their dull and often unimaginative appearances. For starters, we'll modify some of these. Your homework assignment is to discover and modify more of these yourself.

This figure uses two Texture Fills. The first, Patches 5C (Styles Library), was modified (to the right of the red arrow) by altering the colors to a range of ocean hues. A duplicate shape was filled with Rain Drops Soft 2C (Styles Library). Patches was brought to the top and transparency applied, creating the appearance of ripples on water.

This figure began with a shape filled with Rock-Fractal-Eroded 2C (Styles Library) with no modifications. A duplicate shape was created, and a skull and crossbones from the Wing Dings symbols roll-up was centered and Combined, cutting out the skull and crossbones. This shape was filled with a Rock-Speckled-Eroded 2C (Styles Library) fill. Two duplicates of this were created and the outside edges shortened, using the Shape tool, so as not to distort the skull and crossbones. The Brightness setting on one of the duplicate shapes was increased to 20. The Brightness setting on the other was decreased to -20. This created a lighter and darker version of the Texture Fill. The two duplicate shapes were aligned directly under the top layer, with the lighter version moved slightly up to create a highlight edge and the darker version moved slightly down to create a shadow edge. The result is the appearance of a pirate symbol etched in moss-covered rock. I applied the Rain Drops Soft 2C to a rectangle covering the right half of the image and applied transparency. This created a murky and mysterious underwater effect.

I modified the colors of a Mineral Speckled 2C (Styles Library) Texture fill to red and yellow, producing a pretty acceptable image of fire. I made a duplicate shape and filled it with a three-color Radial Fountain Fill, using Pale Yellow, Orange, and Violet, brought it to the top, and applied transparency. I'm sure I did this for a reason, but at the moment the reason escapes me, indicating that it probably was unnecessary.

Using essentially the same fill as for the fire, but altering the Smoothness setting, produced a convincing sunset sky as you can see here. A Firewater Fill (Samples 7 library) produced a rippled ocean surface. I added two wedge shapes on either side, added nodes, and used the Shape tool to ripple the outlines. I filled the two wedge shapes with a darker version of Firewater. The setting sun is a radial-filled sphere, using Deep Yellow to Pale Yellow. The ship silhouette is from the Transportation Symbols Library.

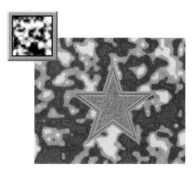

Patches 5C makes a dandy camouflage cloth pattern when the colors are modified to olives, browns, and tans. I added a red and gold star, selected the whole group, converted to bitmap, and added a small amount of noise.

Satellite Photography (Styles) can make a plausible planet Earth, as shown here. I filled a square with the fill unchanged, added a circle with a black-and-white radial fill to which I applied transparency to add spherical shading, selected the square and shading circle, and converted both to bitmap. I applied an effect by choosing 3D Effects, Map To Object, then Spherical to distort the planet. I masked off the right side to show off the new planet, while leaving the left side of the square to show the fill.

Creating the Beautiful Lady Image

My intent in writing this chapter is not to teach you how to make the photo montage that won the Grand Prize in the People, Plants and Animals category at the 1997, World Design Contest. Instead, I want to share with you the several techniques that were used in the creation of the image. In fact, the original purpose of this image was to see if I could re-create a technique I had seen demonstrated in Adobe Photoshop—that of the text contoured to the face of the woman in the picture. I discovered that while it couldn't be done in **PHOTO-PAINT 7** (it can be done in **PHOTO-PAINT 8**) using the same technique used in Photoshop, I could come up with a workaround that did the same thing. After spending all of that time figuring out a way to create the effect, I felt I needed to put it to use. Thus began the image called Beautiful Lady.

NOTE

This chapter is for PHOTO-PAINT 7 and 8.

Here is the original photograph that was used for the centerpiece of the work. Now, let's set the record straight. I didn't select this woman because her haunting eyes represent the soul of the woman searching for her—you get the idea. I chose her because she had a wider-than-usual face, which was perfect for the effect I was trying to accomplish.

STEP

1 Crop the photograph and begin the work of contouring the text (or any other object, for that matter) to her face. The text chosen is from an old nursery rhyme: "Sugar and spice and everything nice, that's what little girls are made of." (By the way, my choice of text was the one thing that the Duke of DRAW didn't like. When I showed him the finished work, he said, "You've got a real winner here, but change the text—it's politically incorrect." I guess that's one of the benefits of being a Texan: nobody expects a Texan to be politically correct.)

STEP

2

Back to the image. The next step is to create the text with the Text tool and use the cut-and-paste features of the clipboard to duplicate the text again and again. Using the Freehand mask tool, make a rough outline of her face; with the text selected, choose the Crop to Mask (Clip Object to Mask in PHOTO-PAINT 7) command in the Object menu to clip the text to the mask marquee boundaries, as shown.

> ### N O T E
>
> In PHOTO-PAINT 8, the Clip Object to Mask command in the Object menu has been renamed Crop to Mask, to avoid confusion with the new Clip Mask commands.

STEP

3

The problem now is that the text is flat—if it were really on her face, it would follow the contours of her face. The method used in Photoshop is to create a contour displacement map that displaces the object as a function of the color value of the map. Well, this presents a problem in PHOTO-PAINT 7, since the Displacement filter cannot be applied to an object. So, use the Mesh Warp filter. While this filter works great for producing that kind of distortion, it presents another problem: the filter can see only the selected object, which means if I select the text to distort it, I cannot see the face. If I can't see the face, then I can't see which parts are supposed to go up and which should go down. Fortunately, I came up with a solution. Create an object out of the masked area (her face), and then duplicate

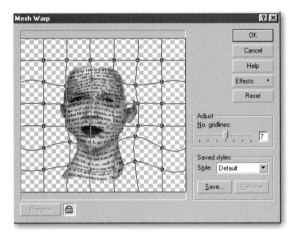

the text. Next, hide the background and the original text object, leaving only the object containing the duplicate face and text visible. Combine these two objects together and apply the Mesh Warp filter (in the 3D Effects option of the Effects menu) to distort the text, as shown. Because the objects are combined, the filter distorts both the face and the text. In applying the filter, it is necessary to focus on the way the text is being distorted and not worry about what it is doing to the other object (in this case, the woman's face).

When satisfied with the resulting displacement of the text, delete the object that was just distorted (trust me). Next, make the original text and background visible, select the original text object, and select Repeat last Effect (CTRL+F). The last effect applied was the Mesh Warp, so it is reapplied to the text, causing the text to be distorted but not the face. The background is removed by selecting the face, inverting the mask, and deleting it.

ADDING A PHOTO

STEP 4

With the woman's face and text in place, we next add an old photograph as part of a series of images that would represent the woman's heritage. I found the type of image I wanted in the PHOTO-PAINT 7 Plus CD. The subject matter was perfect, but the photo was, among other things, too dark. The first corrective step is to make the photograph lighter so the details can be seen. This is done by applying the Gamma filter at a setting of 2.0. The next step is to apply a light brown tint using the Rectangle Shape tool with the color Brown and the Transparency set to 70 percent for the look of an old photograph. I chose not to use a Duotone, since it was going to be in an RGB image and tint was easier to apply with the Edit Fill command. The before and after is shown here.

STEP

5

Next, we need to create a rectangle-shaped object that is large enough to serve as a border for the photograph when placed behind it. I didn't use white, because I knew the photograph would get lost on the white background, so instead I chose an off-gray. Select the Rectangle Shape tool (F6), with Render to Object enabled, to create a long, narrow rectangle. We want to apply a ripple to this shape. To keep the tops from being clipped by the filter, the Lock Transparency checkbox in the Objects Docker window must not be checked (in PHOTO-PAINT 7, the object in the Objects Roll-Up must be in Layer mode). With the rectangle object selected, apply the Ripple filter (located in the 2D Effects category of the Effects menu) at a very low Amplitude setting of 2 and a Period of 5. In PHOTO-PAINT 8, use a Direct angle of 90 degrees; in PHOTO-PAINT 7, select the Vertical button. The resulting red wavy shape (looking a lot like a red lasagna noodle) is shown. This shape is the source of the mask we will use to remove the edge of the photograph's border shape.

STEP

6

With the rippled object selected, click the Create Mask button in the Toolbar (if using PHOTO-PAINT 7, make sure the Preserve Image button is enabled, to prevent the red shape from becoming one with the rectangle). Using the Mask Transform tool, we need to move our newly created mask up to the top edge of the photo border so just the tops of the waves touch the edge. Since only the area inside the mask can be acted upon, we must invert the mask (CTRL+I).

7

In the Objects Docker window, make sure the rectangle object is selected (in PHOTO-PAINT 7, set the Objects Roll-Up to Single mode and select the rectangle object). We could erase the border edge with the Eraser tool, but the shape of the border would remain the same. To change the actual shape of the border, we need to use the Object Transparency Brush tool in the Toolbox. (In PHOTO-PAINT 8, it is located in the Transparency Tools flyout, while in PHOTO-PAINT 7 it can be found in the Object Picker flyout; in PHOTO-PAINT 9, it will probably be located in the Tomb of the Unknown Brush—sigh.) With the tool selected, open the Tool Settings Roll-Up (CTRL+F8) and change the Opacity slider to 0. With this setting, anywhere you click and drag the Transparency Brush will have its opacity changed to 0, meaning it will be completely transparent. In the image on the next page, the top edge has already been modified and the mask (using the Mask Transform tool) has been moved to the bottom of the border shape.

8

The left edge of the border shape is modified by inverting the mask, then selecting the mask with the Mask Transform tool. From the Tool Settings Roll-Up, click on the Rotate tab and rotate the mask 90 degrees in either direction, or you can click on the mask until the Rotate handles appear and click and drag one of the corner handles until it reads 90 degrees in the status bar. Then move it to the edge. (The reason I invert the mask is just a habit, because it makes it more manageable.) Once the border is finished, the photo is centered on top of it and the two objects are combined.

To make it look more like a real photograph, add a date stamp by selecting the Text tool from the Toolbox, changing the size to make it small enough to fit the border, and creating a date. Then select the text object with the Object Picker tool and choose Rotate >90 degrees Clockwise from the Object menu. (I kept the date as a separate object, but it could have been combined.)

ADDING THE "BEAUTIFUL LADY" FRAME

STEP

9

Next, I wanted to add something that would both frame the young woman's face and connect the images thematically. In a Corel CD photo collection, I found a cover to sheet music from the turn of the century that seemed perfect. It is shown here. I have a lot of old sheet music lying around the house, and there were a few I could have scanned in; however, copyrights, even from the turn of the century, can reach out and get you, so I didn't take any chances.

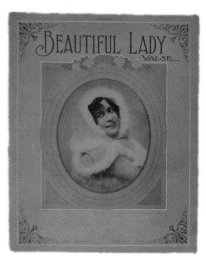

NOTE

If you have any questions about how serious the copyright issues can become, then you haven't been following the World Design Contest very long. Gary's wife, Mary Carter, has written an award-winning book on the subject, entitled *The Wild Women of the Planet Latex*. No, that's not right. Its title is *Electronic Highway Robbery* (Peachpit Press, 1995), and anyone working in this field of digital image manipulation should own a copy. This isn't a blatant plug for the book because Gary's wife wrote it. It is a blatant plug because it is a book that may save you from financial disaster. End of public service message. Back to the sheet music.

STEP

10

The sheet music is placed directly behind the woman's face so the title can be easily read. The photo with border is also placed behind the face but on top of the sheet music. Using the Transparency Brush tool, I removed a portion of the photograph so it would blend into the image. In PHOTO-PAINT 8 (I didn't have it when I made the image), I would have used a Clip Mask so that the portions of the photo I removed would not be permanent. Once satisfied with the photograph, I used the Drop Shadow command in the Object menu to create a simple drop shadow behind the photo, as shown.

STEP

11

After staring at the image for some time, I decided that I wanted to add something on the right side. However, there was no more room. No problem. I selected the Paper Size command in the Image menu and, after unchecking Maintain Aspect Ratio in the dialog box, I added a few inches to the right side of the image. Try that trick with real canvas and you will see why I love electronic art.

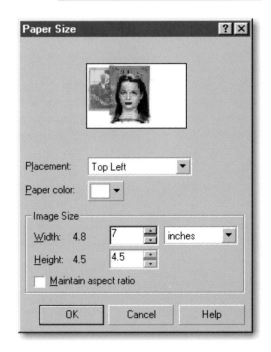

Two more images are next added. The baby picture is also a grayscale that is tinted just as the photograph of the elderly lady was. To improve the blending, use the Object Transparency tool to make the left edge of the photo slightly more transparent than the original transparency of the right edge. I then selected an image of a woman from the Corel CD collection called Cover Girls. I selected the woman from the original background with the Freehand mask tool, made her into an object, and dragged her (kicking and screaming) into the final image shown at the beginning of the chapter. (Did you realize that photo-editing is the only discipline in which you can treat a woman as an object and still be politically correct?)

Variations on a Theme

SAME SONG, DIFFERENT LYRICS

Quite a bit of the time it took me to make this jewel was spent making versions that I later scrapped, returning to the starting point. I have included some of the versions that for one reason or another I rejected. In other words, this is similar to the out-takes that appear at the end of the TV show *Home Improvement*.

In the image shown here, I selected a photo of a statue and used a Lightness Merge Mode (more on Merge Modes later in this chapter), which merges the existing object's colors and combines them with the lightness value of the pixels below it. While I liked the effect, I wanted to add something else.

ADDING A FLAPPER

Next, I added another woman from a magazine cover dated from the mid-1920s. I liked the color she added and began to think the statue was out of place. After all, I was trying to show the woman's heritage and not make a mural of the entire history of womankind. So, back to the drawing board.

REPLACING STATUES WITH COWGIRLS

I found the western lady from yet another magazine cover in the Corel CD. I selected her and used her to replace the statue image. At this point, I was quite happy with the montage as it was, but after a few weeks of opening it and looking at it, I decided that I wanted to make it not so darn square.

The almost-final version is similar to the piece that won, and truth be known, I almost submitted it. The only major difference between it and the final is the amount of transparency around the young woman's hair. In this version, her hair on the right side is nearly transparent and the background figures just kind of blend into one another. Since I couldn't change the transparency of an object once changed in PHOTO-PAINT 7, I made a copy of her and placed it on top, which resulted in the image shown at the beginning of the chapter.

TIP

It is a good idea to use the Save As command to maintain an original baseline image to which you can return (time and time again) when doing this kind of creative work.

You can do some of the wildest and most creative things with the Merge Modes in PHOTO-PAINT. To begin with, we need to create a background to demonstrate the effect of the merge mode. In this image, I have placed the young woman against a background that was created using the Neon Spandex Texture fill from the Samples 7 library. I then applied a Glass Block filter (from the Artistic filter option in the Effects menu) to complete it.

Chewy Cactus Cookies

With each release of CorelDRAW, it becomes easier to create objects in **DRAW** and move and use them in **PAINT** or the other way around— this is the synergy of the Corel suite of products. Synergy is defined as "the interaction of two or more forces so that their combined effect is greater than the sum of their individual effects." In this chapter, you will learn and practice some techniques that combine the strengths of **DRAW** and **PAINT** synergistically to produce results that you may not have believed possible. At the very least, I hope you will be impressed.

Corel has made the pathway between **DRAW** and **PAINT** large and easy enough so there is no longer any excuse for not moving actively between Corel applications. If you have been doing it all in **DRAW** and putting off using **PHOTO-PAINT** (much like the Duke of **DRAW** used to do), then this chapter is for you. All of the techniques demonstrated use built-in **PAINT** commands, so it does not require prior knowledge of **PHOTO-PAINT**.

Many of the rules you may have learned about moving images between applications using previous versions of the CorelDRAW suite have changed. This is good news, since **PHOTO-PAINT 7** makes the movement of images between applications very simple. It is even easier to get objects from CorelDRAW to **PHOTO-PAINT 8** using the clipboard, as we will soon see. To learn about this, we are going to create a mock ad for a cookie that sounds like something a Texan would eat: a chewy cactus cookie.

CREATING THE CIRCLE OF TEXT

To create our cookie ad, we start in DRAW. Follow the step below to first create the circle of text.

STEP

1 Select the Text tool and type **CIRCLE C RANCH CHEWY CACTUS COOKIES**. Change the font to Arial Black at 24 points. Select the Ellipse tool in the Toolbox and, while holding the CTRL key, click and drag a circle that is approximately three inches in diameter. Marquee-select both the circle and the text. From the Text menu, choose Fit Text to Path... and when the dialog box opens, click the Apply button. Press TAB until the control ellipse (circle) is selected, as indicated on the status bar, and then press DELETE. Change the color of the text to Blue by clicking on that color in the onscreen palette. The resulting image is shown. If you are using PHOTO-PAINT 8, select the image and copy it to the clipboard (then continue with step 4). If you have PHOTO-PAINT 7, save the file and name it CIRCLE C.CDR (then continue with step 2). Close CorelDRAW.

Next, we want to convert the vector drawing we just made in DRAW to a bitmap image. When we bring an object from CorelDRAW to PHOTO-PAINT (or any other bitmap application), it is necessary to convert the vector (or line) format into bitmap (or paint) format. This process is called rasterization. It is the rasterization control settings that determine how faithfully the image we import into Corel PHOTO-PAINT is reproduced. The following two steps can be done using either PHOTO-PAINT 7 or 8; however, if you are using PHOTO-PAINT 8, skip them and go directly to step 4.

STEP

2

Launch PHOTO-PAINT. From the File menu, select Open and choose the CIRCLE C.CDR file. When you open the DRAW file, you will be given many choices on how you want to rasterize the image. This action opens the Import Into Bitmap dialog box. Change the Color setting to 16 Million Colors, the Resolution to 200 DPI, and the Anti-aliasing to Super-sampling. Click the OK button. Next, we want to mask the text using the Color Mask. From the Mask menu, choose Color Mask. When the dialog box opens, click the Reset button if there are previous settings. Since the default setting is White, click the checkbox on the first color in the color list (it is indicated with an arrow in the illustration). Click OK.

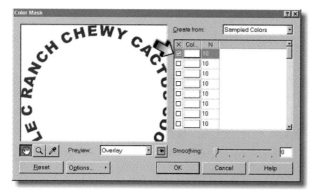

STEP

3

The Color Mask automatically selected the background, so click the Invert Mask button on the Toolbar or press CTRL+I to select the text. With the Preserve Image button off, click the Create Object (from mask) button in the Toolbar. We now have the text as an object, but it fills the image to the very edge. We need to give it some breathing room. So, from the Image menu, select Paper Size. When the dialog box opens, change the Width setting in the Image Size section to four inches and click OK. Skip to step 5.

STEP

4

PAINT 8 Only: Create a new 24-bit color image that is 4 × 4 inches at 150 dpi. Paste the contents of the clipboard (CTRL+V) as an object into the image. Now, wasn't that a whole lot easier? This procedure works with clipboard objects from either CorelDRAW 7 or 8.

5 In the Objects Docker window, enable Lock Transparency (in the Objects Roll-Up in PHOTO-PAINT 7, select the Single button) and select the background. With the right mouse button, click on the color Powder Blue in the onscreen palette (this action changes the Fill color to the Uniform Color of blue). How do you know which one is Powder Blue? With PHOTO-PAINT 8, place the cursor on a color and see the name in the status bar below. If you are using the default onscreen palette in PHOTO-PAINT 7, Powder Blue is directly below Brown. From the Edit menu, choose Fill and click the OK button.

6 In the Objects dialog box, select the text. From the Edit menu, choose Fill. When the Edit Fill and Transparency dialog box opens, choose the Fountain Fill button and click the Edit button. When the Fountain Fill dialog box opens, change the settings until they match the settings in the illustration. The From color is Blue and the To color is Black. Click OK when you are done. The result should look like the next illustration shown.

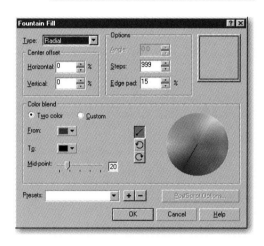

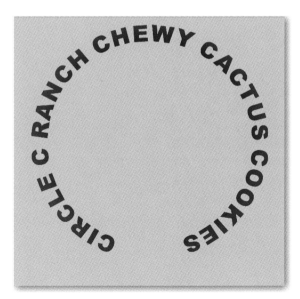

STEP

7   With the object (text) still selected, click the Create Mask button (in PHOTO-PAINT 7, enable the Preserve Image button and click the Create Mask button). Invert the mask (CTRL+I). In the Objects Docker window, uncheck Lock Transparency (in the Objects Roll-Up in PHOTO-PAINT 7, click the Layer button). From the Effects menu, choose 3D Effects (Fancy in PHOTO-PAINT 7) and select The Boss filter. Change the Style setting to Wet and then move the Width setting to 3. Click the OK button. In the Objects Docker window, select the background (in PHOTO-PAINT 7, click the Single button in the Objects Roll-Up and then select the background). From the Edit menu, select Clear, resulting in this image.

STEP

8   From the Edit menu, select Fill. Click the Fountain Fill button. From the Fountain Fill dialog box, in the Presets section, choose Circular— Orange 01. Change the Horizontal and Vertical settings to 0 and the number of Steps to 999. Click OK once to select the fountain fill and OK again to apply it. From the Effects menu, select Noise and then Add Noise. Click the Reset button and click OK. What a mess, right? From the Effects menu, choose Blur and then Radial Blur. Change the settings to an Amount of 40, select Best, and set the mode to Zoom. Click OK. Be advised that this is going to take a little while. I have a very fast machine, and it took almost a minute to process. The result is shown here.

9

Let's clean our text a little. In the Objects Docker window (the Objects Roll-Up in PHOTO-PAINT 7), select the text and deselect the background. From the Object menu, choose Feather. Change the Width to 2 and the Edges to Curved. Click OK. From the Object menu, choose Drop Shadow and change the settings to add a soft drop shadow. For PHOTO-PAINT 8 users, choose the Flat setting, not Perspective. In my example, I used an Opacity setting of 55 and an Average Feather Width of 18. Almost any setting will work, as long as it is soft.

MAKING COOKIES

Now that we've created the circle of text, we're going to add cookies to our cookie ad. While we could have used a photograph of cookies, let's modify one of the images in the DRAW clipart collection.

1

From the File menu, select Open and locate the file on the Corel 7 CD-ROM Disk No. 3 \CLIPART\FOOD\DESSERTS\CCOOKIES .CDR. Click OK. When the Import dialog box opens, change the Resolution to 75 dpi. Click OK. From the Mask menu, open the Color Mask and click OK. The original cookie image is shown here. Invert the mask (CTRL+I). In the Effects menu, choose Artistic and select Canvas. Load the Stucco.pcx file and change the Emboss setting to 25. The result is shown in the next illustration.

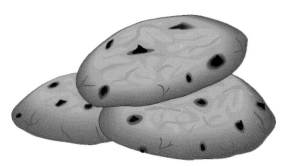

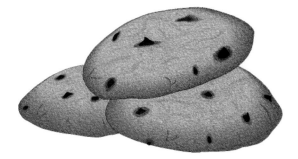

STEP

2

Select Create (Object) from Mask from the Object menu. Click and hold the right mouse button on the cookies and drag it into the original Circle C image. When the menu appears, select Copy here. Grab the handles on the edge of the cookie object and resize them to fit. In my example, I also adjusted the perspective of the cookies, which is done in the perspective transform mode (click on the object until the handles are circles), using the handle on the lower left to make the bottom of the image wider. The result is shown. From the Object menu, choose Feather. Change the Width to 2 and the Edges to Curved. Click OK.

STEP

3

They wouldn't be cactus cookies without the cactus spines, so locate the Line tool in the Toolbox and double-click on it to open the Tool Settings Roll-Up. Change the settings to match those shown in the illustration. Set the Paint to Black. To apply the spines, click on the cookie where the spine is to start and then place the cursor at the point where you want the spine to end. Double-click the mouse to complete the line—and you have a genuine cactus spine. Remember that we set the Line tool to Render to object, so each spine is an object. If you add more than eight to ten spines, you may want to select them in the Objects dialog box, then from the Object menu select Combine and then Combine Objects Together to combine them (alternatively, you can press CTRL+ALT+DNARROW in PHOTO-PAINT 8 and CTRL+SHIFT+L in PHOTO-PAINT 7).

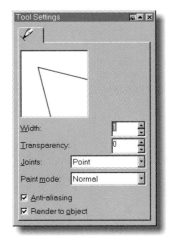

When you have finished adding the spines, open the Objects Roll-Up (CTRL+F7) and select all of the spines, the cookie, and its shadow. From the Object menu, select Combine and then Combine Objects Together. Select the cookies and its spines and apply a drop shadow, using the same settings from step 8 of the "Creating the Circle of Text" section. The result is shown.

4 Add the slogan by choosing the Text tool and typing **The Only Cookie That BITES BACK**. Change the font to Comic Sans MS at a size of 14 points, and make the text bold and centered. Click on the Dark Brown color in the onscreen palette to change the color of the text. Click on the Object Picker tool in the Toolbox to make the text into an object. Apply a Drop Shadow (from the Object menu) to the slogan text. In my example, because the text is small I reduced the Offset of the Drop Shadow to .025 inches, increased the Opacity to 75, and reduced the Feather to 6. The finished product is shown.

Variations on a Theme

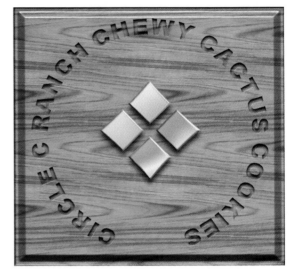

If the Cactus Cookie company became very successful, it would move away from such garish logos and have a sophisticated looking sign on the wall. To do this, take the same circle of text and apply a cutout effect to it. The cutout effect is demonstrated in Chapter 15. Then you could add a gold ornament created using the technique shown in Chapter 14 using a character from the Zaph Dingbats. Next, you could mask the entire image and then reduce the mask by ten pixels (from the Mask menu) before applying The Boss filter to it. You end up with the image shown.

One of the really fun things to do with PAINT and DRAW is to combine clipart with real photography. In the image shown, the photograph of the model is first posterized to reduce the number of colors. You can't reduce it too much, or it will look like the woman has leprosy. Next, select her image with a mask tool and place her as an object on the background of another image. The background and the thought balloon are from the CorelDRAW clipart collection. Using the method described above, you can place and resize the clipart as objects. After everything is in place, combine all the elements with the background. The Halftone filter, located in the Artistic option of the Effects menu, is then applied to the entire image. The last thing added is the caption. If you apply the halftone to the caption text in the balloon, the filter makes it blurry.

There is one more thing I want to show you on the text-in-a-circle thing. If you apply a bitmap fill to something that is circular, like the text, you should know that the bitmap fill in PHOTO-PAINT 7 only goes one way and has a tendency to look unnatural, as shown in this image. It still works, but it is better to use a bitmap fill that doesn't have strong vertical or horizontal elements in it.

Many times it is easy to fall into a "PAINT only" mentality when looking for ways to produce an image. In this variation of the cutout/import technique shown for the Cactus Cookie Company, I have created the word TEXAS in DRAW. This allowed me to make the first letter twice as large as the other and also move the remaining letters along the baseline. The secret to making this image is doing the cutout stars and cutout letters separately. That is, I made the cutout for TEXAS first, flattened it to the background and then made the stars (in PAINT) and created cutouts out of them. I could not have done any of this in PAINT. Before my partner in crime, Gary, begins to chuckle, I am quick to remind the reader and Gary that the cutout effect and all of the other shaded effects couldn't have been done in DRAW.

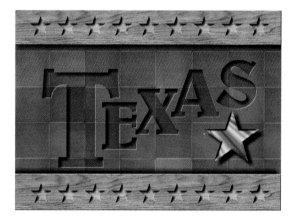

CHAPTER 7

A Logo to Cure an Identity Crisis

When I'm not supplementing my income writing books, I do graphic design. One of the more frequent projects I am asked to do is create an identity program, a fancy term meaning a logo design and stationery application. Good logos, like any good design, rarely appear magically, nor do they come easily, but rather are the end result of a lengthy process of exploration, trial, and error. There is no secret step-by-step process that I know of that explains how to come up with a good design. What works best for me is quantity. I try to crank out as many designs as time and budget allow, often as many as 50 designs. Frequently one idea that appears weak will lead to a better idea, which in turn can lead to a better idea and so on. I also let my right brain—the non-verbal creative half of the brain—work silently, in the background. Often a good idea will come to me in the shower, on the freeway, or when I'm out for a walk. This is the result of the right brain at work and is often the winning solution. When I have enough designs, I cull the number down to the best five to ten designs, clean them up, and present them to the client.

I've got a feeling that my career as a graphic designer is about to take off, big time! I mean, how can it miss with some of the swell designs in this book? To that end, it's become apparent that I'm going to need a logo and some slick corporate identity. And, funnily enough, this chapter is going to be about logos. Coincidence? You decide.

I will use my initials (GWP) for the name of my new company, GWP Design. Where this takes us is anybody's guess, but we'll give DRAW 7 a good workout, and we'll try out a couple of new Distortion effects from DRAW 8 as well.

BEGIN WITH A FLIP FLOP

A font we're all intimately familiar with is Avant Garde, designed in the 1960s by Herb Lubalin. It's the default font in CorelDRAW. I like the round quality of the letters as you see in Figure 7-1. If we flop the lowercase g (click on the Mirror Horizontal icon on the Property Bar), it could make a credible lowercase p. (The original letters are shown in black.) If you can create a unique letterform, such as the flopped g, you're ahead of the game.

Figure 7-1: Three Avant Garde letters will be modified to make a logo

STEP

1

Set the size of the font to 105 points. Convert the letters to curves (CTRL+Q), and from the Arrange menu select Break Apart. Figure 7-2 reveals that when text is converted to curves and broken apart that letters that have an inside shape (such as the g and the p) are also broken into separate objects.

Figure 7-2: The text is converted to curves and broken apart

Select the two elements from the g and Combine them. (CTRL+L) You can delete the p objects.

STEP

Make a duplicate of the g and click on the Mirror Horizontal button on the Property Bar to flop the g. Position the letters together as shown in Figure 7-3, select them, and click the Weld button on the Property Bar, making one continuous outlined object as shown in Figure 7-4.

Figure 7-3: The two elements for the g are re-combined, a duplicate g created and flopped, and the letters moved closer together

Figure 7-4: The letter shapes are Welded into one shape

STEP

Select the welded object and apply a Contour (Effects-Contour) with these settings: Outside, Offset: 0.02", Steps: 2. Click Apply. This produces two increasingly larger outlines as shown in Figure 7-5.

Figure 7-5: A 2-Step Contour effect is applied

STEP

Select the Contour group and from the Arrange menu select Separate. In DRAW 7 you will also need to Ungroup the three outline elements.

6

Select the outer outline and apply a Brick Red fill. Select the center outline and apply a White fill. Finally select the original outline and apply a Khaki fill. Select all three shapes and set the outline to none. Create and position the word design as shown in Figure 7-6, in 7-point, Compacta Lt BT with 430 percent Character Spacing.

Figure 7-6: The three Contour shapes are separated and filled with color and the word design is added

N O T E

There are two ways to add character spacing (the distance between the letters). The first is to select the text with the Shape Tool and drag the right arrow to the right. This method is intuitive but inexact. The second method uses the Format Text (CTRL+T) option. Select the Spacing tab and key in the amount of character space desired.

ATTRACTIVE OPPOSITES

An approach that often works well for me is playing a heavy shape against a thin and elegant shape, as you will witness in this next logo exploration. In this case I've pitted Gill Sans Ultra Bold, a very rugged, heavy font, against Flemish Script, an attractive slender script font.

1

Set GP in 130-point Gill Sans Ultra Bold. Use the Shape Tool to select the letter P and move it a little closer to the P as shown in Figure 7-7.

Figure 7-7: GP is created using an ultra bold font

2

Create a script W in 130-point Flemish Script and position it over the GP as shown in Figure 7-8.

Figure 7-8: A thin and elegant W is created with a formal script font

3

Add the word DESIGN, as shown in Figure 7-9, using 18-point HandelGothic BT with 385 percent character spacing.

Figure 7-9: The word DESIGN is added using an extended sans serif font

4

Select the GP, W, and DESIGN and place a copy (CTRL+C) of the three elements in the Clipboard. With the three elements still selected, click on the Weld icon on the Property Bar (or Arrange-Weld) to make one continuous shape. Fill the welded shape 30 percent gray. Move the shape down and left one point in each direction. Paste (CTRL+V) the elements from the Clipboard back on top as seen in Figure 7-10.

Figure 7-10: The type elements are duplicated, filled gray, and used to create a drop shadow

5

Draw a white rectangle, no outline, around the gray drop shadow element leaving about 1/8 inch all around. Select the white rectangle and the gray drop shadow and Convert To Bitmap, 256 Shades of Gray, 200 dpi Resolution and Super Sampling. Select the grayscale bitmap and apply a Gaussian Blur (Bitmaps-Blur). In DRAW 7, set the Blur radius to 10, in DRAW 8, 3–5 is adequate. Finally, select the script W and fill it White. You can see the final results in Figure 7-11.

The gray drop shadow also helps us see the portions of the White W that would not otherwise be visible. In addition, it adds a nice dimensional quality to the logo.

Figure 7-11: The drop shadow is converted to a bitmap, blurred, and the script W filled White

SPLIT PERSONALITY

A good logo should reflect the nature of the company it is created to represent. As the company in this case is myself, and as I am often characterized as a "cracked egg" it seemed fitting to create this next logo candidate.

1

Create GP using 130-point Gill Sans Ultra Bold. Draw a tall slender rectangle as shown in Figure 7-12. Click twice to toggle Rotate-Skew mode and drag the rotation bulls-eye to the base of the rectangle. Rotate the rectangle by entering 18 in the Angle of Rotation text entry window on the Property Bar and hit the ENTER key.

Figure 7-12: GP is created using a very bold font. A slim rectangle is added and rotated

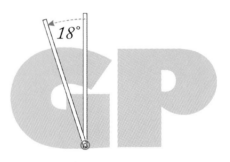

2

Select the rotated rectangle and make a duplicate (+ key). Click the Mirror Horizontal button on the Property Bar to flop the duplicate. Hit CTRL-R (as in Repeat) twice to make two more copies. Position as shown in Figure 7-13. Rotate the third rectangle a little so it dissects the top and bottom of the P as indicated by the yellow colored rectangle.

Figure 7-13: The rotated rectangle is duplicated and flopped producing a W

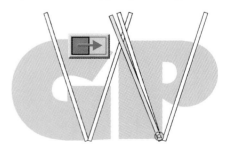

STEP

3

Use the Shape Tool to shorten two of the rectangles as indicated in Figure 7-14. You'll have to Convert the rectangles to Curves (CTRL+Q) first.

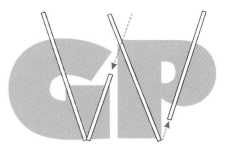

Figure 7-14: Two of the rectangles are shortened so as not to overlap the letters

STEP

4

Select the four rectangles and Weld them (Arrange-Weld). Select the welded shape and then the GP and click the Trim button (shown in inset). Delete the welded rectangles. The results should now look like Figure 7-15.

Figure 7-15: The rectangles are Welded into one shape and used to Trim a W from the GP

STEP

5

Place a copy of the design in the clipboard. Fill the text 30 percent gray. Repeat Step 5 from the last logo to create a Gaussian-Blurred bitmap drop shadow. Paste a copy on top, position it up and left, two points in each direction. With the copy still selected, break the elements apart (CTRL+K or Arrange-Break Apart). Select the individual elements and color them as shown in Figure 7-16. Add the word design in 10-point Rage Italic LET with 375 percent character spacing.

The four rectangles sliced out a subtle W in the GP. This may not be recognized at first to persons seeing the logo for the first time, but it is an interesting conversation starter.

Figure 7-16: A shadow is created, the word design added, and the shape broken apart and the individual objects are colored

Often I like to try something "a little more grand." Corel's new Extrude-Bevel function used in partnership with an elegant Marble fill makes this a piece of cake—marble cake, as you'll see in this next example.

STEP

1

Draw a rectangle 3 1/2 inches wide by 2 inches tall. Create and center within the rectangle the letters GP in Arial XBlk BT to 140 points. Add the word DESIGN in 18-point HandelGothic character-spaced to 385 percent. Add a script W in 130-point Flemish Script and apply a gold type fountain fill to the W and word DESIGN as shown in Figure 7-17. (Refer to Chapter 14 for detailed information about creating gold and chrome fountain fills). Copy the W and word DESIGN to the clipboard. Select the W and DESIGN and apply a 2-point black outline. Paste the copy back on top to create a black outline around the delicate script letters.

Figure 7-17: GP set in very bold type contrasts with an elegant script W, both are centered inside of a rectangle and the word DESIGN is added

STEP

2

Group and set the W's and DESIGN's aside for the moment. Apply a red fill to the rectangle and GP and add a black outline. Select the rectangle and open the Extrude roll-up menu (Effects-Extrude). Click on the Bevel tab and select these options: Use Bevel, Show Bevel Only. Change the Bevel Depth: to .06 inches. Click Apply. Select the GP and repeat the process. Figure 7-18 shows the results of the Extrude-Bevel operation.

Figure 7-18: Bevels are applied to the rectangle and GP in separate operations

IN A PERFECT WORLD

A feature (read bug) in DRAW 7 causes a certain instability in the Bevel Depth text entry window. If you enter the correct amount and then it resets itself to .5, try this. Re-enter the correct figure, .06 inches, then click inside the Bevel Angle text entry box. If the .06 did not reset to the default, you should be OK.

STEP

3

Select the rectangle and click on the Lighting Options tab (the lightbulb). Apply two light sources using the position and intensity settings shown on the left inset in Figure 7-19. Next, select the GP and apply two light sources using the position and intensity settings shown in the inset on the lower right.

Figure 7-19: Lighting effects are applied to the rectangle and GP in separate operations

Intensity:
1=80 2=100

Intensity:
1=75 2=100

STEP

4

Select the rectangle and open the Pattern Fill dialog box. (The checkerboard icon inside the Fill Tool flyout). Click to select the Bitmap option and click Load. From the next menu click the down arrow on the Look In window at the top and from the list select the CD-ROM drive that contains Corel CD-ROM disk #3 (the disk needs to be in the drive first, of course!). Explore the drive, find and click on the Tiles folder. From the contents of the Tiles folder open the Marble folder. Select Marble 21 and click Open. Click OK in the next menu. Select the GP and copy the fill (Edit-Copy Properties From...Fill). Your image should now look like Figure 7-20. All the lighting settings now apply to the marble.

Figure 7-20: A marble fill is applied to both the rectangle and GP

STEP

5

Position the W and DESIGN group as shown in Figure 7-21.

This logo will require CMYK printing which can be expensive. For the modest quantities that I will require, however, I can print the logo on my letterheads, envelopes, and business cards using my ink-jet printer for amazingly professional-looking results.

Figure 7-21: The W and DESIGN type are positioned over the marble GP

Life is not a contest to see how sedate we can be, as this next logo illustrates. Introduced in DRAW 7 were several very jolly and fun type fonts from the Letraset collection, including a splendid font called Arriba Arriba LET.

STEP

1

Set GWP in 100-point Arriba Arriba LET as shown in Figure 7-22.

Figure 7-22: GWP is set in a playful font called Arriba Arriba

STEP

2

Make a duplicate of the text, apply an Electric Blue fill, offset it two points down and left and send it to the back as shown in Figure 7-23.

Figure 7-23: A duplicate of the type is used as a blue drop shadow

STEP

3

Select the original text, Convert it to Curves (CTRL+Q) and break it apart (CTRL+K). Re-combine the inside and outside elements for the bottom portion of the P. Using Figure 7-24 (seen on next page) as a guide, fill the broken sections using the following colors: Tropical Pink, Mint Green, and Turquoise. Select the three sections shown with the checkerboard fill and Combine them into one shape. Open the Pattern Fill dialog and from the 2-Color presets select the black and white checkerboard pattern. Click OK.

Finish the logo by adding the word design in 50 point Telegram LET as shown.

This logo has a casual and colorful Southwestern look and feel. You might consider selecting the blue drop shadow, converting it to an RGB bitmap, and adding Gaussian Blur to soften the shadow.

Figure 7-24: The text is broken apart and various bright colors and fill applied

UPWARD SPIRAL

I used to be able to create a spiral by creating a series of concentric circles, breaking each into a 90 degree arc, and then joining every successive arc. The process took forever and I was forever joining the wrong arcs together. What a mess! DRAW 6 introduced the Spiral Tool into the Polygon Tool flyout and made my life a lot easier. DRAW 7 added a new Auto-Close feature that when used with the Spiral Tool creates a pretty cool effect. Here's what I mean.

STEP

1

Select the Spiral Tool from the Polygon Tool flyout menu and change the Revolutions setting to 6. Hold down the CTRL key (to constrain the spiral to concentric rotations) and drag a one-inch spiral. Select the spiral with the Shape Tool and click the Auto-Close button on the Property Bar. Select the spiral and apply a Brick Red fill as shown in Figure 7-25. On the surface this looks like a series of concentric circles.

Figure 7-25: A six-revolution concentric spiral with the Auto-Close option enabled, then filled

STEP

2

Make three duplicate spirals. Overlap each one so that it covers one filled rotation as shown in Figure 7-26. Flop the third and fourth spiral by clicking on the Mirror Horizontal button on the Property Bar. Apply an Olive fill to the two center spirals and a Sea Green fill to the last spiral.

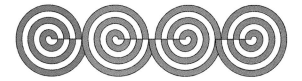

Figure 7-26: Three duplicate spirals are positioned and the last two flopped

3

Create two slim rectangles as shown in red in Figure 7-27. The width of the rectangles should be the exact width of one of the filled loops. Position the first rectangle just above the center of the first spiral so that it covers only the top two loops. Select the rectangle, then the spiral, and click the Trim icon on the Property Bar to remove the section beneath the rectangle. Select the two center spirals and click the Weld button on the Property Bar to make them one unit. Position the second rectangle as shown on the right so that it covers the bottom half of the first loop. Select the rectangle, then the spiral, and click the Trim icon on the Property Bar to remove the portion of loop directly beneath. Select the spiral with the right mouse button and from the flyout menu select Break Apart. Select the small fragment of loop to the left of the rectangle and delete it.

Figure 7-27: Two rectangles are used as cookie cutters to trim off portions of the spirals

4

Move the first rectangle just below where it is now (as shown in Figure 7-28) and shorten the width so that it covers, but does not extend beyond, the three loops. Select the rectangle, then the spiral, and click the Weld icon. Select the second rectangle, then the fourth spiral, and Weld them.

Figure 7-28: The rectangles will be Welded to the spirals

5

Add the word design in 18-point Venetian 301 Dm BT with 650 percent character spacing as shown in Figure 7-29 to complete the logo.

This treatment is quirky and fun, a valid statement about the company. It's also a good demonstration on how to create letters from objects.

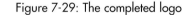

Figure 7-29: The completed logo

FACE TO FACE

We'll revisit Gill Sans Ultra Bold for this next logo. We'll use a W as a cookie cutter to trim out a W in the two Gs. Finally, we'll apply a blue sky texture fill from an unlikely source and add a three-dimensional bevel to the whole thing.

S T E P

1

Create a G in 106-point Gill Sans UltraBold. Flop a duplicate and position it as shown in Figure 7-30. Place a 70-point Gill Sans W as shown. Create a small rectangle 1/2-inch wide by 1/4-inch tall (shown in yellow) and Left Align (CTRL+A) it with the flopped G to form a stylized P.

Figure 7-30: Two bold G's are positioned facing one another and a W and a small rectangle are added

S T E P

2

Select the small rectangle and then the flopped G and Weld the two (Arrange-Weld). Select the G and flopped G and Combine (CTRL+L) them. Select the W, then the combined letters, and click the Trim icon to remove a W shape from the combined letters as shown in Figure 7-31. Use the Freehand Tool to create a small triangle (shown in blue).

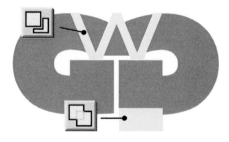

Figure 7-31: The W is used to remove a W portion from the two letters and the rectangle is welded to the flopped G

S T E P

3

When you remove the W and fill the triangle red, your results should match Figure 7-32. Select all the elements and combine them.

Figure 7-32: The object after the rectangle is added and the W trimmed

4 Draw a rectangle (shown in yellow in Figure 7-33) and position it as shown so the top aligns exactly with the top inside section of the G and P. Select all the elements (shown in red) and Combine (CTRL-L) them. Select the rectangle, then the combined shape, and click the Trim icon on the Property Bar. Delete the rectangle. Finally, use the Shape Tool to flatten the top of the shape as shown.

Figure 7-33: A rectangle is used to trim out an even section from the inside of the letters

5 The trimmed out portion should be the same as shown in Figure 7-34. Draw a circle with a .64-inch radius and position it so it is more or less centered on the P as shown. Click on the circle with the Text Tool (the text entry icon will change to indicate Text on a Path mode) and key in **DESIGN**. Switch to the Pick Tool and change the font to Gill Sans and the size to 16 points. Edit the text (CTRL+T) and change the Character Spacing percentage to 60.

Drag two guidelines through the center of the circle. Select the text and path and press CTRL+Q to convert the text to curves. Delete the circle. Click twice on the text to enable Rotate-Skew mode, drag the rotation bull's-eye to the center of the circle, and rotate the type clockwise approximately - 90 degrees as shown.

Figure 7-34: DESIGN is keyed in on a circular path

6 Select the shape and apply an Exhaust Fumes Texture Fill (Samples 6 Texture Fill Library). To achieve the desired blue sky effect, change the background color in the Texture Fill dialog by clicking on the Background colored button and selecting Sky Blue from the palette. Change the Patches color to White as shown in Figure 7-35.

Select the logo and open the Extrude roll-up menu. From the Bevel tab, select Use Bevel and Show Bevel only. Change the Bevel Depth to .05" and click Apply. Add two light sources and modify their settings as shown in the inset.

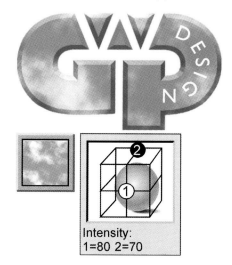

Figure 7-35: A modified texture fill and an Extrude Bevel effect are applied

Intensity:
1=80 2=70

This is a way cool logo. And I could stop here and live with this one for the next month or so. But true to my own teachings, I'm going to wing one more, letting my right brain do the flying.

FLOATING ON AIR

I opened my right brain and found the next logo waiting to escape in a flight of fancy. I also opened DRAW 8 to make use of the fanciful new Interactive Distortion Effects.

STEP

1

Key in GWP in 72-point Arial Black as shown in Figure 7-36. Place a copy (CTRL+C) in the Clipboard.

Figure 7-36: GWP keyed in a medium weight font

STEP

2

With the text selected, choose the Interactive Distortion Tool from the new Interactive Tool fly-out on the main toolbar. Click the Twirl Distortion icon (on the Property Bar) shown in Figure 7-37, and enter a value of 90 degrees. Click the Counterclockwise Rotation icon and hit ENTER to apply the distortion. Figure 7-38 shows the effects of the Twister distortion.

Figure 7-37: A Twister Distortion gives the letters a spin

Figure 7-38: The distorted text

3

Set the distorted text to one side for a moment. Paste a copy of the original text (CTRL+V) on the page, apply a 20 percent Black to 50 percent Black Interactive Linear Fountain Fill as shown in Figure 7-39.

Figure 7-39: A duplicate of the original type is used for a drop shadow

4

Select the gray-filled text and apply a 60-degree, counter-clockwise Twister Distortion as seen in Figure 7-40. Convert the gray shadow to a 256 Shades of Gray Bitmap, and apply a Gaussian Blur with a radius of 5 to soften the shadow.

Select the red distorted type and apply an Interactive Linear Fountain Fill using the following colors: (shown along the bottom of the figure) a.=Red, b.=0 Cyan, 55 Magenta, 45 Yellow and 0 Black, c.=Red, d.=25 Cyan, 98 Magenta, 96 Yellow and 2 Black, e.=0 Cyan, 60 Magenta, 40 Yellow, 0 Black. Drag and modify three solid Red colors onto the path, position them, and then modify the colors as dictated above.

Figure 7-40: An Interactive Linear Fill with several shades of red adds dimension to the letters

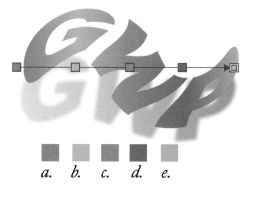

a.   b.   c.   d.   e.

N O T E

To add colors to an Interactive Fountain Fill, simply drag from the Onscreen palette onto the directional fill arrow. These colors can be repositioned by dragging and modified by clicking on the selected color, then clicking on the color on the Property Bar and editing the color.

STEP

5

Create the word DESIGN in 14-point Arial Black. Use the Shape Tool to extend the character spacing to match Figure 7-41. Center the letters between, but not touching, the G and the P. Select the distorted red type and then the DESIGN type. Click the Intersection icon (shown in the inset) on the Property Bar to produce a third object encompassing the area where the two objects overlap. With the intersection still selected, hit SHIFT+PAGEUP to bring the intersection to the top. For the time being, apply a yellow fill.

Figure 7-41: DESIGN is added and an Intersection (shown in yellow) created where the letters on top overlap the letters below

STEP

6

Select the yellow intersection and then the black DESIGN text and click the Trim icon on the Property Bar to remove the section of black text directly under the yellow intersection as shown in Figure 7-42.

Figure 7-42: The Intersection is used to Trim the portion of the letters just below it

7 Select the yellow intersection and change the fill to Black. Apply an Interactive Transparency by clicking on the wine glass icon on the Main Toolbar, then specifying the following, Type: Uniform, Transparency Operation: Subtract, and set the slider amount to 60 percent. Hit ENTER to apply the settings. The final logo is shown in Figure 7-43.

Figure 7-43: The Intersection is filled and Black and Transparency are applied to the Intersection creating the illusion of the word DESIGN passing behind the Red logo

This logo says (to me at any rate) free spirit, which is how I like to think of myself. It possesses a kind of magic floating quality. The right brain has once again worked its magic. And not a moment too soon, as I'm about to run out of space for this chapter.

Variations on a Theme

What I've shown above is literally the tip of the iceberg. When preparing this chapter I created two dozen additional logos, several of which I'll show here, along with a few business card designs. So, which logo is going to be the official logo for GWP Design? If you haven't already guessed, you'll find out in Chapter 8.

I had a photo of myself on my hard disk which I brought into DRAW and Converted to a 1-bit (black or white only) image. I used DRAW's ability to color a 1-bit image by using line and fill colors. The result is a very personal logo which is as timeless as my ponytail.

I used the font American Typewriter to create this low tech, debossed logo. The paper is from the Tiles/Paper folder. This logo is kind of funky and probably does not speak to my technical know-how.

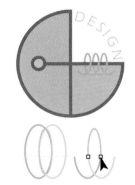

The fun thing about this hand-crafted logo design is the cool spiral that I created for the W. The small inset illustration will give you a rough idea of how I created the spiral.

I used a cutout shapes approach for this next logo as seen on this business card design. For more information on creating cutout shapes, see Chapter 15. The effect is what the French would call *trompe l'oeil* (to fool the eye) as it looks as though the logo is die cut or in relief.

GWP
DESIGN

123 Main Street
Black Point, CA 94945
FAX 415.555.4300
www.ersatz.com

Gary W. Priester
☎ 415.555.1234
gary@ersatz.com

This final illustration shows how spiffy the free spirited twister-effected logo looks on a business card. The true test of any logo, in my opinion, is how well it works on a business card. If the logo looks good on the business card, it will look terrific anywhere. And remember, your business card is your most important piece of advertising.

Gary W. Priester
☎ 415.555.1234
gary@ersatz.com

123 Main Street
Black Point, CA 94945
FAX 415.555.4300
www.ersatz.com

TIP

If you have a color ink-jet printer, you can print your own four-color stationery. Many stationery stores sell matching letterhead, envelope, and 8 1/2 × 11-inch card stock. We print our stationery as we need it, printing quantities of 10 to 20 at a time. When we get tired of the design, we just change it. We print the cards ten to a page and use a metal straight-edge and #11 X-acto knife to carefully trim them out.

Web-Page Magic

Who We Are   What We Do   Contact Us

Elegant Concepts & Design Solutions

Internet capabilities were introduced in DRAW7. DRAW adds to Version 7's capabilities but in ways that are just different enough to be very confusing to the reader. To avoid confusion, I will concentrate on DRAW 7 for this chapter. Since we're going to be concentrating on Web page design in this chapter, we will need to tweak our page layout settings for optimum results. We needn't worry about four-color reproduction, so we can set Color Correction (in the View menu) to None. This will display colors onscreen as they will appear on the Web. From the Color Palette option (in the View menu) select Netscape Navigator. This loads the Netscape palette of 216 nondithering colors. From the Layout menu, select Page Setup. Select the Landscape option and then set the Resolution to 96 dpi. Since 96 dpi (Windows resolution) is not included in the drop-down list of choices, you'll have to key it in. Change the Horizontal resolution to 96 dpi and click the Identical Values options. When you click on the Zoom tool (the magnifying glass icon) and then click on 1:1 on the Property Bar, your screen image will appear the same size as it will in a Web browser. That should do it.

STEP

1

In this chapter, we'll continue solving my identity crisis, as we establish a Web personality for GWP Design. We'll use DRAW's Web capabilities to create a small Web site with a stylish background pattern and an image map using the winner of the logo contest from Chapter 7. I'll cover some basic HTML language and share a few of my tricks for getting around the Web's layout limitations. Ready? Let's get going.

Carpenters have a phrase they repeat over and over: measure twice, cut once. What this has to do with Web design is anybody's guess, but I'd say it means to plan ahead. Figure 8-1 is a simple site map, a Web design term for flowchart. Our site is going to have a Home Page, a Who We Are page, and a What We Do page, which will branch off to Graphic Design and Web Page Design pages. Sounds simple enough, no? But each page is going to provide links to other pages on the site, and every page will have a Contact Us button to enable an e-mail form. Nothing is more annoying than getting into a site with no means of getting out. Bottom line: it's easier to visualize and organize the flow for your site with a site map.

Figure 8-1: A site map makes it easier to visualize the Web site

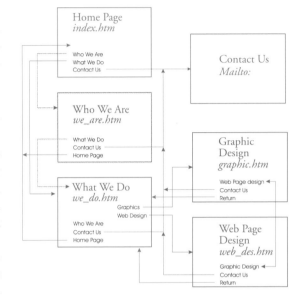

GETTING AHEAD

Among the designs we created in Chapter 7 for the GWP design logo, my favorite is the twisted, that is, Twister-created logo. I like the dimensionality of it and the open airiness of the design. In Figure 8-2, you can see how I've added to the logo to create a simple image map for our site. Image maps are graphic images with designated hot spots, which when clicked will link to other images, pages, sounds, and so forth. DRAW 7 and 8 can create what is known as Client Side Image Maps, which are supported by most recent browsers, Netscape Navigator and Microsoft Internet Explorer being the two most popular. When a visitor's cursor passes over one of these hot spots, the cursor turns into a hand, indicating that something will happen if the visitor clicks here.

Figure 8-2: The winning logo is incorporated into an image map

My personal design philosophy regarding Web page design is: less is more. Sites that have dozens of images and a riot of animations, borders, and buttons are just an impediment to the visitor. So the only element on our home page is the image map/logo and a background design. From here the visitor can visit the Who We Are and What We Do pages as well as bring up a self-addressed e-mail form when he or she clicks on Contact Us.

NOTE

The Netscape Navigator palette of nondithering colors are pure colors that will display solid—with no distracting patterns (dithering)—on both Macintosh and Windows computers capable of displaying 256 (or more) colors. I recommend using these colors for text or solid areas, since they will display cleaner and be easier to view or read. It is necessary to use one of these non-dithering colors if you want a background color to be completely transparent, otherwise the transparency will be spotty and distracting.

In a moment I'll explain how to make the image into an image map, but first I think the site needs texture. We'll accomplish this by creating a repeating GWP pattern, or tile as it's sometimes referred to. I could create a screen-sized image with my repeating background pattern, but that would take a long time to load, and by the time it did load, my visitor with the MTV attention span would be off to other sites. Fortunately, there's an easier way. If you've ever created a repeating pattern in DRAW, then you're already familiar with the technique. Figure 8-3 shows three GWP's equally spaced. The surrounding rectangle represents the tile's border. Note that the rectangle cuts through the middle of both W's. We have one complete GWP and two halves. When the image tiles, the two halves will come together, creating a repeating pattern of offset logos. To preview how the image is going to look when it tiles, PowerClip the logos (by selecting PowerClip in the Effects menu) inside the rectangle and make three duplicates, as shown. You can make adjustments if necessary. I have changed the gray fill to 5 percent Black, because I want the background to be very subtle.

When you're pleased with the results, select the one PowerClip rectangle and set its line width to none and Export the image as a Gif 89a file with the following steps. From the File menu select Export (or click on the Export button on the Property Bar), name your file, from the Save As Type: drop-down box select CompuServe Bitmap (GIF), and click the Export button. This opens the Bitmap Export dialog box. Select 256 Colors, Dithered, Size 1:1, Resolution-Custom 96 dpi (or Windows resolution-72 dpi for Macintosh resolution), and Super Sampling (anti-aliasing). Click OK. A final window appears: the Gif89a Options dialog box. Select None for the Transparency option. A little later on, I'll show you how to create a transparent background color.

Figure 8-3: Three GWP's are PowerClipped inside a rectangle to be used for a repeating background pattern

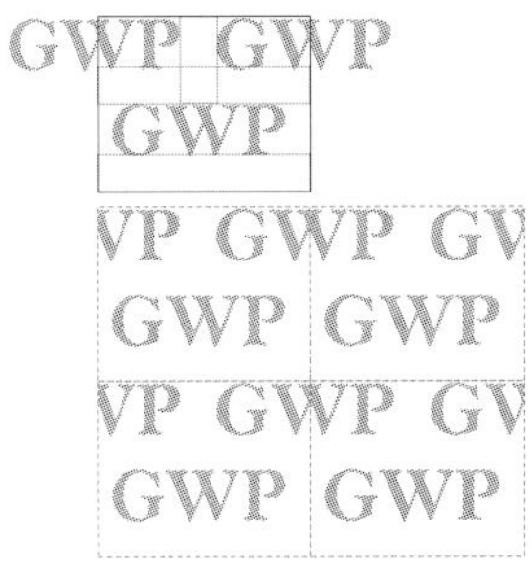

BASIC HTML (VERY BASIC)

4 HTML (Hypertext Markup Language) is a simple scripting language used to define the elements of a Web page. When a browser, such as Netscape Navigator, encounters an HTML document, it uses the HTML script to draw the page on your monitor and place the images and text. Figure 8-4 shows the most basic script. Every HTML script, no matter how complex, has these basic elements. You can write in any text program (but it has to be saved as an ASCII text file). The script begins and ends with HTML; the forward slash (/) closes the script. The head and title sections only appear in the title bar. All material displayed on the page is listed between the body tags. If you save this page as an ASCII text file and name it htmlpage.htm, then open it in your browser, all you would see is the default gray background color. But, hey, you've got to start somewhere.

Figure 8-4: The basic elements of an HTML script

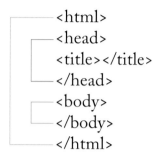

```
<html>
<head>
<title></title>
</head>
<body>
</body>
</html>
```

5 In my opinion, the most important part of the HTML script is the title. Although the text inside these tags (as shown in red in Figure 8-5) never appears on the screen, it will appear in the Bookmarks menu when somebody adds a bookmark to your page. If you leave it blank, the bookmark copy becomes the URL for the page. If we opened this page in a browser, it would still be just plain gray; however, the title text would appear in the title bar. We're making progress.

If we replace the opening body tag with the copy shown in Figure 8-6, our page would now display the repeating background pattern. (The background pattern file and HTML document have to be in the same directory.) There are several additional options for the body tag statement to change the background color, pattern, text, link, and visited link colors, but for this discussion I'm going to keep it simple.

Figure 8-5: Copy inside the title tags will appear in the Bookmarks menu when your page is bookmarked

```
<html>
<head>
<title>GWP Design </title>
</head>
<body>
</body>
</html>
```

Figure 8-6: The HTML command to fill the screen with the background tile

```
<html>
<head>
<title>GWP Design </title>
</head>
<body background="gwpbkgd.gif">
</body>
</html>
```

If our visitors are ever going to get beyond the home page, they're going to need a map. We could add some simple buttons, but an image map is cleaner and more impressive. With DRAW's Internet Objects menu, creating a sophisticated image map is almost easy. Finding the Internet Objects menu is the hard part! Well, not really—simply click on the Property Bar with the right mouse button and select Internet Objects from the pop-up menu. Figure 8-7 shows the Internet Objects menu and the GWP image created earlier. Here's the procedure for creating an image map.

STEP

6

Click on any blank space on the Property Bar with the right mouse button. Select Internet Objects to open the Internet Objects menu pictured in Figure 8-7. Select the first object, which in this case is the first red bullet and the text Who We Are. The Internet Objects menu is now open. In the Location (URL stands for Universal Resource Locator) text box, type we_are.htm, the name of the page we want to link to. You could key in the address of another Web page if you wanted, such as http://www.corel.com, which would link out to Corel's home page, but we won't because we want the visitor to stay on our site. It's important to type in the Alternate text, which in this case is Who We Are. In fact, DRAW 7 will not let you create an image map without alternate text. Alternate text is displayed while the image is loading or if the browser viewing your page does not support image maps. Because the file we_are.htm will reside in the same directory, you can leave out the http://www stuff.

Next, click on the Use Bounding Box to Define Hotspot button (the third button on the Internet Objects menu). The second button uses the objects outline, which would be OK if we had an actual map with irregular shapes. However, the second button also creates a more complex file and is unnecessary in this case. Repeat these steps until all the items have been linked. Click on the first button (Show Internet Objects). This displays a red wire mesh screen over all selected hot spots

Figure 8-7: The Internet Objects menu is used to designate hot spots on the image map

TIP

Calling up an e-mail window, to enable your visitors to send e-mail directly from your site, is a piece of cake. Instead of keying in a URL on the image map for the Contact Us button, simply type mailto:gary@ersatz.com. You can use this command—just substitute your own e-mail address after mailto:—and the browser will do the rest.

STEP

7

Once the image map has been created, we'll need to Open the File menu and select Publish To Internet. This opens a dialog box. Select Corel Image Map from the Save As Type: drop-down list. Name your image map and click Export. This opens another dialog box, shown in Figure 8-8. Unless your image is a photograph, select Gif and click OK. Yet another dialog menu opens, offering Gif89a options as shown in Figure 8-9. In this case, we want the background color (white) to be transparent so we can see the nifty repeating GWP pattern directly behind the image map. Click on the Image color radio button. The easiest way to make sure you have designated the right background color is to simply click the cursor (which turns into a +) on the background in the small preview window. Click OK.

Figures 8-8 (left) and 8-9 (right): Two dialog boxes for specifying file type and transparent background color. The figure on the right is the Gif 89a options dialog box

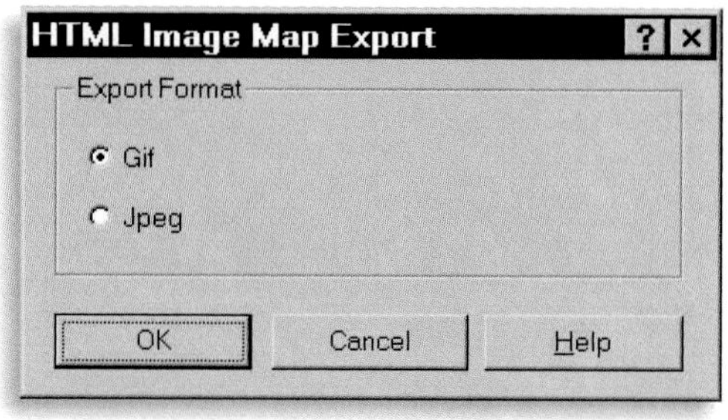

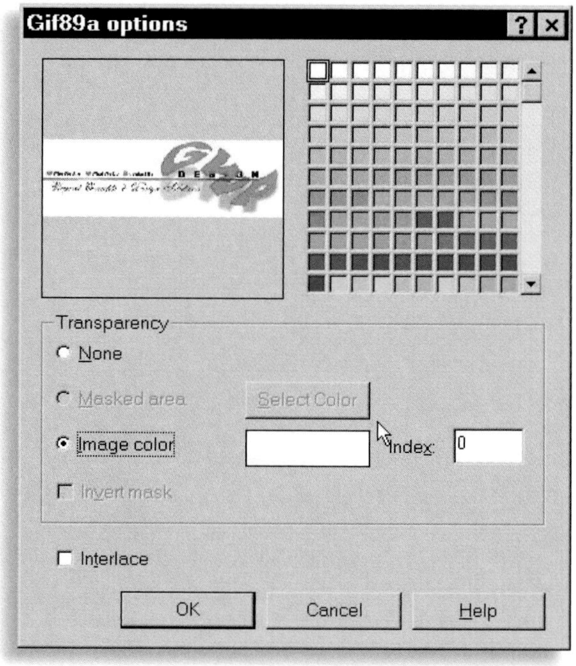

TIP

If your screen background color or pattern is something other than white and you plan to use Gif images with transparent backgrounds, use a nondithering color that is closest to the background color or pattern. DRAW will anti-alias (smooth) a bitmap file when you select the Super Sampling option. This creates a series of intermdiate-colored pixels that visually smooth the transition between objects. If you use a transparent white background, the intermediate pixels will contain some white pixels and appear as fringe against darker colors or patterns.

8 With the help of CorelDRAW, you create a very basic HTML page, which you can simply use as is. If you open the HTML document in a text editor, you'll see the same basic tags that I outlined earlier, plus the image map information shown in Figure 8-10. Here's what it all means. The first line defines the image map and sets the border width to none. The second line opens the map tag and states the name of the image map (imagemap.gif). The third line informs the browser that the hot spot is a rectangle (Area shape=rect) and what action to take (href="mailto:gary@ersatz.com"), the alternate copy (Contact Us), and the pixel boundary for the hot spot (CoOrds="154,63,162,72"). The next two lines define the other two links, and the last line is the close map tag (</map>). This statement goes right after the Body Background= tag in the HTML script. You can view your image map by opening your browser and selecting Open File in Browser. Use the Explorer to find the file's directory and the file. Highlight the file and click Open.

Figure 8-10: The script automatically generated by Corel defining the image map

```
<IMG SRC = "imagemap.gif" USEMAP = "#imagemap.gif" BORDER = 0>

<MAP NAME = "imagemap.gif">

<AREA SHAPE=RECT HREF="mailto:gary@ersatz.com" ALT="Contact Us"
      COORDS="154, 63, 162, 72">

<AREA SHAPE=RECT HREF="we_do.htm" ALT="What We Do"
      COORDS="83, 63, 92, 72">

<AREA SHAPE=RECT HREF="we_are.htm" ALT="Who We Are"
      COORDS="9, 63, 17, 72">

</MAP>
```

TIP

If you want to place an image in your page, simply insert the following text in your script (the quote marks, brackets, and spaces must be in the statement as shown): <img src="filename.gif">. Substitute the name of your image for filename and select the appropriate extension, gif or jpg.

S T E P

9

Figure 8-11 shows the actual Netscape screen with the image map and background pattern. Pretty clean, if you ask me. And the actual file size for the background and image map is very small, which means the page will load quickly. I added one set of tags to center the image, <center> and </center>. These tags precede and follow the image. Note that the text we placed between the title tags shows up on the title bar.

Figure 8-11: The image map and background as it appears in the Netscape browser

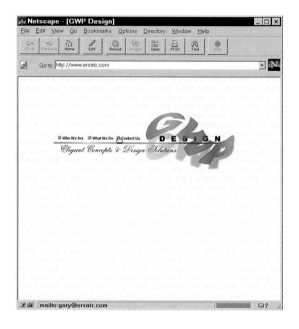

S T E P

10

Also notice that the destination of the hot spot is displayed along the bottom of the frame, in this case the mailto: link, which will bring up the e-mail form seen in Figure 8-12. The e-mail window permits your visitor to communicate with you directly.

Figure 8-12: The e-mail window is called up by the mailto: statement

STEP

11

I use invisible spaces to add air to my page design when needed. Simply create a small 1/4-inch white square, name it, and save it as space.gif. As you're exporting the image, select white as the transparent background color. I use the width= and height= statements to change the size of the square as needed. For example, if I need a space that's 20 pixels wide and 300 pixels tall, I add the following statement: <img src="space.gif" width=20 height=300>. You can change the size of an image using the height and width statements, although I wouldn't recommend it. The space is invisible on most browsers and because the space is one color, the file size is tiny. Figure 8-13 shows the What We Do page with the spacers shown, first displayed in pink and then displayed transparently.

I've also used another tag, <Font Face ="Verdana, Arial, Helvetica" Size="3>, which works with newer browsers and forces the browser to use one of these fonts if any is installed on the host computer. Verdana is a Microsoft font that ships and installs with Microsoft Explorer. It is designed specifically for use on the Web. The size=3 tag controls the size of the type. A larger number increases the size of the type; a smaller number reduces the type size. Finally, browsers do not recognize more than one space between characters or normal paragraph formatting. To force a new paragraph, use the <P> tag where you want the paragraph to end. You can also use a <BR>, which forces a line break with no extra space. In this example, I've used <P> tags to space out the text. I've made a smaller version of the masthead/navigation bar and placed it flush left at the top of the screen. You can easily create another page by simply copying the HTML script and renaming it. If you offer a page forward and page back option, as shown in Figure 8-13, be sure you change the text in the image map portion to reflect the new HTML page numbers.

Figure 8-13: The What We Do page uses invisible spaces (shown in pink) to air out the layout

TIP

Most software used to create HTML scripts offers only a few extended characters, such as the (c) copyright symbol and the (r) registered trademark symbol. You can also use any of the ASCII extended characters in your HTML script by simply pressing and holding the ALT key and entering the ASCII number from the numeric keyboard. (You may have to enable NUM LOCK first). Corel includes a list of these extended characters on the Character Reference Chart included in the Clip Art book. For example, a proper apostrophe is ALT+0146 (the 0 must be included). Open and closed quotation marks are ALT+0147 and ALT+0148. These characters will display properly, as long as your visitor's browser is using the English character set.

STEP

12

Figure 8-14 displays one of the Graphic Design portfolio pages. Each page will contain one image and a small amount of copy to explain the project's concept and other relevant information. I've used two more tricks to get the copy to appear to the right of the illustration and to have a small margin. I inserted an align=left tag into the image statement, which forces copy to appear to the right of the image. By default, the copy would begin at the bottom of the image. I've added another invisible space with the height slightly larger than the image, otherwise some of the copy would appear under the photo. I've added an align=left tag to the space as well. The HTML statement looks like this: <img src="filename.gif" align=left>.

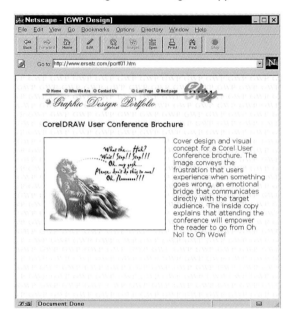

Figure 8-14: A portfolio page displays an image with left-aligned copy

BROWSING AHEAD

STEP

13

DRAW 8 incorporates some exciting new features, which would be a chapter unto itself. The biggest advancement is the new capability to create a page layout and let DRAW convert the images and the text into a complete HTML document, which it does by constructing an elaborate HTML table. This process is very similar to Adobe PageMill and Net Objects Fusion, two object-oriented Web page design programs, adding a giant amount of user friendliness to Web page creation. I've always been a hacker and enjoy the challenge of beating my head against the wall until the HTML script works the way I think it should. Some of you may prefer the less painful method provided by DRAW 8.

Briefly covering what we learned in this chapter, let's begin with some very important observations. People visit Web sites for two reasons: to get information and/or to be entertained. Good Web sites provide content. Life is not a contest to see how difficult we can make our sites to navigate, and life is definitely not a contest to see how many stupid and inappropriate animations we can pepper throughout the site. (OK

Gary, how do you really feel about this?) One of my favorite Web sites is Fedex.com. Why? Because it provides useful content. I can quickly tell not only if my editor has received my chapters, but also the exact time she received them and who at the reception desk signed for the package. That is a valuable service and an excellent use of the Web's capabilities.

First and foremost, we learned in this chapter to plan ahead by preparing a site map, which is an invaluable tool for Web site design. We learned how to create a simple tiled repeating background, how to make a color invisible, and how to prepare graphics for the Web. We learned enough basic HTML commands to be able to tweak Corel's HTML page that we generated when we published our image map to the Internet. And, of course, we learned how to prepare a client-side image map to enable our visitors to logically navigate our site.

Variations on a Theme

CAN YOU REPEAT THAT?

Here are some additional ideas to add pizzazz to your Web site. This first figure shows a variety of Texture Fills that make excellent tiling background images. Some require modification, while others can be used off the rack (as they say in the rag trade). Texture a. is Styles Library, Patches 2-C. The colors have been changed to White and Pale Yellow and the density was increased to 80. Texture b. is Styles Library, Mineral Speckled 3C, using 20 percent Black, 10 percent Black, and White. Texture c. is Styles Library, Recycled Paper, using 80 percent Black and 60 percent Black. Texture d. is Samples Library, Red Brick, using Olive and Pale Yellow. Texture e. is Samples 7 Library, Autumn Cloth, with the Brightness adjusted to 30 percent. Texture f. is Samples 7 Library, Concrete, using Black 50 percent. Texture g. is Samples 7 Library, Wool. Texture h. is Samples 5 Library, Night Sky.

ROCK OUT!

I like to add to a Texture Fill to make a unique tile, as you can see in the image shown here. Tile a. uses Patches 2-C with the addition of a rocking horse from the Holiday Symbols library. Each corner contains one-fourth of the horse; when the image tiles, it will make a subtle repeating rocking horse pattern. Tile b. adds thin, high-tech stripes to the modified Recycled Paper fill. Tile c. uses the Concrete Texture Fill. The Zapf Dingbats decorative heart is the same Concrete fill with the Brightness set to 20 percent, creating a transparent look. Tile d. uses the Night Sky fill with a stylish script W, a circle, and a 45-degree diagonal line.

SET IN CONCRETE

This image reveals one of my favorite tricks. The background is the Concrete tile with the Brightness set to 20 percent. The drop shadow is filled with the Concrete fill, with the Brightness set to -5. When I export this image as a Gif 89a image and make the white background transparent, the gold pen image will look as if it's casting a shadow on the background pattern when it displays on the Web page.

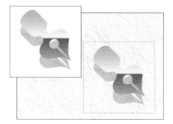

WHAT GOES ROUND

A simple black-and-white Conical Fill makes a swell 3-D round button, as you can see here. The background color is Red=204, Green=204, Blue=204, and a nondithering gray. The smaller circle in the center is 15% Black. If we flop the button and darken the inside circle, the button now appears recessed. The inside circle on the last button has a Linear Fountain Fill from 20 percent Black to 10 percent Black.

BEVEL WITH ME

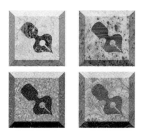

Corel's Color Bitmap fills make cool buttons, as you can see here. I've used four beveled edges with transparency applied to give the button dimension. I've used two fills from the same Library for each button, which are Marble, Wood, Metal, and Paper. Quite handsome, if you ask me. You could also use the Extrude Bevel effect (I just like doing things the hard way).

THE ODD BUTTON

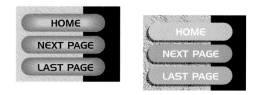

Buttons do not have to be round or square. The image shown on the left uses a blend of two rounded rectangles to create lozenge-shaped buttons. The image on the right uses the same lozenge shape but with solid colorful fills. The background on the left is the Concrete Texture Fill, with the shadows a darker version of the Concrete fill.

CRAZY-MAKING ANIMATION

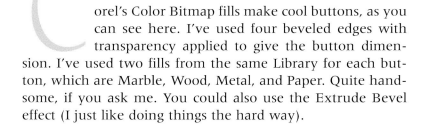

If you want to make me crazy (and why shouldn't you?), you can use the images shown here (note top figure) to make an animation that will pulsate between hot and cold. I applied DRAW 8's Push-n-Pull Distortion effect in 10-degree increments on the left side and in -10-degree increments on the right side. You can make me doubly crazy if you make an animation using the frames in the bottom figure and include it on your page with the animation from the top figure. The word "Whirl" is distorted with DRAW 8's Twister Distortion in 15-degree rotations. The colors begin as a Rainbow Radial Fountain Fill, using 100 percent Cyan for each color. Each successive word uses 10 percent less Cyan in the Fountain Fill.

Well, that covers the World Wide Web. We'll see how easy it is to create a nifty brochure for GWP Design in Chapter 9.

Publishing with DRAW

Things are off to a good start for fledgling GWP Design. I have a zippy new logo and business card, plus a dynamite Web site. But not everybody is online, and even if they are, I can't count on the Web to reach all of my potential market. What's more, GWP Design does traditional design as well as Web page design, so I need a sales piece to communicate this fact. And, wouldn't you know, this chapter is about publishing with DRAW. It's just one coincidence after another. I'll be doing most of this project in DRAW 7, although the illustrations were actually created in DRAW 8. All the features I'll be using in DRAW 7, however, work pretty much the same in DRAW 8; only the Distortion tool's Twister effect cannot be done in Version 7.

IMPORTANT

We'll be preparing a document for commercial four-color printing, so please change your Color Correction to Accurate in the View menu in DRAW 7 and Tools-Options in DRAW 8 to display screen colors as they'll print in four-color process.

WHAT'S THE BIG IDEA?

When I was in art school, times were simpler and everything took longer to do because the computer had not come along to make our lives easier. Back then, I remember an instructor sharing an intriguing piece of information: Every person is exposed to several hundred advertising messages every day. This figure included traditional media—radio, television, magazine advertisements, and outdoor posters—as well as matchbooks, signs on the sides of cars and trucks, and on and on. Given the increase in today's advertising messages, the figure could easily reach into the thousands when you take into account the advent of the Web, cable TV, clothing bearing commercial logos, and such. If there's an opportunity to place an ad somewhere, you can be sure someone will do it.

I've decided to use this fact as the concept upon which to build my advertising message, which as it turns out is going to be incorporated into a direct mail piece. There is currently so much competition in the printing business that I can afford to produce a four-color mailer, and a four-color mailer will make GWP Design look bigger than the one-person company it is. Plus, the mailer will allow me the luxury of enough space to tell my whole story, which is that GWP Design will cut through the clutter and get my client's product or service noticed.

Due to the complex nature of this project, I'm going to modify the step-by-step format. Rather than take you through every step needed to create the brochure in this exercise (enough steps to get you to the top of the Washington Monument), I'm going to concentrate only on the major steps. We'll assume that the major elements already exist and focus on getting them all into the right places.

LAYING THE GROUNDWORK

STEP 1

Set your page size to 11 inches by 17 inches (Tabloid) in the Landscape orientation. This change can either be made by selecting Page Setup from the Layout menu, or by double-clicking on the gray page border on the screen to bring up the Page Setup dialog. Construct a rectangle that is 9 1/2 inches tall by 14 3/4 inches wide. Drag guidelines dividing the rectangle into 4 3/4-inch by 7 3/8-inch quarter sections. Make a folding diagram like the one in Figure 9-1 to help you visualize how the brochure will fold and the orientation of the material on each panel. Panel A is the address portion of the mailer and is backed up by panel B. When the mailer is opened halfway, panels C and D are exposed. Finally, when the entire piece is opened, we see the inside, panel E.

Figure 9-1: A folding diagram for a two-fold direct-mail brochure

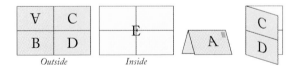

To get the reader's attention and convince him or her to open, and with any luck, read the mailer, place the logo and copy line on panel A (the address side). Place the more elaborate message on panel B as shown in Figure 9-2. Substitute the initial cap I (which mimics the illustration on panel C) for the first letter in the text. PowerClip (Effects-PowerClip) the "ad hype" type illustration (shown in Figure 9-3) inside the rectangle as shown.

Figure 9-3: A graphic heavily cluttered with a variety of advertising "calls to action" illustrates the problem— information overload

Figure 9-2: The front and back covers for the direct mailer

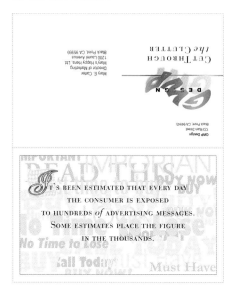

DROP CAPITAL IDEA

STEP

2

Figure 9-4 provides a visual description of the process I used to create the initial capital used in the copy on panel B, which was created in DRAW 8 using the same Twister Distortion that I used to create the logo.

Figure 9-4: A drop cap is created using DRAW 8's Twister Distortion

Begin with a 7 × 8 grid pattern created with the Graph Paper tool, which can be found in the Polygon Tool flyout. Ungroup the grid and then Combine it (not combining the grid makes the grid squares come apart when the Twister effect is applied). Type an uppercase **I** in Flemish Script, center it over the grid, and apply a bright gold-like Linear Fountain Fill. See Chapter 14 for more details on creating gold and chrome fills. Select both the letter and the grid and apply a Twister Distortion with a 30-degree rotation. Copy the twisted grid and letter to the clipboard. Select the letter and change the fill color to 40% Black. Then select the grid and give it a thicker outline and change its line color to 40% Black. After converting the two elements to Bitmap, apply a Gaussian Blur of 5. Paste the originals on top and move them slightly up and to the right. Finally, copy the letter to the clipboard, add a 2-point Black outline to the one onscreen, and paste the original on top.

STEP

3

The initial capital I used on panel B was inspired by the twisted illustration inside the mailer, specifically on panels C and D. Figure 9-5 shows the illustration and the copy, which is set in Bauer Bodoni Roman SC (as in small caps). The italic version of the font is in lowercase, and the combination of both creates an elegant type treatment.

I've used a combination of type and symbols to compose my illustration, as shown in Figure 9-6. The grid, as explained previously, is created with the Graph Paper tool, ungrouped, and then combined. All the illustration elements are grouped and a Twister Distortion is applied with a partial rotation amount of 35 degrees, as shown in Figure 9-7. To add the extra dimension, shown in Figure 9-8, convert a copy of the illustration to bitmap, using the 256 Shades of Gray option. Bring the grayscale bitmap to the top, offset it up about 1/4 inch, and apply an Interactive Transparency, Subtract, amount 30. The illustration represents navigating a daunting variety of advertising images.

Figure 9-5: Panels C and D use a Twister-distorted illustration and a font in caps and small cap letters

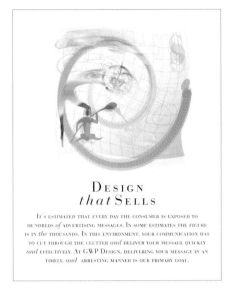

Figure 9-6: Elements for the illustration are assembled in DRAW 8

Figure 9-7: DRAW 8's Twister Distortion applied to an illustration creates a unique effect

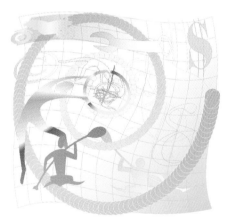

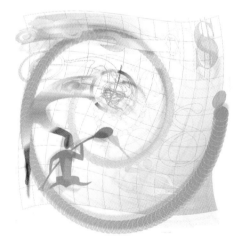

Figure 9-8: Transparency is applied to a grayscale bitmap version of the illustration

TIP

If you have DRAW 7 and want to create the Twister effect, convert your image to bitmap and use the Bitmaps-2D Effects-Swirl. The settings and results are fairly similar.

THE INSIDE STORY—THE BIG PICTURE

STEP

4 The inside of the brochure, shown in Figure 9-9, is laid out in a four-column format with liberal use of images integrated into the copy as "copy warmers." The images represent a variety of GWP Design's recent projects, which are discussed at length in the copy. Small captions are placed under some of the copy warmers to give the casual viewer pertinent information. My whizzy new logo appears at the end of the copy preceded by a paragraph calling for the order (as they say in the ad biz). The basic steps I used to create the inside follow.

Lay out a four-column grid for the inside of the brochure. Determine where the text will begin and end in each column. Leave extra space for the center fold. Arrange the illustrations in an artistic and pleasing manner. Resize the illustrations to accommodate both body copy and captions. Enable the Wrap Paragraph Text option to flow the copy around the illustrations where appropriate. (This process is discussed in more detail further down.) Import your text and position it inside the grid. The next section provides a more detailed description of the type-fitting process. Format the text. Save your file. If you plan to send your file to a service bureau, use the Prepare File For Service Bureau (Edit menu) to create the appropriate file.

Figure 9-9: The inside of the mailer is laid out in four columns of text which wrap around the images

STEP

5

DRAW 7 and 8 make linked multiple columns of paragraph text a
breeze. It's as simple as drawing a
rectangle.

Figure 9-10: Paragraph text can be
linked to a new shape

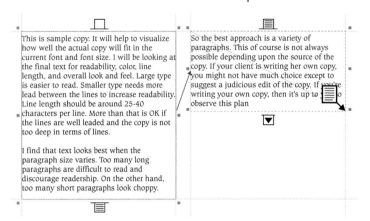

Add guidelines where your columns of text will
be placed. Enable Snap To Guidelines. Click on
the Text tool and drag an outline for your first
column of text, as shown in the first column of
text in Figure 9-10. The small tab at the bottom
of the column contains a down-facing triangle
when there is more text to place. With the Pick
tool, click on the down-facing triangle, and the
cursor changes to the cursor seen in the second
column (it's enlarged for viewing). Click and
drag the cursor to create the next column.
(Don't worry if the rectangle is not the exact size, you can go
back and resize it.) When there is no more text to be placed,
the tab at the bottom will be empty. When you edit your text,
blue arrows will appear to indicate which columns and text
blocks are linked to other columns and text blocks. When you
alter any of the columns or text blocks, the text automatically reflows.

TIP

When working with large amounts of text, consider using styles. DRAW lets you create sophisticated styles with a variety of attributes; then, you
simply highlight your copy, click the right mouse
button, and from the pop-up menu select Apply
Style. You can create separate styles for paragraph text, subheads, captions, page numbers,
and so forth.

STEP

6

Back in the good old days before computers, there existed a breed of professional craftspersons known as typographers. These good folks learned about typography in the traditional way, beginning as apprentice typesetters and perfecting their craft until they became journeyperson typesetters and eventually full-fledged typographers. I could send them marked-up advertising copy, with specified font, desired point size, and amount of leading along with a rough layout, and in a few days, beautifully set type would appear on my desk. Unfortunately, these professionals have gone the way of the pterodactyl, replaced by blundering incompetents such as myself. I'm fortunate to have worked with these skilled professionals, and hopefully a little of their knowledge has been passed down to me. I shall in turn try to pass a little of this precious knowledge along to you.

I prefer copy that is justified "ragged right" as opposed to fully justified (flush left and right). In my opinion, ragged right copy is more inviting to read, and the letter spacing and word spacing is consistent throughout. Fully justified copy can be effective but requires a lot of tweaking to make it look as good as ragged right copy. The important consideration for ragged right copy is that the ragged edge be reasonably tight and not have vast differences between the longest and shortest lines. Some hyphenation is often required to accomplish this, although I prefer to use as little hyphenation as I can possibly get away with. Fully justified copy also requires tweaking to keep the difference in word spacing and letter spacing as unnoticeable as possible. If you want to see a bad example of fully justified type, just look in your local newspaper.

Figure 9-11 shows two paragraphs of text; the first is ragged right, and the second is fully justified. Notice on the left that the difference between the lines is not extreme and the negative shape that appears between the two columns is not unpleasant or jarring to the eye. The second column is fully justified. A slightly longer measure will give you a better chance of a successful justification.

TIP

One good way to learn about type is to learn from the professionals. Tear out ads from magazines that have appealing and imaginative uses of typography and try to re-create the type in DRAW. We used to play a game called Type Detective, in which someone would give us a headline or maybe just a word or two and we'd have to look through all the type specimen books until we could identify the font.

Sometimes you may want to use small type. I won't be able to read it, but I may not be your target reader, either. If you use tiny type, as shown in Figure 9-12, apply a generous amount of leading (distance between the lines). This holds true for copy that has more than 50 characters per line.

I've asked Ms. Squirrel to pop out of the Animals 2 Symbols Library to assist in this next demonstration, shown in Figure 9-13. DRAW's wrap text function tends to look better with fully justified type, as shown on the left, as opposed to rag right justification, shown on the right. There is a workaround for this, which I'll discuss next.

Figure 9-11: Two paragraphs of text-one set rag right and the other with full justification

This is sample copy. It will help to visualize how well the actual copy will fit in the current font and font size. I will be looking at the final text for readability, color, line length, and overall look and feel. Large type is easier to read. Smaller type needs more lead between the lines to increase read-ability. Line length should be around 25-40 characters per line. More than that is OK if the lines are well leaded and the copy is not too deep in terms of lines

This is sample copy. It will help to visualize how well the actual copy will fit in the current font and font size. I will be looking at the final text for readability, color, line length, and overall look and feel. Large type is easier to read. Smaller type needs more lead between the lines to increase read-ability. Line length should be around 25-40 characters per line. More than that is OK if the lines are well leaded and the copy is not too deep in terms of lines

Figure 9-12: Small type requires generous leading between the lines

This is sample copy. It will help to visualize

how well the actual copy will fit in the

current font and font size. I will be looking

at the final text for readability, color, line

length, and overall look and feel. Large type

is easier to read. Smaller type needs more

lead between the lines to increase read-

ability. Line length should be around 25-40

characters per line. More than that is OK if

the lines are well leaded and the copy is not

too deep in terms of lines

Figure 9-13: Two differently justified paragraphs of text used with irregular-shaped symbols with the wrap text option enabled

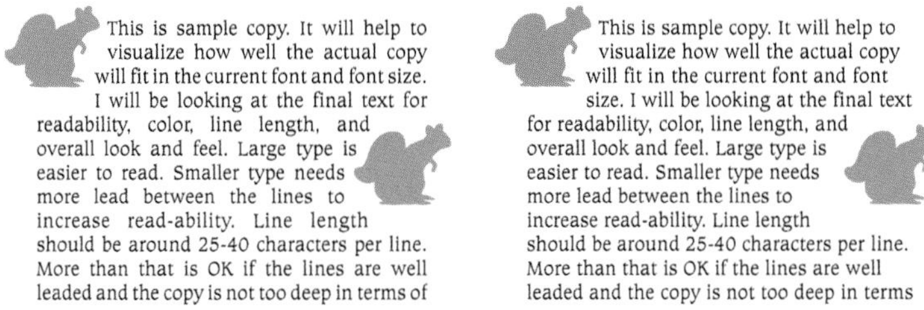

This is sample copy. It will help to visualize how well the actual copy will fit in the current font and font size. I will be looking at the final text for readability, color, line length, and overall look and feel. Large type is easier to read. Smaller type needs more lead between the lines to increase read-ability. Line length should be around 25-40 characters per line. More than that is OK if the lines are well leaded and the copy is not too deep in terms of

This is sample copy. It will help to visualize how well the actual copy will fit in the current font and font size. I will be looking at the final text for readability, color, line length, and overall look and feel. Large type is easier to read. Smaller type needs more lead between the lines to increase read-ability. Line length should be around 25-40 characters per line. More than that is OK if the lines are well leaded and the copy is not too deep in terms

WRAPPING TYPE

STEP

7

I like to place images inside the text blocks and flow the text around these images. In DRAW, you can select an object and "wrap" the text around the object. Here's how.

Click on an object you wish to wrap your text around with the right mouse button; a pop-up menu appears. Click on the Properties option to bring up the Object Properties dialog box with the Wrap paragraph text option. By default, this is set to 0 inches (.1 in version 8), and results in type that is too close to the object. Change the setting to 6 and the units to points, as shown in Figure 9-14. Click OK. Notice that when the object is selected with the Text tool, the repelling outline is displayed. The Wrap Paragraph Text option works OK with simple shapes, but your ability to alter the outline is severely limited. I'll show you a better method.

Figure 9-14: The Object Properties dialog box is used to specify Wrap paragraph text options

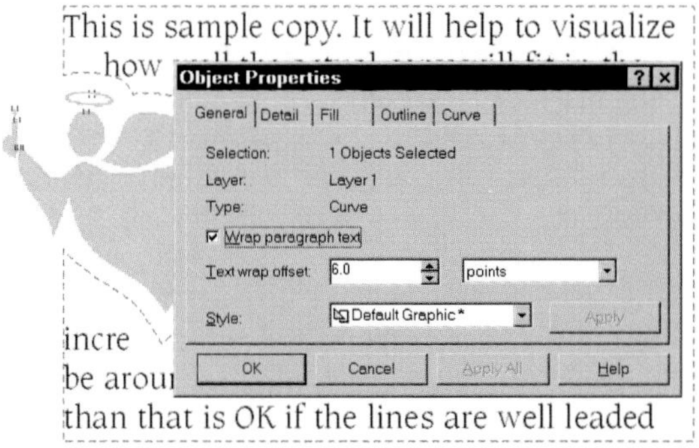

This is sample copy. It will help to visualize

Object Properties

General | Detail | Fill | Outline | Curve |

Selection: 1 Objects Selected
Layer: Layer 1
Type: Curve

☑ Wrap paragraph text

Text wrap offset: 6.0   points

Style: Default Graphic*   Apply

OK   Cancel   Apply All   Help

incre
be arou
than that is OK if the lines are well leaded

CUSTOM WRAPPING

STEP

8 The first paragraph of text illustrated in Figure 9-15 uses DRAW's Wrap Paragraph Text with the offset modified to 6 points. It does an adequate job, but notice the odd break in the word "increase." This is simply unacceptable. When you specify a 6-point offset, DRAW offsets the entire image 6 points. In most cases, you don't want the top or the bottom of your image to have any offset, only the sides. This is where my secret method comes in.

Create an outline with the Freehand tool that conforms to the actual shape you wish the type to wrap around. Apply the wrap Paragraph Text to the outline (with the offset set to 0). Make sure that the object itself has Wrap Paragraph Text disabled by clicking on it with the right mouse button. If Wrap Paragraph Text is checked, click on the option to disable Add and adjust the nodes as necessary until the text wrap meets your approval. Make the outline shape invisible by changing the line and fill to none.

Figure 9-15: A simple outline shape is used to wrap paragraph text, assuring a tight wrap

> This is sample copy. It will help to visualize how well the actual copy will fit in the current font and font size. I will be looking at the final text for readability, color, line length, and overall look and feel. Large type is easier to read. Smaller type needs more lead between the lines to incre   ase readability. Line length should be around 25-40 characters per line. More than that is OK if the lines are well leaded

> This is sample copy. It will help to visualize how well the actual copy will fit in the current font and font size. I will be looking at the final text for readability, color, line length, and overall look and feel. Large type is easier to read. Smaller type needs more lead between the lines to increase readability. Line length should be around 25-40 characters per line. More than that is OK if the lines are well leaded and

IN PRODUCTION

STEP

9 Many of the unemployed typographers are now employed as technicians by service bureaus, which were formerly typesetting establishments. These talented people have learned and mastered the pre-production skills required to take my EPS files and output professional-quality four-color film separations. I tell you this because this is how I deal with the issue of pre-press. I export my files as EPS (Encapsulated PostScript) files and let my service bureau output the film and, when necessary, do the trapping. If you insist on doing this yourself, you're a better and more courageous person than I. For in-depth knowledge about preparing your own material for pre-press, I highly recommend Foster Coburn and Pete McCormick's *CorelDRAW 7 or 8 The Official Guide* (Osborne/McGraw-Hill, 1997 and 1998).

Figure 9-16: 1/10-inch crop marks are colored 100 percent Cyan, Magenta, Yellow, and Black and set back 1/8 inch from the page's outline

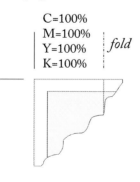

C=100%
M=100%
Y=100%
K=100%
fold

I will share this tidbit with you: I prefer to add my own crop marks, like the ones shown in Figure 9-16 for four-color (CMYK) printing.

Use the default hairline weight of .2 points. Color the line 100 percent Cyan, Magenta, Yellow, and Black so that the crop marks will appear on all four pieces of film. Indicate a fold with a dotted line that stops 1/8 inch short of the page border. Extend objects that bleed (go off the edge of the page) 1/8 inch, to allow the printer leeway when trimming the page.

MAIL IT ALREADY!

In this chapter, we began by making a page diagram for a self-mailer. This makes it easier to visualize and plan a complex printing project. We revisited DRAW 8's Twister Distortion to add a twist to an illustration and drop cap. We had a brief discussion of typesetting and learned how to link paragraph text in DRAW. We also learned how DRAW forces paragraph text to wrap around an object. Then we learned a better way to wrap paragraph text around an object using an invisible shape. The inside of the brochure provided insight into how to arrange type and photographic images to create a compelling layout. And finally, my weakness in electronic pre-press was revealed.

Variations on a Theme

Here are some ideas to spice up your next printed piece. The image here shows a colored circle inside a block of colored text. This is easier than it looks in DRAW. I placed a solid-colored circle behind the text as a template. I used the Shape tool to select the individual nodes of the letters that were in front of the circle template, and with the nodes selected clicked on a color in the onscreen palette. When I was finished, I deleted the circle. This technique works with a variety of shapes, although simple shapes work better.

INNER CIRCLE

This is sample copy. It will help to visualize how well the actual copy will fit in the current font and font size. I will be looking at the final text for readability, color, line length, and overall look and feel. Large type is easier to read. Smaller type needs more lead between the lines to increase readability. Line length should be around 25-40 characters per line. More than that is OK if the lines are well leaded and the copy is not too deep in terms of lines. This is sample copy. It will help to visualize how well the actual copy will fit in the current font and font size. I will be looking at the final text for readability, color, line length, and overall look and feel. Large type is easier to read. Smaller type needs more lead between the lines to increase readability. Line length should be around 2540 characters per line. More than that is OK if the lines are well

A DECORATIVE DROP CAP

I used a large decorative letter for an initial cap as shown here. I merely deleted the first letter in the text and dropped my script initial cap to the back.

This is sample copy. It will help to visualize how well the actual copy will fit in the current font and font size. I will be looking at the final text for readability, color, line length, and overall look and feel. Large type is easier to read. Smaller type needs more lead between the lines to increase readability. Line length should be around 25-40 characters per line. More than that is OK if the lines are well leaded and the copy is not

YOU CAN'T SEE IT BUT IT'S THERE

I used my invisible shape trick (see image here) to produce a rectangular indent for an elegant Onyx initial cap T with drop shadow.

This is sample copy. It will help to visualize how well the actual copy will fit in the current font and font size. I will be looking at the final text for readability, color, line length, and overall look and feel. Large type is easier to read. Smaller type needs more lead between the lines to increase readability. Line length should be around 25-40 characters per line. More than that is OK if

In the image shown here, I PowerClipped a farm scene from the Corel Professional Photos CD, Barns and Farms, inside the text "Farm World" to produce a handsome masthead. Setting the fill on the type to none and applying a thin white outline allowed me to move the type around until I was happy with the placement of the photo. When the type was positioned to my liking, I PowerClipped the photo and set the outline to none.

I selected various words in the paragraph of text in Figure 9-21 and changed the color as well as the font to produce a fun piece of copy with keywords that pop out. This is a useful trick to ensure that critical elements of the copy are noted even if the entire copy block is only skimmed and not read.

This is sample copy. It will help to **visualize** how well the actual copy will **fit** in the current font and font size. I will be looking at the final text for **readability,** color, line length, and overall look and feel. Large type is **easier** to read. Smaller type needs **more lead** between the lines to increase readability. Line length should be around 25-40 characters per line. More than that is **OK** if the lines are well leaded and the copy is not too deep in

The East Indian Rope Trick Company, Ltd.

The image in this chapter can be created only in **PHOTO-PAINT 8**, because it uses many new features that exist only in **PHOTO-PAINT 8**. Gary and I talked about whether this image should have a western or a nautical theme. Having lived in Texas now for nearly 20 years, I found myself longing for the sea (I used to be in the Navy), so that is how we came to choose a nautical theme.

If you have experimented with the Rope preset on the Image Sprayer tool, you may have noticed that the rope image it produces looks more akin to pasta than a rope (but who makes borders and knots with pasta?). In this chapter, we will learn to use many of the new **PHOTO-PAINT 8** features and have a little fun along the way.

NOTE

The techniques in this chapter can only be done with PHOTO-PAINT 8.

The Image Sprayer tool first showed up in PHOTO-PAINT 7. Its sole purpose in life is to paint stored images with a brush tool. In this illustration, I painted the leaves and the butterflies on the background with a brush. In this regard, the Image Sprayer in PHOTO-PAINT 8 stills works the same way. What is new is a feature called Orbits. Orbits, when enabled, control the way in which the brush images are laid down.

Figure 10-1: Orbits give the Image Sprayer tool some real power

For example, look at Figure 10-1. With Orbits disabled, a straight line is drawn across the top, resulting in an almost interesting string of beads. Enable the Orbits (in this case, the Orbit preset is Swirly Wave), and you end up with a pretty wild creation, as shown at the bottom of the figure. What can you do with Orbits? If you combine them with natural objects, such as rocks and grass, you can end up with an image like the one shown in Figure 10-2.

Like many other attributes of the Image Sprayer, the degree of interaction of the Orbits feature is defined by the Tool Settings roll-up. While you can make any combination of effects using the controls provided in the Tool Settings roll-up, Corel has provided some excellent presets. The one we will use to make the rope is, interestingly enough, called Rope.

Figure 10-2: Combining the power of Orbits and natural objects produces images that look like photographs

CREATING A NAUTICAL SIGN

We are going to make a sign for Knotts Nautical Shoppe. (You thought I was going to make it Knotical, didn't you? I thought about it for a moment.) Since chrome and neon effects don't convey the nautical message the customer wants, we will use something that does. That means wood, rope, and beer—well, maybe not the beer.

MAKING THE BORDER AND BACKGROUND

First, we will create a background for the sign. It begins with a simple rope border, and during the course of creating the sign you will be introduced to a lot more of the new tools. While it is possible to draw a border with the rope, the result will be uneven and less than satisfactory. We will use the Stroke Mask command to make the border. Follow these steps.

STEP

1

Create a new image that is 5 × 3 inches at 96 dpi. Select the Ellipse Mask tool and create a mask that looks like the one shown.

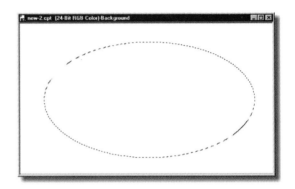

STEP

2

From the Objects Docker window, make sure Lock is not checked. From the Object menu, select Create and then choose New Object. Open the Brush Tools flyout at the bottom of the Toolbox and select the Image Sprayer tool. Open the Tool Settings roll-up (CTRL+F8). Select the Brown Rope preset at the bottom. From the Edit menu, choose Stroke and select Stroke Mask. When the Choose Stroke Position dialog box opens, choose Middle of Mask Border and click OK. The result is shown. The great part about this rope is that it is an object. We will discover the great advantage of this as we proceed.

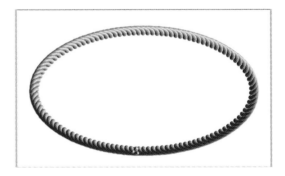

3 Remove the mask (CTRL+SHIFT+R). Now the rope looks more like pasta than rope. To correct this, select Artistic from the Effects menu and choose Canvas. When the Canvas dialog box opens, click the Load button and open the file STUCCO.PCX. With the default settings, the results look like a circle of sand. Change the Emboss setting to 35 percent and leave the Transparency setting at 100 percent and the X and Y Offset at 0 percent. Click OK. Our rope now has a realistic texture to it.

4 Now we need a drop shadow—no problem with PHOTO-PAINT. Select the Object Picker tool and make sure the rope object is selected. From the Object menu, choose Drop Shadow and find a shadow that you like, or select the following Drop Shadow settings: Flat, 270 degrees, Offset of 0.035, Opacity of 100, Feather Width of 17, and Average Direction. Click OK.

Now for the background. In the Objects Docker window, click on the background to select it. From the Edit menu, choose Fill and then click the Bitmap fill button. Click the Edit button, and when the Bitmap dialog box opens, click Load. On the CD, locate the tile labeled WOOD07L.CPT in the folder \TILES\WOOD\LARGE\. Click OK three times to apply the fill to the background. That completes the background. You may want to save the file at this point.

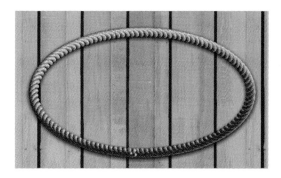

TYING THE KNOT

The next stage is to create a knot. Hey, the company's name is Knott, so why not use a knot? Making knots can be a little tricky, but once you get the hang of them, you will start doing all kinds of things with them.

The rope we use to create the knot needs to be a little smaller than the rope we used to make the border. This presents a problem. If the size of the Image Sprayer is changed, the Rope preset changes shape. To make the Rope setting smaller, you must reduce the Radius setting on the Orbits tab proportionately to the change you make in the Size setting of the brush. Alternatively, because the rope is an object, you can resize it to the desired size. Since we are going to be adding a Canvas filter to it and the Canvas bitmap is a fixed size, we will get the best results from the latter method. Let's tie a knot.

STEP

1

Create a new image that is 3 × 2 inches at 96 dpi. From the Object menu, choose Create and then New Object. Using the Image Sprayer (still set to the Brown Rope preset), click and drag a rope that looks like the one shown here. This can be done with a mouse, but it is difficult. Most of the rope techniques work better with a stylus. I use a Wacom ArtZ II, and whether I am roping or masking, I find it is a lifesaver. The created image does not have to be exactly like the one shown, but you should attempt to get it pretty close. Use the Undo tool and try, try again. That is what I had to do to achieve the one shown, even with a stylus.

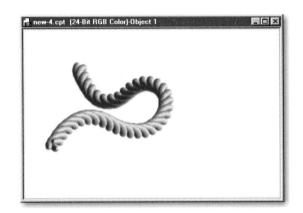

STEP

2

Again, from the Object menu, select Create and then New Object. With the Image Sprayer tool, create the image shown here.

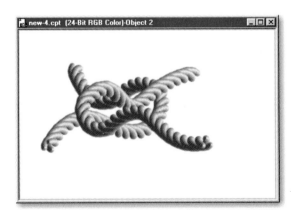

3 Select the Object Picker tool. In the Objects Docker window, make sure that the top object (the one you just created) is selected. From the Object menu, choose Clip Mask, then Create, then From Object Transparency. This action creates a Clip Mask that perfectly coincides with the top object, which I have named Top Knot. The Clip Mask is indicated by the symbol shown in the illustration.

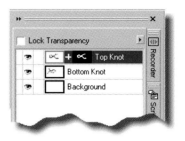

The Clip Mask is a wonderful new addition to PHOTO-PAINT 8. In PHOTO-PAINT 7, the only way we could make the rope do the over-and-under thing would be to use the Object Transparency brush to make portions of the rope invisible. Changes to the object (rope) using the Transparency brush are permanent. Using the Clip Mask, we make changes to the mask, which is clipped to the object, and the mask determines what we can and cannot see. So, if at a later time you need to use the knot again but want to change parts of it, you can remove the Clip Mask, and the original object (rope) is restored. Pretty slick stuff.

4 In the Objects Docker window, click on the object on the bottom and click the Create Mask button in the Toolbar. This creates a mask, which we will use in a moment. Now click on the Clip Mask of the top object to make it selected. It will have a red square to indicate the selection. From the Brush Tools flyout, select the Paint tool, and from the Tool Settings roll-up (CTRL+F8), change the brush tool to the paintbrush tool, as shown in the illustration, and select Quick Doodler as the Type. With the Paint color set to Black, begin to paint the areas of the rope indicated by the circles in the next illustration. Everywhere you paint, the Clip Mask becomes invisible. When you have finished this end, go and do the same thing to the other end of the knot. The finished knot is shown.

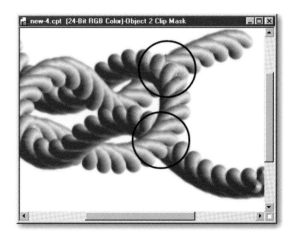

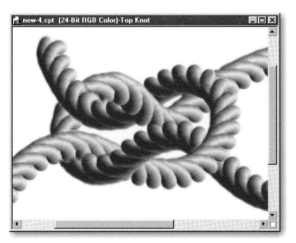

STEP

5

With the Clip Mask thumbnail still selected in the Objects Docker window, click on the thumbnail of the mask with the right mouse button and select Combine Clip Mask. This will make the transparency of the Top Knot permanent. If we were going to use this again, we would save it before combining the Clip Mask. Our next step is to do something about the two points where the Image Sprayer brush has stopped, which leaves something similar to one of those soft-serve ice cream cones. Remove the mask and select one of the objects. Select the Effect tool from the Brush Tools flyout and choose Smudge, then choose the Smudge A Little for the Type setting. Adjust the brush size to 24 (pixels). Place the brush tool on the tips of the rope, as shown. Click and hold for a moment, and the end of the rope will fuzz out. Select the other object and smudge its ends.

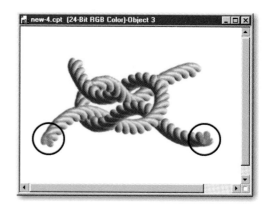

STEP

6

SHIFT-select both objects and combine them (CTRL+ALT+DNARROW). From the Effects menu, choose Artistic and then Canvas, as we did in the first part of the exercise to create the rope border. I recommend reducing the Emboss setting to 24. Copy the knot object to the clipboard (CTRL+C) and close this image. You can save the individual knot image if you want, but we won't need it again in this exercise.

PUTTING THE PIECES TOGETHER

The hard part is over, and this is the fun part. The last stage puts all of the elements together. So let's get started.

STEP

1

With the original background file open, paste the contents of the clipboard onto the image as an object (CTRL+V). With the Object Picker tool selected, click and place the knot at the top of the image, as shown. If your knot isn't the same size, click on the image until the handles are small squares (scaling mode), then click on one of the handles and drag it until it is the right size. When you like the size, double-click the object to apply the transformation.

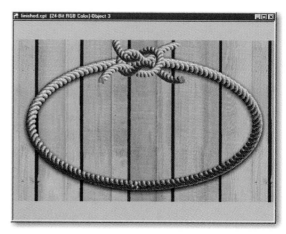

2 Select the Text tool and type **Knotts Nautical Shoppe**. The text in my example is Playbill BT at a size of 60, centered, bold, and with a line spacing of 65 percent. I used Blue for the Paint color. To give the letters some texture (so they don't look so computer-generated), click the Lock Transparency checkbox in the Objects Docker window, and from the Effects menu, choose Noise and then Add Noise. Select Gaussian Noise at a Level of 20 and a Density of 30. Click OK. Uncheck the Lock Transparency option in the Objects Docker window and select Emboss in the 3D Effects option of the Effects menu. Change the settings to the following: Original Color, Direction of 135, Depth of 4, and Level of 100. Marquee-select both the knot and the text objects. From the Object menu, choose Drop Shadow. Change the Presets to Flat-Bottom Right. After that, change the Opacity to 65 and the Width to 12. A drop shadow is added to both objects, as shown.

3 The last step is to add shadows to the edge of the sign. This is the easiest part. With the background selected, open the Effects menu, choose Artistic, and select Vignette. Change the settings to the following: Color of Black, Shape of Ellipse, Offset of 120, and Fade of 60. The resulting image is shown.

Variations on a Theme

Congratulations. You made knots and rope borders and learned a little about Clip Masks along the way. Now let's look at some of the other rope tricks we have in our hat.

This was the original idea I came up with when working on this chapter, and it is also the one that Gary liked best. Go figure—I live in Texas and love things nautical, and Gary lives near San Francisco and likes the dusty western look. The text in the image shown was created by selecting it with Lock Transparency enabled and applying a wood Bitmap fill to it. The edge on the text was then created using the Emboss filter with Lock Transparency disabled. The boots are floating objects from the Objects folder in the CD. The original is loaded and placed on the left side. It is then duplicated (CTRL+D). The duplicate is flipped by choosing Flip, then Horizontal in the Object menu. Drop shadows are added to both.

The photograph on the text in this image was created by placing a photograph on top of the text and then, with the photograph object selected, clicking in the empty column in the Objects Docker window between the eye icon and the name. This enables Clip to Parent, which allows only the portions of the photograph directly above the text to appear. The rope was drawn on top and then, using the Clip Mask technique described earlier in this chapter, I removed the parts of the rope that were to appear behind the letters. Drop shadows were added using the Drop Shadow command in the Object menu; the tips of the rope were blurred with the Smudge Effect tool.

To write a name in rope (in this case, for Doug Chomyn, product manager for PHOTO-PAINT), you must have a stylus. Now, there may be some of you out there who can actually write with a mouse. To you I say: well done, and you need to get out more. The stylus is really helpful, if not necessary, to write names or accurately control the rope brush for this type of work. The background fill was one of the Bitmap fill tiles from the Tiles folder on the Corel CD, to which I applied an Emboss filter. It makes most of the wood fills appear to be raised and more rustic.

I was surprised by how many people asked me to include a noose. Maybe it's because Halloween is only ten days away at the time of this writing. Anyhow, the noose is composed of three parts. The actual noose is drawn as an object. A new object is created, and the shank of the noose is made by starting on the bottom and spiraling upward. As in the previous exercise, a stylus is almost mandatory to get the control needed. I know it should have 13 spirals (don't count—there are only 9), but it conveys the idea. The last piece is the end of the rope placed on the top. With this piece, it was necessary to use the Clip Mask command to remove the part where it is supposed to look like it is going into the shank. I also used a Clip Mask on the shank to remove a small portion at the top so it would look more rounded. The Clip Masks were then combined with their respective objects, and then the three objects were combined together (CTRL+ALT+DNARROW); texture was applied using the Canvas filter, as previously described. The shadow was created with the Drop Shadow command using the Perspective setting. After making the shadow, I ungrouped it from the noose, applied a Gaussian blur to it, and moved it away from the noose. The only problem I see with this noose is the shank. The Rope setting of the Image Sprayer doesn't corner very well, and the tight angles of the shank don't give a look I am overly fond of. Regardless, it is a noose and that's it for now.

Creating Dynamic Text Effects

Nearly every time I create something in **PHOTO-PAINT**, I also add a title, logo, slogan, or what-have-you to the image. Over the years, I have collected—in the part of my brain normally dedicated to watching the Cowboys win football games (it is currently vacant)—an assortment of techniques for making text look good with sometimes little to no effort. So there are no fancy or complex projects in this chapter. In fact, it is more like a cookbook of text recipes. As a bonus, I may include my famous recipe for rum cake. On with the text. Let's begin with a real no-brainer.

NOTE

This chapter is for use with PHOTO-PAINT 7 and 8.

This technique has become quite popular in the magazines in the past few years. Notice in the image that the text, while readable, gets lost in the crowd. To make it stand out, select the Drop Shadow command in the Object menu and use the following settings: Distance: 0, Opacity: 100%; Width: 12, Average. The result is shown next. I told you it was a no-brainer.

QUICK AND EASY BRASS

Here is a recipe for brass that is easy and works well for most occasions.

STEP

1 Create a 5×3 inch image at 120 dpi. Enter the text you are going to use. For the example, I used Futura XBlkCn BT at a size of 72 points and interline spacing of 75. Select the Object Picker tool and enable Lock Transparency in the Objects Docker window; PHOTO-PAINT 7 users, ensure the Objects Roll-Up is in Single mode. The image shown is in blue text, but that is only because I want to take advantage of a full-color book.

THE SOUND OF SMOOTH JAZZ SILKY BRASS

STEP

2 Let's make brass. From the Effects menu, choose Fancy and then select Julia Set Explorer. Click the Presets menu at the middle-bottom of the dialog box and choose Corel Presets. Move down the list until you reach Totally Tubular. We now have the correct pattern but the wrong color. Click on the Color Outside box (lower right of the dialog box) and choose Metallic from the list that just appeared and then choose Gentle Gold from the secondary list. Click OK. The results are shown here.

THE SOUND OF SMOOTH JAZZ SILKY BRASS

3 PHOTO-PAINT 7 users should click the Layer mode in the Objects Roll-Up. PHOTO-PAINT 8 users should uncheck Lock Transparency in the Objects Docker window. From the Effects menu, choose 3D Effects and select Emboss. Click the reset button to restore defaults and change the color to Original color. Click OK, and you have brass. For an added touch, select the Drop Shadow command in the Object menu and change the Direction to lower right (225 degrees), the Offset to 0.04; Opacity: 80; Feather width of 6 Average. The resulting image shown has a wood bitmap fill for the background with a Vignette filter (from Artistic in the Effects menu) applied.

WOOD LETTERS MADE EASY

Now here's one we hope you'll really like. (Did that phrase sound familiar? Watched a lot of Rocky and Bullwinkle, didn't you?) Although the steps may appear complicated, you can create very realistic-looking wood characters in one minute, leaving you 29 minutes to watch Rocky and Bullwinkle (sigh).

1 Create a new 24-bit color image that is 4×3 inches at 120 dpi. Click the Text tool in the Toolbox and from the Property Bar select the font CroissantD at a size of 96 with Bold enable and interline spacing set to 68. Type **SAM'S WOOD SHOP** as shown. Again, for those just tuning in, don't be concerned about the color of the font in the example.

STEP

2 Select the Object Picker tool. If you are using PHOTO-PAINT 7, change the Objects Roll-Up to Single mode and ensure the object is selected. In PHOTO-PAINT 8, enable Lock Transparency in the Objects Docker window. From the Edit menu, choose Fill and select the Bitmap fill, and then click the Edit button. In the Bitmap fill dialog box, click Load and then locate a light-colored wood. I used the Wood13l.cpt in the \TILES\WOOD\LARGE folder of the Corel CD. Click Open and then click OK each time to apply the fill. The image should look like the one here.

STEP

3 PHOTO-PAINT 7 users should ensure the Preserve Image button is enabled before doing this step. Create a mask from the object (CTRL+M) and invert the mask. From the Effects menu, select 3D Effects (Fancy for PHOTO-PAINT 7) and select The Boss. Change the Style to Wet and change the following settings: Width: 5; Height: 50. Click OK. That's it. Add a drop shadow and a background, and you are done. Now where is the *TV Guide*?

TIP

Technically, the above technique will work with any font, but I recommend using a broad sans serif rather than a thin, anorexic one. The key to adjusting The Boss filters for different fonts is in the Width setting. In PHOTO-PAINT 8, it is very simple to set up onscreen preview, change the settings, and watch the results. Not so in PHOTO-PAINT 7, where you must squint at a microscopic nonzoomable image in the Preview window and wonder what the different settings will look like.

MAKING A PLAQUE FOR A MONUMENT

This is one of those neat things that you can do with PHOTO-PAINT that you can't do with any other program. I love going to museums, and if there is one common element, it is copper or bronze plaques. Just so we can have a little class in this chapter, I chose for the text on the plaque a famous quote of Caesar's (not Caesar's Palace): "Vini, Vidi, Vici," which means "I came, I saw, I conquered." This exercise is a little complicated, but if you have half as much fun as I did creating it, you'll enjoy it.

STEP

1 Create a new 24-bit color image that is 3×3 inches at 150 dpi. By now you should know where Edit Fill/Texture Fill is located (Edit-Fill). Open the Texture Fill dialog box and change to Moss in Samples 7. Change the first Mineral color to Mint Green and the second Mineral color to Murky Green. Change the Light to Pale yellow. Click OK and OK again to apply the fill. From the Effects menu, choose 2D Effects and select Wet Paint. Change the settings to Percentage: 75; Wetness: 50. Click OK. The result is shown.

STEP

2 Select the Text tool and change the font to Garamond at a size of 72 with Bold enabled. Select Center alignment and change interline spacing to 80. Type in our Latin quote of the day: **VINI, VIDI, VICI** and click the Object Picker tool. Align the text to the center of the image (CTRL+A, or CTRL+SHIFT+A in PHOTO-PAINT 7). Now create a mask from the object (CTRL+M), and from the Objects Docker window (Objects Roll-Up) select the background and make the text invisible by clicking the eye icon.

S T E P

3

From the Effects menu, choose 3D Effects (Fancy in PHOTO-PAINT 7) and select The Boss. Change the settings as follows: Width: 15; Smoothness: 50; Height: 125; Brightness: 25; Sharpness: 0; Direction 135; Angle: 45; Drop off: Mesa. Click OK. The image should look like the one shown here. We could call it quits right here, but let's not.

S T E P

4

Remove the mask. In the Objects Docker window (Objects Roll-Up), make the text visible again and select it. Enable Lock Transparency and use the Edit Fill tool to apply the Texture Fill to the text. Now, select the Emboss filter (in 3D Effects of the Effects menu) and change the settings to the following: Original Color; Depth: 3; Level 60; Direction: 135. Click OK, and the resulting image is shown.

5 For our last, finishing touch we are going to make four mounting blot heads to hold our plaque wherever it will be mounted. It is very simple. Select the Ellipse Shape tool and ensure it is set to Render to Object. While pressing and holding the CTRL key, drag a small circle like the one shown; when you let go of the mouse button, it becomes an object. With Lock Transparency still enabled and the new circle object selected, go to the Effects menu and from the 3D Effects choose Map to Object. Change the settings to Spherical, 12, and Best and click the OK button. With the object still selected, enable the Drop Shadow command with an Offset: 0; Opacity: 100%; Average Feather width: 14. Finally, add just a touch of an airbrush (Black) to the bottom side of the circle. Now combine the shadow and object together into one object. Duplicate it three times and place one in each corner. The completed image, with the added but necessary marble is shown next.

A WORD OF WARNING

As you begin to create your own text designs, I advise that you keep a notepad nearby. As you are working, jot down the steps as you go through them and store them somewhere safe. Remember, when it comes to techniques and procedures, the weakest pen is superior to the best mind.

Variations on a Theme

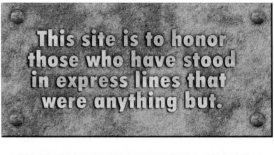

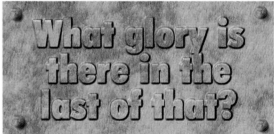

There are several variations to this copper theme and the ones that follow show only a few of them. Whether you are making copper plaques, tape labels, or quick chrome, the techniques that follow will allow you to make publications and Web pages that really demand attention.

Starting with the technique we just completed in the preceding section, here are some variations you can try when you make your own plaque. In this image, the text that was placed on top had the Motion Blur filter applied to it (at a setting of 30 and a direction of 135). Then the text had a -10 hue and a +10 brightness applied to it. It gives it the appearance of a style of casting where the surface of the letters is ground off after it is cast. In the next image, a broader typeface was used and instead of Embossing the letters, the Wet Paint was applied at a lower setting (Percentage: 50; Wetness: 40) to give it the weathered appearance at the top of each character. The bolts on the corners had the Swirl filter applied instead of the Map to Object filter, and in place of the Drop Shadow command a light shadow was created to the lower right of the bold with an airbrush (set to Wide cover).

Making tape labels is fun. To create the tape, just make a red rectangular object like the one shown here. The Fountain Fill for the tape is made by selecting Custom with Red on each end and placing a light pink in the center. Type the text you want (white), create a mask, and use The Boss filter to emboss the tape. The settings are: Width: 3; Smoothness: 50; Height: 24; Brightness and Sharpness: each 100; Drop off: Mesa. Click OK and remove the mask. If you have ever used these labels, you know that the actual tape turns white when stretched. For that reason, the edges of the text on the real tape have a white feather around them. Use the Drop Shadow command, using white for the shadow and a distance of zero. Adjust the feather width and opacity until you achieve the effect you want. For the final touch, use the Page Curl filter and apply it to the end of the tape, as shown above.

ry applying the same technique used to make the wood letters to thin or hollow text. The word "Bold" had a Texture fill (Rainbow blend) applied to it, and the text below it had a Fountain Fill applied to it. The only difficulty I have discovered to date with using thin or hollow text is the difficulty of seeing any patterns due to the thinness of the font.

QUICK CHROME FOR PHOTO-PAINT 8 USERS

ere is a technique to easily create some excellent chrome. (I discovered this technique while rechecking this chapter. Time did not allow me to include it in Chapter 18, our mutual chrome chapter.) While it could be done in PHOTO-PAINT 7, theoretically, it requires a Julia Set Explorer fill/setting, which doesn't exist in that release.

First, create a new 24-bit color image (I used 6×2 inches at 120 dpi). Select or create the object you want to make into chrome. In this example, I used the Text tool to create the word "Mustang" using the font Revue BT at a size of 96. Select the Object Picker tool and then center the text on the image (CTRL+A) and in the Objects Docker window and enable Lock Transparency.

From the Fancy category in the Effects menu, choose Julia Set Explorer 2.0. When the dialog box opens, choose Totally Tubular from the Corel Presets in the middle-bottom portion of the dialog box. Now, click on the Color Outside box, and a large drop-down list appears with Metallic already checked. Click and drag the mouse down the list until Metallic is highlighted. Yet another list appears. Don't let go of the mouse button. With the mouse button still held down, move over to this new list and select Silvery Sheen; the list closes. Click the OK button in the lower-right corner of the dialog box, resulting in the image shown.

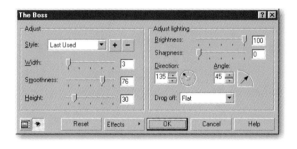

Then, create a mask from the text (CTRL+M) and then invert the mask (CTRL+I). From the Effects menu in 3D Effects, choose The Boss. Change the settings to match those shown and click OK. Click the Remove Mask button in the Toolbar. The resulting image is shown next.

Finally, in the Image menu, choose Adjust and then select Tone Curve. In the Curves section of the dialog box, click the Open button. In the next dialog box, choose Solarize.crv and click Open and then OK. To make it look even more like chrome, from the Effects menu choose Sharpen and then Directional Sharpen. Change the slider to 75 percent and click OK. There you have it—chrome. To add that finished look, I added a drop shadow and applied a Fountain Fill background, as shown.

PAINT Bucket to the Metal

As a judge in several of the Corel Design contests, I always admired the metallic effects people were able to create using CorelDRAW. The only problem with all of them was that they didn't look real. I would study these shrines to metallic effects that were composed of literally thousands of blends and wonder why they just looked like illustrations and not photographs. With all of the detail, shadows, and the reflections, I never asked myself, "Is it real or is it...?" Finally, I realized why they looked like drawings and not photographs. They were too perfect. There are generally two things you can say about real objects as opposed to created or drawn objects: real objects are rarely symmetrical, and more important, they are never perfect. As I began to create original work with **PHOTO-PAINT**, I discovered that there were a lot of ways to mimic the imperfection of the real world. So what follows in this chapter are a few of the tricks I have learned over the past few years about creating metallic effects that will hopefully cause the viewer to ask, "Is it real?"

N O T E

Note: This chapter is for use with PHOTO-PAINT 7 and 8.

I really had fun creating this exercise. My wife thought it was because of my years in the U.S. Navy, but I doubt it. Of all the things I worked with while in the canoe club, I never ever worked with anchor chains. This type of chain is a marvel in design. It has been designed with the single purpose of never getting tangled when laid in a pile (as in the anchor locker). It is also a great spot to begin to work with metal effects, because anchor chains rust (if not properly maintained), and we are going to learn a lot about rust and corrosion in this chapter. The first part is to make the link in the chain.

STEP

1 Create a new 24-bit image that is 4×2 inches at 120 dpi. From the Tools menu, choose Grid and Ruler Setup and change the Grid Spacing to 0.25 in horizontal and vertical and enable both Show Grid and Snap to Grid. Change the Fill color to Black by right-clicking on it in the onscreen palette. Next, select the Rectangle Shape tool (F6) in the Toolbox. Open the Tool Settings roll-up (CTRL+F8) and click the Uniform Fill button. Make sure that the Width is set to 0 and the Roundness is set to 100 and enable the Render to Object feature.

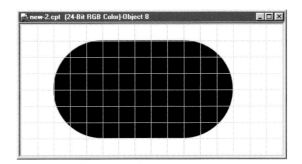

To make the link, click and drag the shape shown. It is 11 squares wide in the middle and 6 squares in height. Change the Fill color to White and click and drag to two shapes, as shown in the next illustration. We now have three objects that look like a link in an anchor chain. At this point, you can turn off the Grid in the View menu and disable Snap to Grid (CTRL+Y). From the Toolbox, select the Magic Wand Mask tool and click anywhere on the black part of the link. A mask now surrounds the link both inside and out. From the Object menu, choose Select All and then select Delete from the same menu. All that is left is the mask. From the Mask menu, save the mask to a channel, naming it Chain Link. In PHOTO-PAINT 8, from the Object menu choose Create Object-Copy Selection; in PHOTO-PAINT 7, from the Object menu choose Create from Mask. If you cannot see the object, turn on the Object Marquee in the Toolbar.

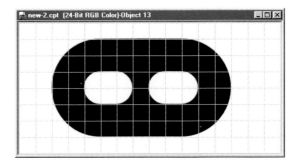

STEP

2 In the Objects Docker window, enable Lock Transparency; for PHOTO-PAINT 7 users, select Single mode in the Objects Roll-Up. From the Edit menu, choose Fill. When the Edit Fill and Transparency dialog box opens, choose Bitmap fill and click Edit. Click the Load button in the Bitmap Fill dialog box and locate the file Wood08l.cpt in the \TILES\WOOD\LARGE\ folder. Click Open, then click OK to select the Fill and click OK again to apply it. The result, which at this point doesn't look much like anything, is shown.

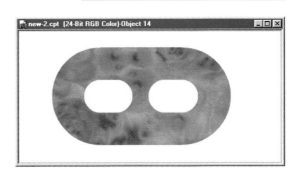

3 From the Image menu, choose Adjust and then select Auto Equalize. From the Effects menu, choose Noise-Add Noise, and Gaussian at a Level of 20 and a Density of 50. Click OK. Now apply the Emboss filter (in the 3D Effects option of the Effects menu) at the default settings with Original Color. The result shown is a rusty look, but the link looks as flat as a playing card—we will fix that next.

Choose Load in the Mask menu and load the channel named Chain Link. PHOTO-PAINT 8 moved the location and method of operation for the Stroke Mask tool. So, here is how to apply this step in PHOTO-PAINT 8: Select the Brush tool in the Toolbox. Open the Tool Settings roll-up (CTRL+F8). Change the selected brush tool to the airbrush and choose Wide Cover as the Type. Make sure the Paint color is still black. From the Edit menu, choose Stroke, then Stroke Mask. In the resulting dialog box, select Middle of Mask Border and click OK. In the Tool Settings roll-up, change the Type to Medium Cover and select Repeat Brush Tool (CTRL+L). In PHOTO-PAINT 8, we select the brush and then apply Stroke to Mask.

In PHOTO-PAINT 7, we select the brush from within the command. From the Mask menu, select Stroke, then Stroke Mask. Choose Middle of Mask and then select the Wide Cover airbrush. Click OK to apply, and then repeat the process with the Medium Cover Type.

Remove the Mask. The result is shown.

4 While fresh rust may appear bright, the colors in our link look too saturated. From the Image menu, choose Adjust and then Hue/Saturation/Brightness and change the Saturation to -50. The resulting image is shown.

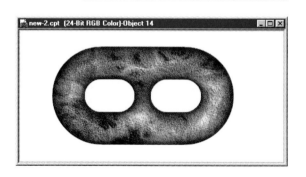

Now we need to make a side view of the link (it is easier than the first link). Turn on Snap to Grid (CTRL+Y), select the Rectangle Shape tool, and drag a shape like the one shown. The color of the fill doesn't mean anything—I used yellow to make it stand out. Select the Object Picker tool and create a mask (CTRL+M) from the new shape. Save the mask as a channel named Side Link and remove the mask. Turn off Snap to Grid (CTRL+Y). Now repeat steps 3 to 7. In the image shown, I have moved the new link over to the side so it appears to be hooked to the original link. Duplicate the link (CTRL+D in PHOTO-PAINT 8 or CTRL+SHIFT+D for PHOTO-PAINT 7). From the Object menu, choose Flip Vertical and then repeat with Flip Horizontal.

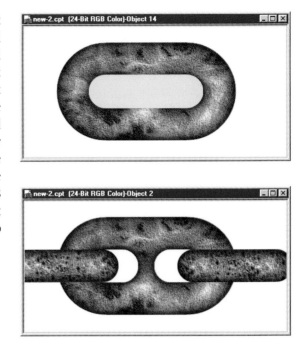

To complete this part of the exercise, select all three objects and group them together (CTRL+G). Select the wide link and, using the Wide Cover airbrush, paint a shadow beneath the two thin links, as shown. Now, click the corner handle and reduce the size of the group until it fits into the image. From the Object menu, combine the grouped objects into a single object and then place a drop shadow below it, as shown. Save the File as CHAIN.CPT and don't forget where you parked it.

MAKE A LIST

What can you do with the anchor chain? More than you might first imagine. While there are some examples in the "Variations on a Theme" section later, here is one that we can do now: make an image list for the Image Sprayer. Since people who smoke are having more and more difficulty finding places where they can enjoy a smoke with their meal, I thought it would be appropriate to make a sign for chain smokers.

STEP

1

Open the file CHAIN.CPT that you made in the previous section. Select the Image Sprayer (press the I key in PHOTO-PAINT 8). Open its Tool Settings roll-up (CTRL+F8) and click the small options button located in the upper-right portion of the first tab. Select Save Objects as Image List. When asked about the Directional Image list, choose Yes; when asked for the number of images, enter 4. This makes four copies of the objects, each one rotated 90 degrees. When asked for a name for the new file, call it CHAIN.CPT. Let's take the new brush out for a spin.

STEP

2

Open a new image that is 6 × 4 inches at 96 dpi. Using Fill in the Edit menu, select the Bitmap fill and select the file METAL01L.CPT in the \TILES\METAL\LARGE folder on the CD. Click Open, then click OK twice to apply to the background. Now we have an uninteresting rectangle of deck plate (metal flooring to you landlubbers), as shown. Please note that I have dragged the image window so it is wider than the image.

STEP

3

Our goal is make an Image Sprayer brush that appears to be a solid chain. Select the Image Sprayer tool again. The Chain file should still be selected. In the Tool Settings roll-up, change the brush size to 300 (mine was originally over 500), and on the middle tab change the Spacing to 55. At the bottom of the middle tab in the Image Choice section, select By Direction and change both the From and To values to 2. Click the third tab and make sure that the Orbits option is not enabled. Whew! Now we are almost ready.

Since we want the resulting chain to be an object, uncheck the Lock Transparency box and click the New Object button at the bottom of the Objects Docker window. If you are using PHOTO-PAINT 7, you will need to make sure the Objects Roll-Up is in Layer mode. Beginning outside and to the left of the image, while pressing and holding CTRL, click and drag the mouse horizontally across the top of the image. The CTRL key is the constrain key that keeps the brushstroke in a straight line. The result should look something like the image shown. If the distance between the links doesn't overlap well, then change the Spacing setting. If your links are pointing up like a picket fence, change the To/From to 1 in the Image Choice section. Use Undo (CTRL+Z) to remove a chain you are not satisfied with. Once it is working correctly, click the New Object button again and create a second chain just like and below the first, as shown next.

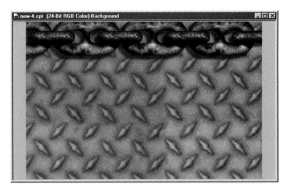

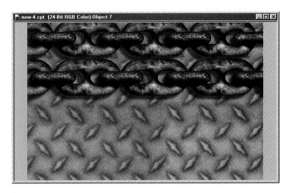

Now for the fun part. With the Object Picker tool, click on the bottom chain until the rotation handles appear. Click and grab a corner rotation handle until the chain is at an approximate 45-degree angle. The chain looks a little jaggy at this point, but once you are satisfied with the rotation, double-click on the chain object to apply the transformation. Then drag the chain down and off the image until the two ends are out of sight, as shown.

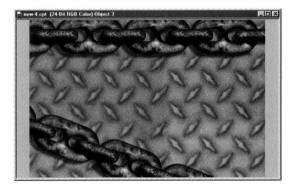

Now for the text. Select the Text tool and change the font to Kabel Ult BT, with a size of 72, Bold enabled, and interline spacing at 75 percent. Type **CHAIN SMOKER'S SECTION**. I used spaces to offset the second and third line. Select the Object Picker tool to make the text an object. Enable Lock Transparency in the Objects Docker window. PHOTO-PAINT 7 users, choose Single mode in the Objects Roll-Up.

STEP

7 Let's give the text some texture. Use the Fill command in the Edit menu to select the burled wood we originally used for the chain and apply it to the text. Now we apply the steps used to create the original rust. Select Auto Equalize-Add Noise, and apply the Emboss filter (see step 4 in the preceding "Anchors Aweigh" section). We won't be applying the Stroke Mask. Add a Drop Shadow using the Drop Shadow command, and you have the finished image.

NOTE

Research indicates that 99 percent of all people who claim to be chain smokers actually do not smoke chains.

WHEN CORROSION IS PRETTY

One of my favorite things to see in a building is green copper. Of course, copper isn't green, and in fact when the copper is first installed it looks like copper. After it is exposed to the elements, it begins to oxidize (rust) and turn that lovely shade of pale green. The two major differences between the rust of iron and that of copper are the color and the name. The color of rusted copper is a faded green, and the rust of copper is called patina. Another major difference between the two is the emotional response they evoke in a viewer. Rust is generally associated with age and neglect, while patina evokes the image of something distinguished and usually expensive. So, let's learn how to make the distinguished and expensive stuff.

MAKING A GREEN PATINA (NOT GREEN PEACE) SIGN

Every town I have lived in has a first church of whatever and a first bank and a—you know what I mean. What I have never seen is a last bank. So we are going to make a sign for the Last Bank of Dallas.

STEP

1 Create an image 6 × 2 inches, 24-bit color, at 120 dpi. You can use a lower resolution if it doesn't fit in your screen at 100 percent. Click the Text tool in the Toolbox and change the font to Bremen Bd BT. Change the font size so it fits in the image. I am using a size of 72, Bold enabled, centered, and intercharacter spacing of 75. Type **LAST BANK OF DALLAS** and click the Object Picker tool in the Toolbox to change the text into an object. Align the object to the center of the image.

STEP

2 Enable Lock Transparency in the Objects Docker window. PHOTO-PAINT 7 users, select Single mode in the Objects Roll-Up. Select the text object. From the Edit menu, choose Edit, and when the Edit Fill and Transparency dialog box opens, click the Texture Fill button (last one on the right) and then click Edit. This action opens the Texture Fill dialog box. Change the dialog box to Samples 7. From the Texture list, select Moss. We are going to change some colors to get the effect we want. To find the specific named colors called for, click the down-pointing arrow in the color swatch indicated and then click the Others button. When you select a color from the palette, the name appears. Make the following changes to the Moss setting: change the first Mineral to Mint Green, the second Mineral to Murky Green, and the Light to Pale Yellow. Now click the + button up by the Texture library and name this setting Patina. Click OK to select the fill and OK again to apply it.

3   Duplicate the Text object (CTRL+D in PHOTO-PAINT 8 or CTRL+SHIFT+D in PHOTO-PAINT 7). Select the original object (bottom) and make the top one invisible by clicking on the eye icon. The bottom object will form the edge that we can see, so we need to make it look three-dimensional. From the Image menu, choose Adjust, select Brightness-Contrast-Intensity, and change the Intensity to -50. Click OK. Make the top object visible by clicking on the eye icon. With the bottom object still selected, use the arrow keys on the keyboard to move it down three pixels. Each keystroke moves the object one pixel. In the Objects Docker window (Objects Roll-Up in PHOTO-PAINT 7), select the top object. The resulting image is shown.

4   Change the Paper color to Black by clicking Black in the onscreen palette while pressing and holding CTRL. This is necessary to keep the Wet Paint filter from dripping white paint on our image. From the 2D Effects option of the Effects menu, choose Wet Paint and change the settings to Percentage 100 and Wetness 45. Click OK. Next, apply the Hue/Saturation/Lightness filter again, using the following settings: Hue -10, Saturation -20, and Lightness 0. Click OK. Select both of the objects and combine them into a single object (CTRL+ALT+DNARROW in PHOTO-PAINT 8 or CTRL+SHIFT+L in PHOTO-PAINT 7). The resulting image is shown.

5

Select the Drop Shadow command from the Objects menu and change the following settings: Offset bottom-right button (270 degrees in PHOTO-PAINT 8), Distance 0.1, Identical Values checked, Feather 12, and Opacity 100. The resulting image is shown.

6

Select the background in the Objects Roll-Up (Objects Docker window in PHOTO-PAINT 8) and select the Fill command in the Edit menu. Click the Bitmap fill button and then Edit. In the Bitmap Fill dialog box, click the Load button and choose a background tile from the Corel CD (the one shown in the illustration is TILES\MARBLE\LARGE\MARL06L.CPT. Click OK to load the bitmap fill and click OK again to apply it. Final touch: from the Effects menu, choose Artistic and select the Vignette filter. Change the settings to the following: Color Black, Shape Ellipse, Offset 130, and Fade 75. The result is shown here.

While the Last Bank of Dallas sounds like the bank that the Dallas Cowboys used during the last losing season, the technique can be used anytime you want your text to project an image of either tradition or something above retail.

Variations on a Theme

LINKING THE CHAIN

In this illustration, I took the links we made in the first exercise, duplicated them, and formed the chain. Next, I made the deck plate as an object in the background. I made it larger than the image so I could apply perspective to it later. To get the rusty deck (floor) look, I applied the same wood bitmap fill, using the Overlay Merge Mode. Only the dark areas showed through, giving the appearance of rust. The last thing was to apply perspective transform to the back object to give the deck some visual perspective.

REAL RUST

The next example is a chain again, but this time I painted some of the areas on the link with the Sponge Effect tool. This reduced the color saturation in those areas but allowed it to remain in others. The result was a heightened appearance to the rust on the chain. A photo was placed in the background to give the illusion that the chain is real.

For this image, the bottom layer of the patina layer is lighter, to give the effect that the light is shining from underneath. The ridges on the letters came from creating a mask from the text, deleting the object, and then applying the Impressionist filter to the mask in PAINT on Mask mode. This gave the text mask a rippled edge. Next, the rippled mask was made into an object and the texture fill (with a brighter green) was applied. The marble is a bitmap fill that had The Boss filter applied to a rectangle mask surrounding the text. The finished image looks less like weathered copper, but it really looks three-dimensional. The next image used the same technique to ripple the edge.

Well gang, it's time to move on. I leave you with this bit of wisdom: If at first you don't succeed, then skydiving is not for you.

BACK TO ꓘƆA乇

I was not surprised to learn that my young colleague, Mr. Huss, and I have both at some time created actual leaded glass art. Although we approach a problem from different directions, PAINT vs. DRAW, using different techniques and methods, our results are often quite similar. Creating leaded glass art is both rewarding and frustrating. Unfortunately, the computer monitor cannot match the richness of light streaming though pieces of colored glass, although it can come close.

I've always believed that glass can sense one's confidence, or lack of same, when it is being cut with a glass cutter, a small tool with a tiny roller at one end that scores the surface of the glass, creating a slight fracture at the point of the score and permitting the glass to be snapped apart at the score. It's this snapping apart which the glass uses to gauge one's confidence level. If the snap is done in a positive manner, the glass breaks cleanly. But hesitate, show the slightest degree of fear, and the glass, sensing this, is likely as not to break into several pieces, none of which is the desired shape.

Fortunately, creating leaded glass art in DRAW or PHOTO-PAINT is far more forgiving (Undo is not an option when breaking glass). Staring into your monitor is not as harmful health-wise as breathing the fumes put off by the flux when applying lead solder to the lead cams. And I'm happy to say that after a decade of using a computer, I've never received a nasty cut from my mouse. If you want to change the color of glass, you either have to create the glass yourself, fire on color (this is the stained-glass process), or pick out another piece of glass. So, all things considered, creating leaded glass art with DRAW or PAINT is more rewarding and less dangerous using the techniques that Huss and I will offer in this chapter. The only decision you have to make is which technique works best for you.

Stained Glass
IN COREL **PHOTO-PAINT**

Stained glass has a long and rich history. While many tend to associate it with either majestic church windows or the lamps of Mr. Tiffany, it embodies the two most important qualities of any work of art, that of color and light. In that, stained glass serves as a medium, both in the electronic images we create in this chapter or the real thing, to convey powerful images. If there is a limitation to stained glass, it is found in the preconceived ideas of the viewers. While a flower may look wonderful, the same stained-glass window with a picture of a jet plane does not seem to work. With that one minor limitation to this technique understood, let's begin to explore some of the stained glass we can make with Corel.

N O T E

This chapter covers PHOTO-PAINT 7 and 8.

MEMORIES OF GLASSES STAINED AND OTHERWISE

Creating stained glass using PHOTO-PAINT brings back memories for me. I was working at the offices in Ottawa trying to get the Corel PHOTO-PAINT 5 Plus manual finished so I could go home. Many of the features in PHOTO-PAINT were in flux, and I was trying to figure out activities that would demonstrate the program, when I discovered that I could make a close approximation of stained glass. That was using PHOTO-PAINT 5 Plus, many millions of pixels ago. It wasn't until the Duke of DRAW (Gary Priester) told me he wanted to use DRAW to create stained glass that I realized how long it had been. I saw the stained glass that Gary made—not too shabby for a vector drawing—but we pixel pushers always think that we can outdo the bezier benders. You be the judge.

We'll start with a simple stained glass to learn the technique.

BASIC STAINED GLASS

STEP

1

Create a new image that is 24-bit color, four inches wide and seven inches tall, at 72 dpi. Select the Rectangle Shape tool (F6) and open the Tools Setting roll-up (CTRL+F8). Change the fill to No Fill (last button on the right) and change the Width to 4. Ensure the Roundness is set to 0 and Render to Object is enabled. Click and drag a rectangle that goes to (but does not touch) the edge of the image. Select the Ellipse Shape tool (F7). From the Tool Settings roll-up, change the settings so they are the same as the Rectangle Shape tool. Beginning in the upper-left corner, click and drag an ellipse that fills the inside and just touches the rectangle we made. In the Objects Docker window (Objects Roll-Up in PHOTO-PAINT 7), select both objects and use the Combine command in the Object menu to combine them together. The resulting image is shown.

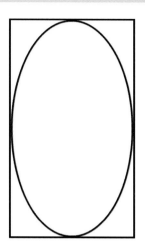

STEP

2

Select the object and click the Create Mask (from object) button. Using the Save Mask as Channel command in the Mask menu, name the mask Lead. Remove the Mask by selecting Remove from the Mask menu. Now combine the object with the background by clicking the Combine Objects button at the bottom of the Objects Docker window (Objects Roll-Up). From the Effects menu, choose 3D Effects and then Emboss. Click the Reset button and then click OK. The resulting image is shown.

STEP

3

From the Mask menu, reload the mask from the channel named Lead. From the Effects menu, choose 3D Effects in PHOTO-PAINT 8 and Fancy in PHOTO-PAINT 7 and then select The Boss. When the dialog box opens, select the Wet setting. Change the Width in the Adjust section to 3 and click OK. Remove the mask. The results are shown.

4 Let's make the glass. Double-click the Fill tool in the Toolbox (which opens the Tool Settings roll-up), change the Tolerance setting to 1, and select the Texture Fill button (last button on the right). Click the Edit button, opening the Texture Fill dialog box. From the Styles Library, select Swirls 2. Change the first Color to a Dark Green and the second Color to a bright Yellow-Green. Now, the key to creating different patterns is to change the pattern by returning to the Texture Fill dialog box and clicking the Preview button. Each time it is clicked, the pattern changes. Find one you like and click OK to apply the colors to all four corners. The result is shown.

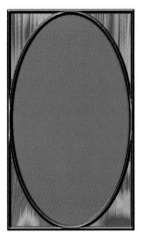

TIP

I recommend saving patterns you like in their own library. I have one called Stained-Glass Patterns. (Wow! What an original title!) When you find a pattern you like, click the + button up by the Texture Library name, which opens the Save Texture As dialog box. Give the texture a descriptive name, and if you want to make a dedicated library for these patterns, make a name for the new library. From that time on, you can save the patterns in the new library. A quick thought about the names you choose: Stained glass patterns tend to be horizontally or vertically oriented (like the one we are using). Calling the pattern Screaming Gonzos is cute, but Bright Green Vertical I, II, III, and so on is much easier to organize and will help you locate individual patterns. But, hey, if Screaming Gonzos works for you, go for it.

STEP

5

Now we will change the orientation of the image. From the Image menu, select Rotate, 90 degrees clockwise. Reload the mask channel named Lead, and from the Mask menu choose Shape and Expand. Choose a Width of 3 (pixels). We need to expand the mask if it is to include the portion of the leading that was created by The Boss filter. Save the expanded mask as a channel named Big Lead. Invert the mask. For the oval background, we will use a different pattern. Select the Fill tool; from the Texture Fill dialog box choose the Styles menu, and from the Texture List select Swirls. Change the preset colors using Pastel Blue for the first color and White for the second Color. To get the pattern shown in the illustration, use Texture # 20623. Click OK, and then click the Fill tool inside the oval. Remove the mask.

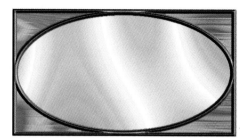

STEP

6

For the centerpiece of the stained glass, we are going to use clip art from the CorelDRAW collection. The one used is CLIPART\FLOWERS\FLOWR025.CDR. For PHOTO-PAINT 8 users, this step is pretty simple. From CorelDRAW 7 or 8, open a new image and import the clip art. Copy the image to the clipboard. In PHOTO-PAINT 8, paste the contents of the clipboard as an object. It will be placed as an object without a white background. If you are using PHOTO-PAINT 7, open the CDR file in PHOTO-PAINT and use the Color Mask to isolate the white background. Use the mask to make the flower clip art into an object. Either drag the object into the stained glass or copy it to the clipboard and Paste it into the stained glass image so it looks like the one shown.

7 The flower doesn't look translucent, so we are going to make it appear so. The flower is an object, so make a duplicate of the object (CTRL+D in PHOTO-PAINT 8 and CTRL+SHIFT+D in PHOTO-PAINT 7). The top (duplicate) object is automatically selected. PHOTO-PAINT 7 users need to ensure the Single mode is enabled in the Objects Roll-Up. Create a mask of the object (CTRL+M). Invert the mask. From the Effects menu, choose 3D Effects (Fancy in PHOTO-PAINT 7) and select The Boss. Change to Wet and click OK. Remove the mask. The image is shown. OK, now this is the neat part. In the Objects Docker window (Objects Roll-Up), change the Merge Mode of the object to Hard Light. For users of PHOTO-PAINT 7, the closest I can get to Hard Light is the Subtract Merge Mode, with Opacity changed to 50 percent. Combine the two objects to the background. The result is shown next.

8 To really make this look three-dimensional, we need to add shadows to the lead. This used to be a laborious effort with the airbrush. Now it is simple. From the Mask menu, load the mask channel named Big Lead. Create an object from the mask using Create Object: Copy Selection. PHOTO-PAINT 7 users should create an object with the Preserve Image button enabled. From the Object menu, choose Drop Shadow. We want to keep the shadow we create physically close to the lead, so I have picked the light source coming from the upper left, meaning the shadow needs to be in the lower right. Use a Distance setting of 0.07, Opacity of 100%, and an Average Width of 10 for the Feather setting. Click OK, and you have a realistic-looking piece of stained glass—almost. If you are satisfied with the shadow, combine the lead and the shadow (they are both objects) with the background.

FINISHING TOUCHES

While we are done at this point, there are a few finishing touches you can add to make it look more realistic.

The most important part, which Gary has already pointed out, is the appearance of solder joints, which are easy—but time consuming. Each joint requires three steps, so do the Henry Ford thing by setting up an assembly line and performing the first step on all of the joints before performing the second.

MAKING SOLDER

STEP

1 Double-click the Brush tool in the Toolbox. From the Tool Settings roll-up, choose the Brush tool and change it to a square nib. Change the Paint color to a 30% gray by clicking on the onscreen palette. Set the Nib size to 15 and the Soft Edge to 60. Load the mask channel Big Lead again. This keeps the solder off of the glass. Paint each joint until it looks like the one shown. Admittedly, it doesn't look much like solder at this point.

2 Now we are going to add some depth to our solder. From the Tool Settings roll-up, choose the Air Brush with a round nib. Select a Black Paint color. Change the Transparency to 95, Soft Edge to 100, and click to apply black paint in the lower-right corner of each joint. We are applying it at that point, since the shadows on the caming (lead) appear in the lower right.

Now add the highlights. Change the Paint color to White, Brush size to 7, and Soft Edge to 60. Click in the upper-left corner—just a little bit, since we are tricking the viewers' eyes so they think they are looking at reflections off of shiny solder. The result is shown. I must confess that although this can be done with a mouse, I used a stylus.

Variations on a Theme

AN EASIER WAY TO MAKE STAINED GLASS

If you are like me, the idea of creating an intricate pattern for a stained glass project can be really time consuming. There is an easier way. You can legally scan a pattern from one of the many stained glass pattern books on the market, as I have done on a work-in-progress, shown here.

SCANNING AND PATTERNS

The patterns that I have found in the stained glass books are usually quite large. Logically, you would scan these images in using a Line Art (black-and white) setting. After all the patterns are just black and white, right? Actually, you will get a better result scanning them in as grayscale images. This will make the curved and diagonal portions of the lines smoother. Don't be concerned if your scan has a slightly off-white or light gray cast to it. When it is embossed, it will be gone. This is another one I got out of a Dover Publication of glass patterns (they have several books of stained glass patterns), which was completed in less than 30 minutes. This image was scanned in vertically and then I used the Rotate command in the Image menu to rotate it.

NOT ALL THAT IS DULL IS LEAD

It is not necessary for the lead in your stained glass to look like a lead fishing weight. In the image shown, I used the same technique we used earlier, except that the lines that made up the lead lines were much wider (8 pixels) and were made with 70 percent black, and I didn't need to use The Boss filter after applying the Emboss filter. It gives it a flatter look.

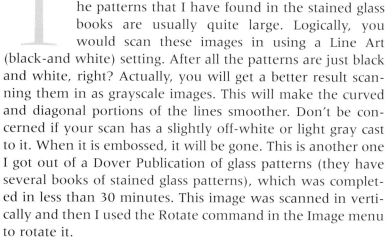

Another variation is shown in an image similar to the one we made in our earlier exercise, as shown here. The title is "Last Call," and it was created in several stages. To begin with, the photograph in the center began as a daylight scene that I darkened using the negative Gamma effect. Next, since streetlights are generally on at night, I created the streetlight glow by applying just a spot from a wide white airbrush (transparency set to 95).

The viewers also need visual clues that they are looking through glass. In this case, I have distorted the glass by applying a Displacement map from the Effects menu to the image before placing it in the stained glass. It is important that you not apply it when it is part of the image, as Displacement maps use colors surrounding the photograph and actually add them to the edges. Not a pretty sight.

The red circles are then created with Texture Fill using the Ripples Hard Embossed-2C preset. The wood on the side is a Bitmap Fill. When making frames always remember to use a Rectangle Mask tool and have the wood running in different directions. The lighting is made using the Lighting Effects filter located under Render in the Effects menu.

CAUTION

The Lighting filter does a wonderful job of creating lighting effects, but it does not have the most intuitive interface in the world. Be prepared to spend some time experimenting with it.

BE AFRAID, HALLMARK

So what can you do with a stained glass once you have made it? The image shown here is the original one I made with PHOTO-PAINT 5. It is essentially created the same way as described earlier. In this case, I used the image to make a Christmas card. With an inexpensive color printer readily available, it is possible to make custom holiday greeting cards for loved ones and also for those whom you are trying to impress. Another neat thing to try with your stained glass creation is to print it on transparency film and sandwich it between two pieces of glass. I have purchased several different frames made this way—they have clips on the edges. After mounting the transparency this way, I hang it by a window. The sun shining through it looks really great.

In case you can't tell, I love this stuff. So, good old Gary "Mr. Etch-A-Sketch" Priester and his mighty vector will probably get to bed before me (he's older and needs the sleep), but I am having a blast.

Stained Glass
IN COREL**DRAW**

GET THE LEAD IN

I had fully intended to do this simulated leaded glass illustration using Corel's PowerLines, only to find that PowerLines was cut after version 6. Shows how much I use PowerLines. Fortunately, I discovered an easier way to accomplish what I had in mind.

The appearance of leaded glass can be effectively replicated in DRAW using blends (the new discovery I alluded to) and Texture Fills, both of which have been a staple of DRAW for many versions. If you've ever created a real leaded glass object, you'll appreciate that my technique is relatively safe, with no danger of nasty glass cuts and no noxious, carcinogenic-inducing fumes from the soldering flux. Plus, with my technique, the glass always cuts just right. I created a circle and star design to illustrate the technique; it's shown in Figure 13-1. For this exercise, I'm going to reduce the number of shapes to make it easier to grasp the technique.

Figure 13-1: An example created with the leaded glass technique

STEP

1 Draw a rectangle. Add two line segments. Select each line and use the Shape tool to change the line To Curve. Gently shape the lines by dragging them with the Shape tool, as shown in Figure 13-2. Set a Copy of the rectangle and lines aside (we'll need them in step 5).

Figure 13-2: Two gently curving lines divide a rectangle into three shapes

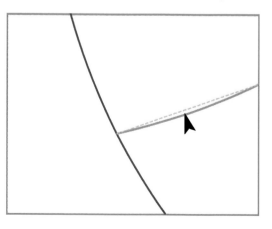

2 Convert the rectangle to curves (select Convert To Curves in the Arrange menu). With the Shape tool, click on each place on the rectangle's outline where the two curved lines touch. Click on the Break Curve button on the Property Bar to break the lines. Then select Break Apart from the Arrange menu. Repeat this process on the curved vertical line, breaking it at the point where it meets the horizontal curved line. Using the lines and open shapes (and copies of these where necessary), make three shapes, as shown in Figure 13-3.

Figure 13-3: The curved lines are used to separate the rectangle into three shapes

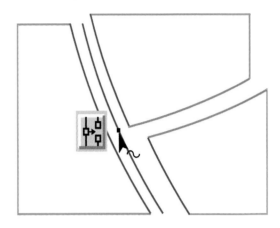

3 Individually select all of the line segments in each group and Combine (CTRL+L). Marquee-select the common end nodes where the different line segments meet with the Shape tool. Click the Join Two Nodes button on the Property Bar. Repeat this everywhere until two separate line segments come together, as I have done in Figure 13-4.

Figure 13-4: The Shape tool is used to join the loose line ends

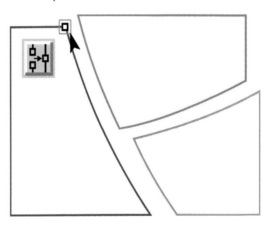

TIP

When you marquee-select a corner node with the Shape tool, the Property Bar will enable the Break Curve icon if the lines are already joined or the Join Two Nodes if the nodes are not joined.

S T E P

4
When you've joined all the nodes, fill each shape with a color, as I have done in Figure 13-5. If you cannot fill a shape, there might be a pair of nodes unjoined or a line segment or segments not Combined properly. If this is the case, marquee-select the line segments again. If the status bar reads "2 (or more) Objects Selected," then Combine them again and repeat this step.

Figure 13-5: The three shapes are filled

S T E P

5
The funny H-shaped thing in the left corner of Figure 13-6 is a cross-section of the channeled lead strip that holds the glass in place. The top and bottom are rounded. The pieces of glass fit into the openings on either side—I bet Huss doesn't know that! (Actually, it turns out that Huss did know this!) To emulate the dull gray look of these lead channel strips, take the copy of lines from step 1 (you did make a copy, didn't you?). Select all the lines and Combine them. Apply a line color of 60 percent Black and a line weight of 8 points to the combined outline. Make a Duplicate (+ key). Change the line color to 20 percent Black and the line weight to 3 points. Move this shape up and left a few points. (I set the Nudge amount in Options to 1 point.) Your drawing should loosely resemble Figure 13-6.

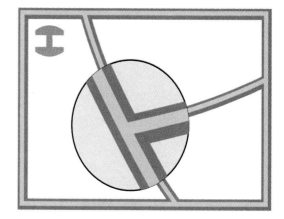

Figure 13-6: The lines are combined and a duplicate set made for blending

Select both outlines and apply a 20-Step Blend. Moving the lighter line shape up and left adds a highlight and gives the lead dimension, as shown in Figure 13-7.

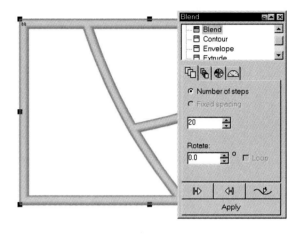

Figure 13-7: Blending the two sets of lines creates a rounded lead effect

With all of our lead channel strips cut perfectly, we need to apply solder to the joints. If we were doing this with real lead solder (if they wanted us to pronounce it "sodder," then why spell it "solder"?), we'd apply flux to the joints, then use a red-hot soldering iron to apply a small glop of solder. My technique is easier, as you'll witness in Figure 13-8.

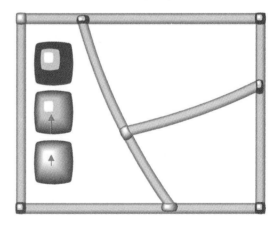

Figure 13-8: Another blend is used to create the lead solder joints

Draw a square in one corner and apply a 60 percent Black fill. Slightly round the corners with the Shape tool, then Convert the square to Curves (CTRL+Q). Marquee-select the shape with the Shape tool and click on To Curves on the Property Bar. Use the Shape tool to drag the square's sides slightly outward. Make a medium and a smaller Duplicate, filled 20 percent Black and White, respectively. Position the duplicates up and left. Apply a 10-Step Blend to the two larger shapes. Deselect all by clicking off the image. Select the middle shape and smallest shape and apply another 10-Step Blend. Repeat this process until you've soldered all the joints. Alter the shapes to conform to the angle of the lead channel strips.

STEP

8

The kinds of glass used in leaded glass art comes in many vibrant colors and types, some highly transparent, some mysteriously milky and opaque. We'll use Draw's Texture Fills to help us make our own custom glass, like the three pieces shown in Figure 13-9.

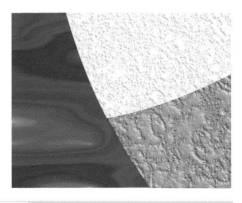

Figure 13-9: Three modified Texture Fills create the look of colored glass

STEP

9

Select the left piece of glass. Open the Fill Tool fly-out and click on the Texture Fill icon (it's fourth from the left). Change the Texture Library, as shown in Figure 13-10, to Samples 6 and select Evening Ripple from the Texture List. Click on the Bottom button and change the color to pale blue. Without closing the palette, click on the Other button (bottom of the palette) and adjust the pale blue until it is almost white. Click OK. Click on the Surface button and pick a very bright and deep blue from the menu. Click OK. Change the setting for Waves softness % to 80 to soften the overall pattern. Change Wave Density to 30 percent. This makes the overall pattern larger. Click on the Preview button to view the new pattern. You can name and save this setting so it will be available in the future. Click on the + next to the Texture Library drop-down list. Name and save your new fill.

Figure 13-10: The Texture Fill settings for producing the blue glass fill

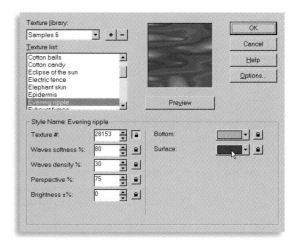

STEP

10

The red glass we'll create is known as cranberry glass, a nubbly cranberry red, transparent glass. Select the lower-right shape and open the Texture Fill dialog box again. Choose Purple Brain (don't you just love it?) from the Samples 5 library, shown in Figure 13-11. We'll modify several settings to create our cranberry glass effect. Select the Shade button and change the color to deep purple. Change Mid-shade to red. Click on the Light button and select a pale pink, then click on Other and modify the pink until it's almost white. Set Brightness to 10% to brighten the fill a touch. Change the Softness % value to 60. Change Density % to 70. Finally, increase Volume % to 20. Click on Preview to see the results.

Figure 13-11: The Texture Fill settings for producing the cranberry glass fill

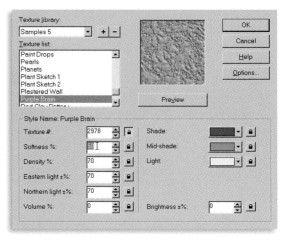
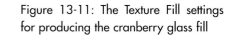

STEP

11

To prove that Purple Brain is not just a one-trick pony, we'll use it for the white-stippled clear glass as well. Select the remaining shape and change the following settings: Shade to very, very, very pale blue, Mid-shade to 10 percent Black, and Light to white. Change Softness percent to 50 and Density percent to 80, and click Preview (see Figure 13-12). If this meets with your approval, click OK.

Figure 13-12: The Texture Fill settings for producing the white glass fill

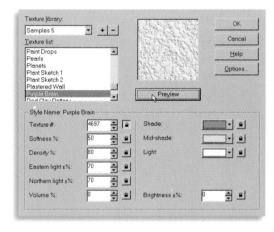

STEP

12

Select the three sections of glass, position them over the lead, and send them to the back (SHIFT+PAGEDOWN), as shown in Figure 13-13.

Looks pretty convincing, don't you think? And not a single nasty glass cut. Use this technique to create more complex designs. Corel's Texture Fills are terrific for replicating all kinds of surfaces. All it takes is a little imagination and experimentation. This leaded glass technique works swell with logos, signs, and homemade greeting cards.

Figure 13-13: The final result

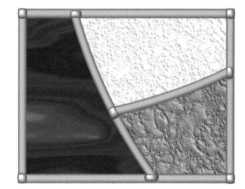

Variations on a Theme

WHEEL OF FORTUNE

I feel compelled to leave you with a few more examples of my leaded glass technique. I know for a fact, that my youngish counterpart, Huss, will probably have three or four pages of sample images he's created using all his layers and channels and trick filters. So as not to appear parsimonious, here are some further examples using the leaded glass techniques discussed in my half of this chapter.

This first image provides a fine example of just how convincing this technique can be. The image uses the same technique covered in this chapter but is more energetic in it's approach. I added clear glass jewels to the design for a finishing touch, as they were frequently used in many leaded glass windows created earlier in the century.

GLASS PALETTE

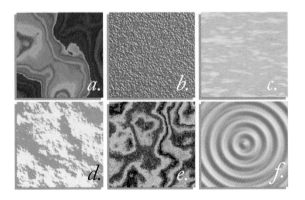

This next image illustrates the Texture Fills used to create the image above. Here is a listing of the Fills used (and modified) in that illustration: a. Styles Library, Mineral Fractal 3C; b. Styles Library, Putty 3C; c. Samples Library, Ocean Water; d. Styles Library, Surfaces 3C; e. Samples 6 Library, Islands in the Stream; f. Styles, Ripples Soft Embossed 2C.

An angel symbol from the Festive Symbol Library (shown in inset) was modified to create the image shown here. A gray 4-point line was used to provide a simplified leaded-glass look. The flame was modified and a circle placed behind the candle to add a glowing effect.

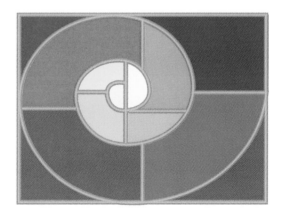

The image here began with a Logarithmic Spiral, three rotations. The spiral was broken into sections and straight line segments were added and combined with the spiral sections to make the individual colored areas of the nautilus shell design. A colored 6-point line with two lighter duplicates of diminishing point size were placed on top, imparting a rounded quality. Flat fills, instead of texture fills, give the composition a contemporary look.

BACK ᴛᴏ ꓘƆAꓭ

Huss and I got our first driver's licenses way back around the 1950s. I got mine the second time I took the test, having ruined an almost flawless first performance by narrowly avoiding a collision with another vehicle (which also had the right of way) in an intersection. I suspect that Dave maxed his the first time out—he's like that. The 1950s was the era of the big car, with big chrome bumpers weighing almost as much as one of today's small compact cars. Back then, the bumpers were made of iron with heavy chrome plating, unlike today's plastic equivalents. There was magic in the chrome. Kind of like a fun house mirror. Depending on which part of the chrome you looked into you could be tall and skinny, short and squat, or distorted in a multitude of shapes and sizes.

Around this time, I had the opportunity to visit a jewelry store and see renderings made by the jeweler of fanciful pieces of gold jewelry. The renderings were done on black paper using colored pencils, and the result was magical. I immediately purchased some black paper and a set of colored pencils and set about figuring out the techniques the jeweler had used to create his renderings.

Fast forward to today. I'm still working at rendering gold and chrome, using the computer and CorelDRAW in place of colored pencils and black paper. Several decades of practice in observing gold and chrome, as well as creating illustrations of the magical metals, has enabled me to pass along some of the tips and tricks I have learned along the way. Huss has his own story, no doubt, which you will hear as you discover his techniques for creating gold and chrome.

Gold & Chrome

IN COREL **PHOTO-PAINT**

Gold and chrome share common attributes: they are bright and shiny. There is just something about text or objects created in chrome that immediately gets the readers' attention. In this chapter you will discover that gold and chrome, while not easy, add a quality to your work that demands attention from the viewer.

NOTE

This discussion works with both PHOTO-PAINT 7 and 8.

ALL THAT GLITTERS IS NOT CHROME

Chrome is what I was raised on in the 1950s and 60s. Everything was chrome in those days, so it is something with which I am very familiar—so much so that I am pretty particular in making an effect that actually looks realistic. The Duke of DRAW will tell you the secret of chrome: it has no color but instead reflects the colors of its surroundings. Chrome is a marvelous study in reflections, which has caused me to spend too much time photographing and studying real chrome. The technique for creating chrome using PHOTO-PAINT falls into two general techniques: either using merge modes and tone maps or using displacement maps. I covered the displacement map method in my book, PHOTO-PAINT 8: An Official Guide (Osborne/McGraw-Hill, 1998). We are now going to discover the tone map technique. This technique works with both PHOTO-PAINT 7 and PHOTO-PAINT 8.

CREATING CHROME WITH TONE MAPS

The following technique is one of the easiest and best I know for creating a realistic chrome effect. If you find you like making chrome, you can save the steps as a script using the Command Recorder and then create it with the touch of a button.

STEP

1 Create a new image that is 4 × 2 inches at 150 dpi, 24-bit color. Click the Text tool in the Toolbox and change the font to Bremen Bd BT at a size of 72. Enable Bold inside the image and type **TURBO**. Click the Object Picker tool (the font becomes an object). Select Arrange from the Object menu and choose Align and Distribute (CTRL+A). Select To Center of Document. In PHOTO-PAINT 7, use CTRL+SHIFT+A to open the Align dialog box and center the text on the page.

TURBO

STEP

2 Next, we need to make a mask of the text for use later, so click the Create Mask button on the Toolbar (make sure the Preserve Image button is enabled if using PHOTO-PAINT 7). Save the mask to the disk by selecting Save from the Mask menu and choosing Save to Disk. Name the mask Temp Chrome Mask.CPT. This action saves a temporary copy of the mask. Click the Remove Mask button on the Toolbar or from the Mask menu.

3 Merge the text with the background (CTRL+DnArrow). From the Effects menu, choose Blur and select Gaussian Blur. Apply the blur with a setting of 4. Mask the entire image by selecting Select All from the Mask menu. Create an object from the masked area (CTRL+UpArrow). With the object selected, change the Merge mode in the Objects Docker window (Objects Roll-Up in PHOTO-PAINT 7) from Normal to Difference. The image will become black. Choose Offset in the 2D Effects of the Effects menu and set the Shift values (both Horizontal and Vertical) to -4. Make sure that the Shift value as % of dimensions checkbox is not checked. Click OK, and we have a ghostly image.

4 Choose Combine from the Object menu and then Combine Objects with Background. Invert the image, selecting Transform from the Image menu and choosing Invert. From the Image menu, choose Adjust and select Auto Equalize. The image shown is beginning to look more like chrome.

STEP

5
Now comes the good part. We need to apply a specialized tone map to create the reflections. Select the Tone Curve (CTRL+T). Click the Open button in the Curves section of the dialog box and load the Solarize Curve as a starting point. Next, we need to modify the curve so it looks like the one shown in the dialog box. Adjusting the curve is a little tricky. When you place the cursor on a point in the curve, it changes into a hand shape. Make sure it is a hand before you begin dragging the cursor, or you will place another node on the Tone Curve, which you do not want to do. If you accidentally create a new node, just reload Solarize. Once you have it so it looks like that shown in the dialog box, save it as Chrome using the Save button. Click the OK button to apply the Tone Curve. The result is shown in the next illustration.

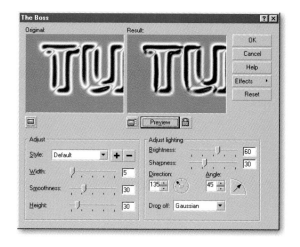

STEP

6
From the Mask menu, load the Chrome mask we saved previously (Temp Chrome Mask.CPT). To include some of the reflection effect we have created that is outside of our original mask, select Shape in the Mask menu and then Expand, using a Width of 5 (pixels). Now, invert the mask (CTRL+I), and from the Effects menu choose 3D Effects (PHOTO-PAINT 8) or Fancy (PHOTO-PAINT 7) and choose The Boss filter. When the dialog box opens, as shown here, select the Default settings and change the Width to 3. Click OK.

To make the text an object, invert the mask (CTRL+I) and click the Create Object: Cut Selection button in the Toolbar. In PHOTO-PAINT 7, select Create Object from the Object menu. The text is now an object floating above the background. In the Objects Docker window, click the background to select it. (If you have PHOTO-PAINT 7, click the Single button in the Objects Roll-Up. Click in the column between the eye icon and the word background and then click on the thumbnail of the text object to deselect it.) Select Clear from the Edit menu, and the background is removed, as shown here.

This type of chrome tends to have a prism-type reflection. To create that, select the Text tool in the Toolbox and duplicate it (CTRL+D in PHOTO-PAINT 8 or CTRL+SHIFT+D in PHOTO-PAINT 7). From the Effects menu, choose Fancy and select the Julia Set Explorer. At the bottom of the dialog box, click and hold on the black triangle and select Corel presets and then choose 60's Wallpaper from the list that appears. Click the OK button in the lower-right corner. The result will be a rainbow-like reflection on the duplicate, as shown.

To make the reflection usable, we need to change the Merge Mode in the Objects Docker window (Objects Roll-Up in PHOTO-PAINT 7) to Soft Light (select the Color Merge Mode in PHOTO-PAINT 7) and reduce the Opacity until only a hint of the rainbow remains. It was about 40 for PHOTO-PAINT 8 and 25 for PHOTO-PAINT 7. Leave a little more of the rainbow reflection than you think you might need. Against a white background, it will look like it is too much, but when you place a colorful background behind it, you will see it really enhances the effect. When you have the Opacity setting you like, combine the objects by marquee-selecting both of them and choosing Combine Objects Together in the Object menu.

STEP

10

Select the background in the Objects Docker window (Objects Roll-Up in PHOTO-PAINT 7). From the Edit menu, choose Fill. When the Edit Fill and Transparency dialog box opens, choose the Fountain Fill button. From the Presets, choose Red Wash. Change the Steps settings to 999. In the color blend section, change from Two color to Custom. At this point, the left-most spot is black and the right-most color is Red. Create a point on the color map by double-clicking just above it. Change the color of the new point to the lightest shade of pink you can find in the palette on the right side of the dialog box. Now drag the point until it reads 50% in the Position box. At 35% and 65%, add a Red point and then change the point at the far right to Black. The dialog box is shown here. Click OK to return to the previous dialog box and click OK again to apply the fill.

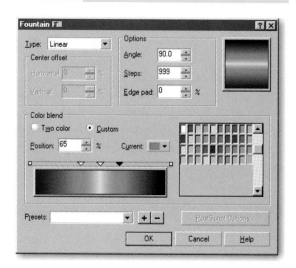

STEP

11

With the Object Picker tool, select the Chrome text. Choose Feather from the Object menu and select a feather setting of 3 and Curved to take the ragged edges off of our chrome.

12

To make the shadows for the chrome text, select Drop Shadow from the Object menu and pick out a shadow that suits your fancy. Click OK. The finished product is shown here. If you want to apply effects or make other adjustments to the image, you should first combine the objects with the background.

T I P

Does this seem like a long, complicated process to make chrome? I think it does. To make the process simpler, open the Command Recorder and record each step. When finished, make sure it works and then assign a button to it using Customize in the Tools menu and the Toolbars tab. Make sure you save your script in the Scripts folder, or you will not be able to assign a button to it.

Variations on a Theme

ADDING THE LENS FLARE FILTER

Whenever you are working with something reflective, you should train yourself to immediately think about the Lens Flare filter, located in the Render option of the Effects menu. In this example, I applied a 35mm Prime setting at the left end of the background fill we created.

USING DIFFERENT FONTS

By applying the same technique to a font with a greater width and size, we end up with an effect that looks more like stainless steel than chrome. The rainbow effect is very strong when you use a broad sans serif like the one shown (Stencil). In this case, the rainbow effect was subdued using the Sponge (desaturate) brush tool, located in the Effects tools.

LIQUID METAL

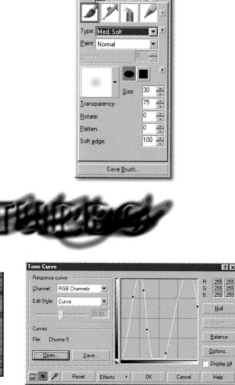

One of my favorite effects is to make the letters look as if they were made of liquid metal. The effect is quite simple to achieve by adding only one additional step to the technique described earlier in the "Creating Chrome with Tone Maps" section. After completing step 4 of that section, select the Paintbrush tool; then, in the Tool Settings roll-up shown, choose Med. Soft as the Type. Click and drag the brush across, as shown in the next illustration.

OK, it looks really ugly and you think you could never make anything out of it—but trust me. Now select Tone Curve (CTRL+T) and change the curve so it looks like the one shown in the Tone Curve dialog box. Complete the steps as previously described in the "Creating Chrome with Tone Maps" section. To make the metal stand out, I placed a wood bitmap fill for the background, as shown here. The raised portion of the wood is created by surrounding the text with a Rectangle mask, inverting the mask (CTRL+I), and applying The Boss filter to it using the Wet preset.

Making gold is simpler than you might first imagine. Follow the instructions described earlier in the "Creating Chrome with Tone Maps" section through step 7. Select the text object and make sure the Lock Transparency checkbox is enabled (in PHOTO-PAINT 7, you must be in Single mode). Choose the Fill command in the Edit menu. Click the Uniform Color button, click the Edit button, and set the fill color to Chalk or Pale Yellow. In the Uniform Fill dialog box in PHOTO-PAINT 8, click the Custom Palettes button in the upper-left area of the dialog box and select the named color. In PHOTO-PAINT 7, click the Other button at the bottom of the palette and select the named color. With the color selected, click OK. In the Edit Fill and Transparency dialog box, change the Paint Mode to Multiply. To complete the job, uncheck Lock Transparency (click the Multi button in PHOTO-PAINT 7) and apply the Directional Sharpen filter from the Effects menu to smooth the edges a little. Select Feather from the Object menu and apply a Curved feather at a setting of 3 or 4. The resulting image is shown with a drop shadow against a bitmap fill background to show it off a little. The top letters were created using Chalk, the bottom one using Pale Yellow. Many discussions ensued as to which one looked like gold—I prefer the bottom one.

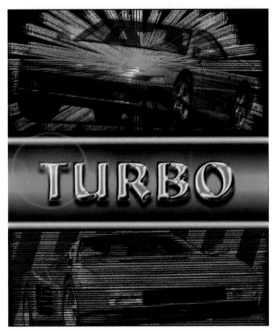

Our last variation on this bright and shiny subject is in the area of application. In our last example, I have placed the TURBO gold text in a car ad. The cars at the top and bottom are individual photographs that I applied to the image using a Clone tool with one of the preset brush types. The secret to this technique is the straight lines. In case you didn't know, you make straight lines in PHOTO-PAINT by clicking the first point with the brush tool (the Clone tool is a brush tool) and then, while pressing and holding the ALT key, click the end point. PHOTO-PAINT will apply the currently selected brush in a straight line between the two points. In the top part of the image, I clicked at a point in the center (grids are very helpful) and then placed the end point at the outer edge of the image. I kept doing this until I had the starburst effect. The bottom one was easier. Beginning in the upper-left corner, I clicked the Clone tool brush and then at the same point on the other side ALT-clicked the end point. This one definitely required that the grid be visible so the lines would be straight. The gold and red behind TURBO is a combination of fills. I made the gold cylinders first and then made the red background. For a finishing touch, I applied a light Lens Flare on the T of TURBO.

Gold & Chrome

IN COREL**DRAW**

ROAD GLOW

Chrome, like a mirror, is clear and colorless. The only thing that informs our senses that this is metal is its reflections. We're used to seeing chrome outside, where it reflects the blue sky (except in Los Angeles, where I grew up, where the sky is naturally brown) and the ground, so we tend to think of chrome as blue and gray. As we usually see chrome on automobiles, the gray represents the reflection of the highway. This perception is almost instinctual.

Continuing down this road, the sky is brighter and lighter on the horizon and deeper overhead. You can think of it as Nature's greatest Fountain Fill. With this in mind, let's do chrome.

STEP

1

Draw a 2" x 2" rectangle.

STEP

2

Create an Interactive Linear Fountain Fill as shown in Figure 14-1 using the following colors:

a = 60% cyan, 40% magenta

b = 20% cyan, 10% magenta

c = white

d = 75% cyan, 70% magenta, 75% yellow, 20% black

e = 23% cyan, 31% magenta, 36% yellow, 5% black

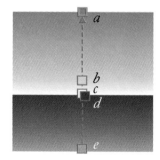

Figure 14-1: A simple chrome fill that reflects the sky and earth

Set the word **CHROME** in 72-point Breman Bd BT (the BT stands for Bitstream, the type foundry that created the font) and copy the chrome fill to the type as shown in Figure 14-2. You can either select Copy Properties From...Fill from the Edit menu, or drag the chrome-filled rectangle over the type using the right mouse button and selecting Copy Fill Here from the flyout menu.

Figure 14-2: The sky/earth chrome fill applied to the word "CHROME"

S T E P

Convert the text to Curves (CTRL+Q) and break the letters apart (CTRL+K). This causes the inside sections in the R and O to become filled in.

S T E P

Marquee-select the R and combine the parts (CTRL+Q), restoring the dropped-out inside sections. Repeat the process on the O.

S T E P

Apply a Contour effect by selecting Contour in the Effects menu to each letter individually.

CONTOUR	
To Outside	
Steps:	1
Offset:	.05

S T E P

With the contour selected, separate and ungroup it by selecting Separate in the Arrange menu. The results of the Contour can be seen in Wireframe view in Figure 14-3.

Figure 14-3: To create a better contour shape (shown in Wireframe view for clarity), the type is converted to curves and broken apart and the contour is applied to each letter individually

STEP

8

Select the letter shapes for the contour (the larger letters), group them, and nudge them away from the filled letters.

STEP

9

Create a dark, custom Conical fill, as shown in Figure 14-4, and apply it to each of the contour shapes. The Conical fill is comprised of these colors:

a = 46% cyan, 37% magenta, 36% yellow

b = black

c = walnut (20 %M, 40%Y, 60%K)

d = black

Figure 14-4: A warm black conical fill for the contoured shape

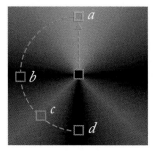

STEP

10

Return the contoured shapes to their position under the bright chrome letters, as shown in Figure 14-5.

Figure 14-5: The bright chrome and dark metal with a starburst highlight

STEP

11

For the finishing touch, use the Polygon tool to create a 16-point starburst. Double-click on the Polygon tool and choose the Polygon as Star option, 16 points, and a Sharpness of 70. For the starburst's fill, create a Rainbow Fountain Fill, using Orange, Pale Yellow, and white, as shown in Figure 14-6.

Figure 14-6: A 16-point starburst created with the Polygon tool

Use the Shape tool to extend the four nodes in the starburst before placing it strategically over the O.

BLEND AMBITION

Unfortunately, DRAW's Envelope Effects have no effect on Fountain Fills—the outline of the shape changes, but the fill remains the same—and for this next example I so wanted to have a gently curved horizon. No problem! I re-created the chrome effect from Figure 14-1, using a 2-part Blend (by selecting Blend in the Effects menu). Here's how it is done.

Use four 2-point lines, color each line the same as in Figure 14-1 (see Figure 14-7).

Figure 14-7: Two blends are created using two pairs of 2-point colored lines

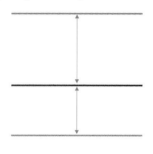

Apply a 50-Step Blend to the top two lines. A 50-Step Blend produces a smooth, nonbanding Blend. Select the bottom two lines and apply another 50-Step Blend. Figure 14-8 shows the results of the two blends.

Figure 14-8: The blend created with the colored lines is virtually the same as a Fountain Fill

STEP

Select the pen symbol from the Zapf Dingbats section in the Symbols roll-up menu and place it over the blended lines.

STEP

4

Group both blends and apply a Double Curve Envelope Effect by selecting Envelope in the Effects menu, dragging the top node upward as shown in Figure 14-9.

Figure 14-9: An envelope is applied to the line blend and distorted, producing a curved horizon line

STEP

5

PowerClip (select PowerClip in the Effects menu) the fill inside a pen symbol.

STEP

6

Make a duplicate of the pen symbol, apply a 30 percent Black fill, offset it down and left two points in each direction, and send it to the back (SHIFT-PAGE DOWN) for a drop shadow as shown in Figure 14-10.

Figure 14-10: The chrome blend is PowerClipped inside a Zapf Dingbats pen symbol

Corel has just the right colors for creating effective-looking gold Fountain Fills in the default onscreen color palette. Figure 14-11 shows the colors, and their proper Corel onscreen palette names, used to create the gold images in this section: Gold, Chalk, Pale Yellow, and Walnut. The three adjoining rectangles demonstrate gold-type fill variations.

The first filled rectangle (just to the right of the color named-rectangles) in Figure 14-11 shows a combination of all the colors. The second rectangle (middle) uses Chalk and Gold. The third (far right) uses Gold, Pale Yellow, Gold, and Chalk. Because the colors on the Fill Path are spaced apart from each other, the third blend is soft, giving the impression of a dull, burnished gold.

If we move the Walnut and Pale Yellow colors almost on top of one another, we get the impression of highly polished gold caused by the sharp horizon line, which is illustrated in the first of the three rectangles shown in Figure 14-11. In this next section, we'll create an embossed shiny gold letter on a shiny gold square.

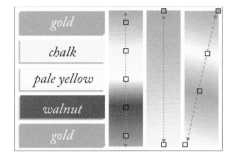

Figure 14-11: Colors used to create three different gold-type fountain fills

NOTE

As you move your cursor over the colors on the onscreen palette, the names appear in the lower-left status bar.

QUINTESSENTIAL Q

STEP

1 Draw a 2 1/4-inch square. Create a capital letter Q, 200 points high, in Jazz LET (or a similar heavy font. Center both elements.

Make two duplicates of the Q.

Apply a solid Pale Yellow to the first duplicate and move it up and left one point.

Apply a Walnut fill to the second duplicate and move it down and right one point.

Bring the original to the front (SHIFT+PAGEUP), to create the embossed look seen in Figure 14-12.

Figure 14-12: A letter Q set in Jazz LET is filled with a shiny gold fill, with a lighter and darker duplicate used to create an embossed look

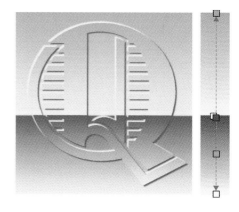

SIMPLY ELEGANT

The CorelDRAW 7 software package sports very handsome black letters with elegant gold borders. The look is easy to replicate.

STEP

1 Draw a 2 1/4-inch square. Create a capital D in 200 point Futura Extra Bold Condensed and center it over the square. Use the same colors from Figure 14-12 to create a Custom Interactive Conical fill as shown in Figure 14-13.

Figure 14-13: A similar type treatment to the lettering on the CorelDRAW 7 package

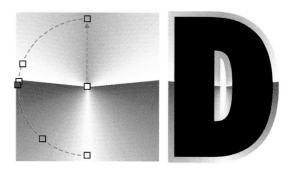

2

To create the outline shape for the gold fill, apply a Contour, To Outside, 1 Step, Offset .05".

Separate the contour (by selecting Separate in the Arrange menu), Ungroup it, and copy the gold fill to the wider contour shape by selecting Copy Properties From...Fill from the Edit menu.

Fill the original letter solid black.

This is the basic technique for creating chrome and gold fills. The following examples use variations on these fills. For the sake of brevity (something that does not come naturally to me), I'll just give you the highlights and spare you the details.

Variations on a Theme

HOWL HIGH THE MOON

Here's a nifty way to achieve both a realistic chrome look and a spherical distortion. For openers, I applied a Custom Radial Fountain Fill to a square, added a howling wolf from the Animals 2 Symbols roll-up, and added a white sphere to which a horizontal Linear Transparency was applied. All the elements were selected and converted to bitmap (select Convert To Bitmap in the Bitmaps menu) at 300 dpi, 16 million colors, Super Sampling.

The square bitmap was selected, and a spherical distortion at 25 percent was created by selecting 3D Effects, then Wrap To Object from the Bitmaps menu. I could have stopped there, but nooooo! Knowing young Huss would be staying up all night trying to one-up me with all his magic filters, masks, and layers, I pushed on.

I filled a rectangle with a Linear Fountain Fill, using the same fill from the sphere, only linear. I placed a rectangle over the sky blue portion and filled it with a Texture Fill called Stormy Sky, from the Samples 6 Library. To add a little magic of my own to the sky, I applied a Linear Transparency to the texture fill, beginning with opaque on top (no transparency) and 100 percent transparent on the horizon. I used the Graph Paper tool (inside the Polygon flyout) to create a 5 × 50 grid. Perspective was applied to add convergence. I used the Polygon tool to create a 16-point starburst, which was converted to curves and whose vertical and horizontal nodes were pulled outward. A sensuously subtle Rainbow Radial Fountain Fill, using baby blue and white, was applied to the starburst.

The wolf/sphere was flopped and squashed for a reflection. The Brightness and Contrast was adjusted using the Color Adjustment option, which is in the Effects menu. Finally, everything was PowerClipped inside the original rectangle. The result is shown here.

TIP

Many of these complex Fountain Fills present a terrific challenge to PostScript output devices (read: won't print) when they are used to fill complex shapes, such as type. PowerClipping a fill inside a complex shape works somewhat better than filling the shape. Better and safer still, convert the image to a bitmap, or export the image as a TIFF or JPEG bitmap image.

To create a wavy horizon, three separate Blends were created using different colored duplicates of a single 2-point line, which was shaped into a subtle S shape using the Shape tool and the To Curve command in the Node Edit roll-up. The resulting blend was PowerClipped (by selecting PowerClip in the Effects menu) inside a heart ornament from the Zapf Dingbats Symbols library. A duplicate of the same heart was filled with 40% gray and Converted To Bitmap, with 256 shades of gray, 300 dpi, Super Sampling, and a Gaussian Blur, value 5 applied, to create a soft drop shadow. Note the image here.

I selected a graceful G from the Rennie Macintosh Ornaments font (from Image Club Graphics) and applied the same Conical fill from Figure 14-13. The Rennie Macintosh Ornaments are based on architectural lettering and symbols of the Arts and Crafts Movement from around the 1930s. I placed a rectangle in the back of the G and filled it with a Mineral-Swirled 2-Color fill from the Styles Texture Fill library. I changed the colors to black and green, producing a dark green marble quality. I selected the symbol and opened the Extrude roll-up (by selecting Extrude from the Effects menu). I applied a Bevel, Depth 0.03", Angle 45 degrees. I used all three light sources to add realism. The finished product is shown here.

In the above image, you can see the mother of all lens flares, which I created for the big finish. Once again, I should have stopped and gone to bed, but Huss is much younger than I am and can stay up all night trying to upstage me! But age and cunning will triumph over youth and enthusiasm any day. I created a circle and applied a Rainbow Fountain Fill, with an Edge Pad value of 10 percent, using pale yellow and tropical pink. I applied a Radial Transparency, reversing the default transparency settings to 0 percent in the center and 100 percent on the outside. To soften the edge, I pulled the end toward the center. I created a four-point star using the Polygon tool and applied a Custom Radial Fountain Fill, Edge Pad value of 15 percent, using pale yellow, (center) chalk, deep yellow, and purple, as shown to the right.

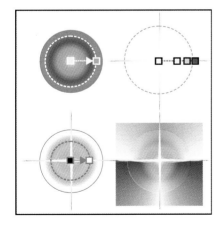

BACK to BACK

Learning to use a drawing software program like CorelDRAW is like learning a foreign language. At first everything is confusing and clumsy. Like foreign words and phrases, you repeat the same moves again and again. It might be a page full of overlapping rectangles or circles with a smattering of text, or it might be a learned trick or two. Nothing fancy and nothing very challenging. Little by little, your Corel vocabulary begins to grow. The breakthrough comes when you find yourself dreaming about Corel moves in your sleep.

Cutout shapes were not part of my early CorelDRAW vocabulary. Like language, you invent words to describe objects or emotions. One day I was designing a logo for a working ranch. I planned to use their existing brand. As the brand was registered, there could be no deviation. But I thought it might be cool to make the brand look like it was branded right into the envelope, letterhead, and business

cards. I wanted the brand to appear to have been burnt directly through the paper. Placing a soft shadow under the opening added dimension and believability. Today, the cutout shape is a frequently used part of my design vocabulary. DRAW's vector and bitmap tools make it the perfect application for articulating cutout shapes. I use the effect often, frequently adding new accents and intonations, as you'll see in the following section.

Cutout Shapes

The appeal of cutouts lies in their visual trickery. The viewer is looking at something that he or she knows is two-dimensional but appears to have depth. If cutouts are done with proper attention to shadow and light direction it will have the same effect on a viewer that a wet paint sign has on someone standing near it. In both cases they will want to reach out an touch it to see if it is real or wet.

Mr. Etch-A-Sketch will show you some nifty ways to make things that appear to be cutouts in DRAW, let's learn how to make some cutouts with PHOTO-PAINT that will tempt your viewers to touch the image to see if it is actually cut out. (Wow, after rereading that last sentence, I can hardly wait to see what I am going to do next!)

Everyone, it seems, likes the effect of cutouts when working with text and other objects. While cutouts look difficult to create, they are in fact simpler than you might imagine. The techniques described in this chapter can be used with PHOTO-PAINT 7 and 8 (but not PHOTO-PAINT 10, since it won't be out until the year 2000).

NOTE

This chapter uses PHOTO-PAINT 7 and 8.

IS IT IN OR IS IT OUT?

There are basically two styles of cutouts. The cookie-cutter style, shown here first, removes a portion of the object floating above the background, as if it had been removed with a cookie cutter. The traditional cutout, shown next, makes it appear that the letters or objects are cut out and their portion of the background has been removed. This traditional style of cutout is what we see every day on bank and university buildings. While this style is a little more complex to construct—it involves several object layers—it isn't all that difficult.

We will begin by learning how to construct the cookie-cutter style of cutout. I once stayed in an executive-level suite and noticed that all the room numbers had stars on them. So we are going to make a duplicate of one of those room number plates. If you do a good job, you could print it out, fly over to the hotel (it's in London), and show it to the manager, who might give you a free biscuit (cookie) for the effort (who says this business doesn't pay the big bucks?).

STEP

1   Create a new 24-bit image that is 5 × 7 inches at 80 dpi. From the Edit menu, select Fill. In the Edit Fill and Transparency dialog box, click the Bitmap fill button and then click Edit. When the Bitmap Fill dialog box opens, click the Load button, opening the Import dialog box. On the PHOTO-PAINT CD-ROM, locate the file \TILES\WOOD\LARGE\WOOD23l.CPT. Click the Open button and, if you are using PHOTO-PAINT 8, change the Rotate value in the Transform section to 45 degrees. Click OK, then click OK again to apply the fill. The image background is shown. If you are using PHOTO-PAINT 7, don't be concerned about the angle of the background produced with PHOTO-PAINT 8. It does not affect the image we are creating.

2

We begin by setting up the grid. From the Tools menu, choose Grid and Ruler Setup. Click the Grid tab and enable Show Grid and Snap to Grid. Change both of the Spacing settings to 0.5 inches and click OK. Select the Rectangle Shape tool (F6). Click the Edit Fill button on the Property Bar, which opens the Select Fill dialog box. Click on the Fountain Fill button (second button from the left) and click Edit. From the Fountain Fill dialog box, choose the Presets setting of Cylinder - Gold 02. This serves as the foundation for making our object, but we need to make a few adjustments. The first is to click on the down-pointing arrow above the horizontal color bar in the Color blend area at position 25 (%). The current color is white; change it by clicking on a pale yellow in the color palette (not the onscreen palette) in the dialog box. To locate specific colors, click on the color swatch of the Current color, click Other, and then click Custom Palette. Locate the color in the named palette box (I am using the default PHOTO-PAINT palette, corelpnt.cpl) and click OK to return to the Fountain Fill dialog box. Change the Steps in the Options setting from 256 to 999 and the Angle to 135. If you want to use this fill again, type Brass (or whatever name you like) in the Presets area and then click the + button. Click OK to close the dialog box and click OK again to close the Select Fill dialog box. Click the Render to Object button on the Property Bar.

3

Starting at a point in the upper-left corner one square down and to the right, drag a rectangle that comes within one square of the image border, as shown. From the Tools menu, choose Grid and Ruler Setup. Click the Grid tab and uncheck Show Grid and Snap to Grid. Select the Object Picker tool from the Toolbox and then click the Create Mask button (if you are using PHOTO-PAINT 7, click the Preserve Image button to enable it). From the Mask menu, choose Shape and then select Reduce. Ensure the Width value in the Reduce dialog box is 10. In the Objects Docker window, check the Lock Transparency checkbox; if using PHOTO-PAINT 7, open the Objects Roll-Up

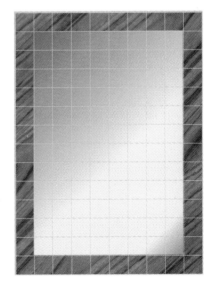

(CTRL+F7) and click the Single button. From the Effects menu, choose 3D Effects (Fancy in PHOTO-PAINT 7) and then select The Boss. Use the Default Style setting in the Adjust section of the dialog box and click OK. Select Remove from the Mask menu to remove the mask. We now have a simple brass plate, as shown next.

S T E P

4 Select the Text tool in the Toolbox and click near the upper-middle area of the brass plate. In the Property Bar, change the font to Zapf Dingbats BT with a size of 150. Type the letter **H** (must be uppercase). This will create a star. Select the Object Picker tool to make the star into an object. Select the Text tool again, change the Font to Garamond, and enable Bold. Click on the image and type the number **23**. After selecting the Object Picker, marquee-select both text objects in the image. Now we need to line up the star with the numbers, so open the Align dialog box (CTRL+A, or if you are using PHOTO-PAINT 7, use CTRL+SHIFT+A) and align all of the objects to vertical (not horizontal) center, as shown.

With both text objects still selected, click the Create Mask (from object) button. From the Objects Docker window (Objects Roll-Up in PHOTO-PAINT 7), make sure the two text objects are selected and the brass plate isn't, and click the Delete Object(s) button at the bottom of the roll-up. All that remains of the text is the mask. Click the Invert Mask button in the Toolbar. Select the brass plate object in the Objects Docker window (Objects Roll-Up in PHOTO-PAINT 7).

From the Object menu, select Crop to Mask (Clip to Mask in PHOTO-PAINT 7). A note about Crop to Mask: just before PHOTO-PAINT 8 shipped, the developers at Corel decided that people would confuse Clip to Mask with the new Clip Mask command, so they renamed it Crop to Mask. This decision was made after both my PHOTO-PAINT 8 book and the PHOTO-PAINT user manual were at the printer—sigh. What's in a name? Regardless of the name of the command, the result is shown here.

S T E P

7

Well, even though the cookie-cutter holes are in brass plate, it still doesn't look real. There are several techniques that allow the plates to appear three-dimensional. The first one we will use is to make the star and the numbers have a beveled edge. I hope you kept your mask. Click the Invert Mask button. From the Mask menu, choose Shape and then Feather (in PHOTO-PAINT 7, just choose Feather). In the Feather dialog box, enter a Width setting of 5 (pixels), Direction Outside, and Edges Curved. Click the OK button. From the Effects menu, choose 3D Effects and then Emboss to open the Emboss dialog box. Change the Emboss color to Original Color, Depth 4, and Direction 135. Click the OK button. Click the Delete mask button in the Toolbar. The resulting image is shown.

S T E P

8

The effect that gives the viewer a sense of depth is shadows. This is quite easy with PHOTO-PAINT. From the Object menu, choose Drop Shadow and choose the Flat-Bottom-Right preset. In PHOTO-PAINT 7, change the settings to: Offset lower-right button, Horizontal and Vertical 0.18, Feather 10, Opacity 100, and Direction Average. Click OK. The resulting image is shown. The first time I showed this image to the Old Man of DRAW (Gary), he commented that the plate could use a couple of screws to hold it up to the wall. Rather than make the screw heads (which would take a few extra steps), next is a quick-and-dirty way to make rivets.

9 Select the Ellipse Shape tool and make sure that Render to Object is enabled. Open the Fountain Fill dialog box and change the Fountain Fill type from Linear to Conical. Back to the brass plate: click and drag a tiny circle (pressing and holding the Ctrl key while you drag makes a circle). Now we need to add a little darkening on the lower-right side. Enable Lock Transparency in the Objects Docker window (in PHOTO-PAINT 7, go to Single mode in the Objects Roll-Up). Select the Paintbrush tool from the Toolbox, and from the Tool Settings roll-up change to Wide Cover with a Transparency of 70. Ensuring the Paint color is Black, slightly darken the lower-right portion. These "rivets" are too bright and attract attention, so in the Objects Docker window (Objects Roll-Up), change the Opacity to 50%. Duplicate the rivet (Ctrl+D, or in PHOTO-PAINT 7 use Ctrl+Shift+D). Place the duplicate directly below the original, near the bottom of the plate—and there you have it. The one I made is shown here.

In summary:

- Create an object out of the image you want to make into a cutout.

- Get (import or produce) the cutout shape and convert it to a mask.

- Invert the mask.

- Select the object and choose Clip Object to Mask (Crop to Mask in PHOTO-PAINT 8).

CREATING COOL CACTUS COOKIE-CUTTER CUTOUTS

*Try saying the above three times really fast. Using the techniques previously described, it is simple to create the cactus cookie image shown. The background is a rectangle that was made using a Fountain Fill called Sunset2. The cactus was made by loading the Symbol font PLANTS and using the Text tool, applying it several times. After the text **CACTUS COOKIES** was entered, it was converted to a mask and then inverted. With the rectangle selected using the Object Picker tool, Clip to Mask (Crop to Mask in PHOTO-PAINT 8) removed the parts of the object overlapped by the cactus. The texture on the rectangle came from applying a light (9 at 75) amount of Gaussian noise and applying the Emboss filter to it. A bonus received from using the Emboss filter is that it applied a light highlight on the edges. The text had Spike noise applied as well as being embossed. There are two drop shadows in this image. One was applied to the text at a large feather setting and a zero offset, and the other, a normal drop shadow, was applied to the cactus cutout.*

N O T E

PHOTO-PAINT 7 users must be in Single mode.

CARVED LETTERS AND SUCH

Here is a variation of the technique shown earlier in the chapter, to create the effect that something has been carved out of a material.

STEP

1 Make your original fill out of the material. In the image shown, I have created a 6 × 4-inch image and used one of the light-colored wood fills rotated 45 degrees (Rotated fills is only available in PHOTO-PAINT 8). Next, place the text or other object that is to be carved into the background. I have used the font GlaserSteD at a size of 72. Create a mask from the object (PAINT 7 users, keep Preserve Image enabled, or the object will merge with the background). In the Objects Docker window (Objects Roll-Up), delete the object from which you created the mask. At this point, all that remains is a background and a mask.

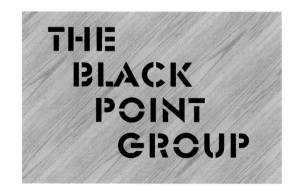

2 Invert the mask, select the background in the Objects Docker window (Objects Roll-Up), and choose Create Object: Copy Selection (PHOTO-PAINT 7 users, use Create Object with Preserve Image enabled). The image appears the same, but an object now appears in the Objects Docker window that is a copy of the original background with a hole in it the shape of the area selected by the mask.

3 Duplicate the object you just made (CTRL+D for PHOTO-PAINT 8 and CTRL+SHIFT+D for PHOTO-PAINT 7). You should now have a background and two objects with a mask-shaped hole in them. The top object is already selected, so choose the Drop Shadow command from the Object menu. You will need to adjust the shadow you create to fit the font and type size you have chosen for your text. After doing this for several years, I have learned to keep the feathering values and offset distance values relatively small. The shadow shown in the illustration is 315 (lower right) with a Distance of 0.083, an Opacity of 100%, and a Feather width of 6. While this looks OK, we can improve on it.

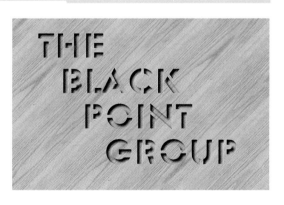

4 We are going to create a light highlight to the opposite edge of the engraved text. Select the middle layer and choose Gamma from the Adjust option in the Image menu. Set the Gamma to 1.7 (makes it much brighter) and click OK. Again, it appears nothing has happened, because this layer is hidden behind the top layer. Use the arrow keys on the keyboard and nudge the middle object one or two keystrokes up and to the left. The lighted edges of the middle become slightly visible and appear to be edge highlights. Don't go overboard on this—a little highlight goes a long way. Select the background and apply from the Hue/Saturation/Lightness filter (in the Adjust option of the Image menu) the following: Hue -5, Saturation -5, and Lightness -5. The result is shown. Once you are satisfied with the results, you can choose the Combine all objects with Background in the Objects menu. The result is shown here.

Variations on a Theme

MAKING BRUSHED METAL CUTOUTS

There are many variations to the cookie-cutter theme. The image shown is almost identical to the previous step-by-step exercise, except that I have used one of the marble papers available in the \TILES\PAPERS folders in both PHOTO-PAINT 7 and 8 to create the background. The plate also has a slight brushed-metal appearance, which is created by applying a small amount of either Gaussian or Uniform noise to it (in the Effects menu, choose Noise, then Add Noise) and then applying the Motion Blur filter (in the Effects menu, choose Blur, then Motion blur). This streaks and blurs the noise. I recommend applying this effect after you have applied the Emboss filter, otherwise it tends to turn the fine brush streaks into ridges.

CUT OUT THE ROUGH STUFF

It isn't necessary to stick with shiny and smooth textures, as shown in this illustration. The technique is the same as demonstrated earlier, except in this case a two-color Fountain Fill was used (Sunset 2 was the preset), and then a small amount of Gaussian noise was applied to the rectangular object. Next, the Emboss filter was applied to give it the textured look. After that, you would follow the steps in the previous section to end up with this cool-looking cutout.

STAINLESS STEEL CUTOUTS

All that glitters is not gold—sometimes it's stainless steel. In the image shown here, the gold was made as in the previous exercises. The only difference was that after it was complete, its Saturation (under Hue/Saturation/Brightness in the Adjust option of the Image menu) was reduced to -75%.

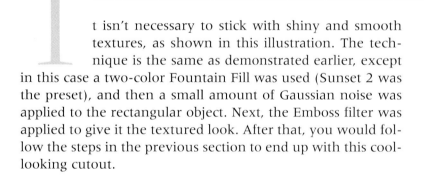

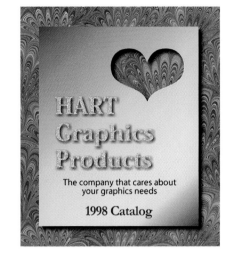

Up until now, the use of cutouts was limited to text. In the image shown, a character from the Zapf Dingbats BT typeface is used to create a heart-shaped cutout for the cover of a graphics catalog. These characters are just like normal type but to view them you need to use Character Map, located in the Accessories of Windows95. If it is not there, open the Add/Remove Programs in the Control Panel and click the tab labeled Windows Setup. Under Accessories, choose Character Map. Many times you will need to enter the character's ANSI number. For example, if the character number shown in the Character Map is 0197 you must enter all four characters (including the leading zero) from the numeric keypad of the keyboard while holding down the ALT key.

Well sports fans, there's much more we could do. In the image shown here, I have used the Image Sprayer brush and applied some of the new image lists from PHOTO-PAINT 8 to add that special touch. The darkened edge of the image was created with the Vignette filter. There is so much more we could explore, but we should move along to the next section.

Cutout Shapes

IN COREL**DRAW**

VERY SIMPLE CUTOUT SHAPES

Creating cutout shapes in DRAW is a no-brainer. It's not that much more complicated in PAINT, unless young Huss creates it, and then you've really got your work cut out for you. Walk this way, and I'll step you through the easy way.

STEP 1

Draw a rectangle 3 1/2 inches wide by 1 1/4 inches tall. Create the word **CUTOUT!** in Futura Extra Bold Italic (or a similar heavy font) as shown in Figure 15-1.

Figure 15-1: The text "CUTOUT!" centered over a rectangle

STEP 2

Select the type, and then the rectangle, and Combine (CTRL+L). This physically removes the text as shown in Figure 15-2. The type cannot be edited once it and the rectangle have been Combined, so check your spelling before you perform the Combine step.

Figure 15-2: The type and rectangle are Combined making the type portion transparent

S T E P

3 Make a Duplicate (+ key on the numeric key board). Fill the duplicate 30% Black. Move the duplicate down and left about two points in each direction, as indicated in Figure 15-3.

Figure 15-3: A 30% Black duplicate is created

S T E P

4 Send the duplicate to the back (SHIFT+PAGEDOWN). This is cutout shapes in a nutshell, as Figure 15-4 affirms. To hide the edges that have been nudged into view, select the shadow portion and use the Shape tool to select the left side and bottom side nodes and drag them behind the front shape. It's cleaner that way. The 30% Black duplicate is moved down and left and sent to the back

Figure 15-4: A simple cutout effect

N O T E

Use the Shape tool instead of the Select (Pick) tool to adjust the sides of the shadow. If you use the Select tool, you'll make the whole image smaller. Selecting the outside nodes with the Shape tool only changes the position of those nodes selected.

ALMOST SIMPLE CUTOUT SHAPES

We could leave it at that, but you didn't shell out your hard-earned money for this book just to have me stop here. We can take this technique another step further by making the shadow diffused. In addition, we'll add a slightly darker color behind the cutout portion to impart a visual cue that the cutout area is farther back.

S T E P

1 Add a smaller rectangle, slightly larger than the cutout section, fill it 5-10% Black (or a slightly darker shade of whatever color or surface is underneath), and send it to the back, as shown in Figure 15-5. Making the cutout area slightly darker gives the viewer a visual cue that this darker surface is slightly lower. Our brains are programmed to perceive this. Conversely, if we want to make an object appear to be raised, we make it slightly lighter than the surface.

Figure 15-5: A slightly darker rectangle placed beneath the cutout shadow enhances the cutout effect

 We can make the shadow more realistic if we blur it. The easiest way to do this in DRAW is to Convert the shadow to Bitmap (by selecting Convert to Bitmap in the Bitmaps menu) and apply a Gaussian Blur.

S T E P

2 Select both the cutout shadow (30% Black) and the lighter rectangle behind the cutout shadow and convert them to a single bitmap. As this shadow is gray, you can make the shadow bitmap grayscale. The results are shown in Figure 15-6. If you are creating an image for printing, set the resolution between 266 and 300 dpi. For Web graphics, 96 dpi is sufficient.

Figure 15-6: The cutout shadow and rectangle are converted to bitmap

N O T E

In DRAW 8, you can eliminate the white rectangle by using the Auto Inflate Bitmap option (select Inflate Bitmap in the Bitmaps menu). This automatically adds extra space to the bitmap as required.

3

Select the grayscale bitmap and apply a Gaussian Blur (in the Bitmaps menu, select Blur, then Gaussian). The results are shown in Figure 15-7. The higher the amount, the greater the blur. Try not to go overboard—an amount of 3 to 5 is more than enough. Shadows get sharper the closer they are to the object casting the shadow, so we don't want the shadow to be too soft.

Figure 15-7: A Gaussian Blur adds a realistic softness to the cutout shadow

4

If you haven't already done so, send the blurred shadow to the back, as shown in Figure 15-8. If you color the top element (shown in orange) white, or your background color, the top element becomes invisible, leaving only the cutout letters.

Figure 15-8: The Gaussian-blurred shadow is sent to the back

MORE COMPLEX CUTOUT SHAPES

Next, we'll create a logo for Dave's Woodworking by building on the techniques we've just learned. For a radial saw blade, we'll use a letter O from Adobe's Toolbox font. If you do not own this font, substitute a symbol from Corel's Symbols Library roll-up.

1

Draw a rectangle 3 inches wide by 2 inches tall. Resize the saw blade symbol (or round symbol of your choice) to about 2 1/2 inches and center it over the rectangle.

Figure 15-9: The saw blade and rectangle are combined and a metal fill applied

Combine the radial saw blade with the rectangle. Open the Pattern Fill menu (inside the Fill Tool flyout). Apply a bitmap metal fill (Metal06.cpt) from METAL\LARGE in the Tiles folder on CD-ROM #2. Figure 15-9 shows our progress thus far.

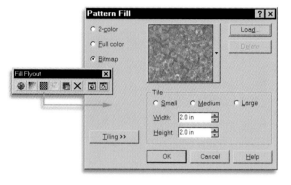

N O T E

To access the bitmap fills, click on the Load button in the upper-right corner. This brings up the Explorer window. Locate the drive with CD-ROM #2 and then locate the Tiles folder. Open the Tiles folder and then open the Metals folder, then the Large subfolder. The fill is the last one in the list, Metal06.cpt.

Gary's Trivial Information: This fill is the finish found on machine surfaces, where a high degree of flatness and accuracy is required. The texture of the surface is produced by a series of small, circular strokes made with a very sharp chisel and applied by hand by skilled craftspersons.

STEP

2   Make a copy of the radial saw blade/rectangle image and fill it black. Drop a 70% Black rectangle behind. Select both and Convert to Bitmap. (use the settings from step 2 in the "Almost Simple Cutout Shapes" section earlier). The result is shown in Figure 15-10.

Figure 15-10: A dark copy of the combined saw blade/rectangle and a black rectangle are converted to curves

3 Place a rectangle filled with the metal fill behind the bitmap shadow you just created. Select the bitmap shadow and apply an Interactive Transparency, Uniform, Multiply, 40%. Figure 15-11 shows how the layers structure.

Figure 15-11: A representation of the top metal-filled cutout shape, the transparent shadow layer, and the metal-filled back layer

4 Copy the main metal image to the clipboard (CTRL+C), fill the main metal image white, and then Paste the metal version directly on top (CTRL+V). Apply an Interactive Linear Fountain Transparency, as shown in Figure 15-12. Begin the transparency at 20% (top left) and end at 85% (bottom right). This imparts the impression of a light source to the metal. The white copy we placed underneath the main shape confines the transparency to just the main shape. You should now have four layers: the linear transparency on top, the white plate second, the gray-level bitmap shadow third, and the metal-filled rectangle on the bottom.

Figure 15-12: Linear transparency is applied to the metal-filled top layer

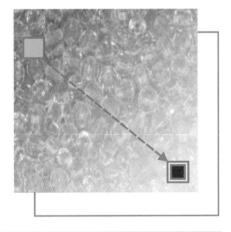

5 Draw a circle slightly larger than the radial saw blade, centered on the blade. Convert the circle to Curves (CTRL+Q), click on the circle's outline with the Text tool, and type **DAVE'S WOODWORKING**. Change the font to Enviro. Figure 15-13 shows the finished logo.

Figure 15-13: The finished illustration with type added

A VERY COMPLEX CUTOUT SHAPE

We'll modify the cutout technique a bit for this next example by creating a carved marble cutout effect.

STEP

1

Draw a rectangle 2 inches wide by 1 3/4 inches tall and center a capital letter in the middle. I've used a capital G set in 150 point Engravers Old English Bold, shown in Figure 15-14.

STEP

2

Make a copy of the letter; we'll need it later. Combine (CTRL+L) the rectangle and the letter and apply a marble bitmap fill (I've used Marble21.cpt). The marble bitmap fills are in the Pattern Fill section of the Fill Tool flyout in the Tiles folder, which as you remember is on CD-ROM #2.

Figure 15-14: An Old English letter combined with a marble-filled rectangle

STEP

3

Make a duplicate of the letter/rectangle, fill it black, drop a 50% Black rectangle in back, and convert the two objects to bitmap, as in Figure 15-15. Apply a Gaussian Blur to the bitmap, as shown in Figure 15-16.

Figure 15-15: A duplicate combined shape filled Black

Figure 15-16: A 50% Black rectangle is placed behind the Black cutout duplicate, both are converted to bitmap, and a Gaussian Blur applied to soften the bitmap

4 Place the bitmap shadow over a rectangle with the same marble fill. Apply Transparency using the following parameters: Type Uniform, Transparency Operation, Multiply, Amount 50%. Position the original shape on top, as shown in Figure 15-17.

Figure 15-17: The cutout shadow placed over a rectangle filled with the same marble fill and transparency is applied

5 This effect is pretty subtle. To help define the outline of the opening, we'll create a shadow and highlight edge with the duplicate letter G. Create an additional duplicate. Offset it one point up and one point left. Make another duplicate and nudge it down and right the same amount. You should now have three letters, as shown in Figure 15-18.

Figure 15-18: Three duplicates of the Old English G offset diagonally in one point increments

6 In Wireframe view, use the Zoom tool to get in real close. Bring the middle letter G to the top (SHIFT+PAGEUP). Select it, and from the Arrange menu select Trim. Make sure the Other Object box is checked and Target Object is unchecked. Click on the Trim button and use the big arrow cursor to point to the upper-left duplicate. This will trim all but the exposed portion of the letter. Uncheck Other Object, then with the middle letter selected, click on Trim and use the big arrow cursor to click on the lower-right copy. If you did this correctly, you'll have two edges left, as shown in Figure 15-19.

Figure 15-19: The center letter G is used to Trim all but the exposed edges of the two duplicate letters

7 Fill the top edge dark red and fill the bottom edge a very pale pink. Position the two edges over the original image, as shown in Figure 15-20.

Figure 15-20: The light and dark edges add dimension to the cutout marble effect

Variations on a Theme

MULTILINGUAL CUTOUT

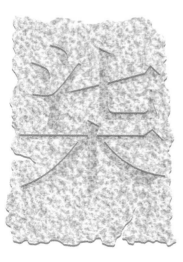

Young Huss is ruthless and will stop at nothing to one-up me. With this in mind, I've cranked out some additional examples of the cutout shapes effect.

I selected a Chinese calligraphic character from the Symbols roll-up (I hope it doesn't mean anything offensive). I constructed a rectangle around the character and used the Eraser tool to draw a very ragged, torn-paper outline around the Chinese character. When I finished using the Eraser tool, I selected the shape, selected Break Apart from the Arrange menu, and deleted the outside portion. I applied an Oatmeal texture fill (Samples 6 Texture Fill Library) to give the shape a rice paper look. I made a shadow shape using solid purple. Another rectangle shape went to the back and was filled with Oatmeal but was altered thus: the Light value of white was changed to Ice Blue, and the Brightness value was set to -15%. This produced a darker value of the rice paper.

VIRTUALLY TRANSPARENT

White on White cutout shapes look cool on Web pages. I took two symbols from the Common Bullets Library in the Symbols roll-up and centered them over a rectangle. The bullets were combined with the rectangle, with a duplicate created for a shadow. I made a simple Linear Interactive Fountain Fill using 20% Black and white and applied it diagonally. The shadow- and fountain-filled areas were converted to bitmap and Gaussian Blurred. I made the rectangle white with no outline, effectively making it invisible, so all you see are the two cutout shapes.

The cutout shapes technique can create very distinctive business card and stationery designs, as you can see here. The cutout shape creates a *trompe l'oeil* (French for to fool the eye) illusion that is sure to make recipients of the cards and stationery to look twice to see if the paper has actually been die-cut.

BUREAU
of **MISSING**
CHICKENS

1234 Cockerel Way
Orpington, CA 94945

Mario Gallo
Special Investigator
Voice: 555-555-1212
FAX: 555-555-2121
gallo@bomc.com

We Strive to Eliminate Foul Play

This final example gets a little tricky, so bear with me. This logo for Wenzel construction, shown here, contrasts diamond plate industrial metal construction material with an elegant script W. The W was Combined with the diamond plate Bitmap Pattern fill. A shadow section was created, converted to bitmap, Gaussian-blurred and sent to the back. The diamond plate portions was converted to bitmap, and a 3D Effects Emboss added to create the highlight and shadow edges. The construction warning stripes are red and yellow skewed rectangles. A rectangle the same size as the striped area was filled with the diamond plate fill, positioned over the stripes and Uniform Transparency, Operation: Subtract, Amount: 50% added. A duplicate of this rectangle was made, and the Operation changed to Add, Amount: 50%. The same process was used for the type.

Well, I hope you got your money's worth. The cutout shapes technique is perfect for logos and Web graphics. For example, you can create a cool cutout shape for a business card, using the last technique, which will look as if it were die-cut. If you create Web graphics, be sure to enable Super Sampling when you export the image, to anti-alias (smooth) the image.

BACK TO KCAB

Hard-edged drop shadows are a bore and totally unnecessary, because creating soft-edged drop shadows is really a piece of cake. In DRAW, that is. But I didn't come here to have a contest with Huss and PHOTO-PAINT. Or did I? I'll share with you my techniques, and you can compare them with young Dave's and draw your own conclusions.

Before DRAW 7, I created soft shadows by using Blends and Contour effects. I would begin with a small area of darker shadow color and then Blend or Contour to the background color, usually to white. This technique was OK for simple shapes but had several drawbacks, the greatest of which was the lack of transparency which limited the Blending or Contouring to solid backgrounds. DRAW 7 coupled the ability to create a Gaussian-blurred bitmap with transparency, making

soft shadows almost easy. DRAW 8 introduced Interactive Drop Shadows, making the process easier still. In spite of the ease of DRAW 8's Interactive Drop Shadows, I still prefer to create my own soft shadows, mainly because I think they look better overall. In this chapter I'll cover the Blend and Contour methods and the bitmap methods as well.

The Shadow Knows

NOTE

This chapter works with PHOTO-PAINT 7 and 8.

SHADOWS, PHOTO-PAINT, AND ALL THE REST

I must give the Duke of DRAW credit for doing a commendable job over the years making vectors look like real shadows. As Gary will soon point out, PHOTO-PAINT 7 and 8, like DRAW 7 and 8, have an automatic Drop Shadow generator. The major difference between the two releases is that PHOTO-PAINT 8 has the ability to make both a flat and a perspective shadow. What I appreciate most about the drop shadows created by PHOTO-PAINT is that they are objects. In previous releases, the making of a drop shadow was somewhat complicated, involving as it did the creation of a blurred object and Merge Modes. So, how good are these "machine made" shadows? Pretty darn good, but even they can be improved, as we will soon see. Let us begin with some shadow basics.

SHADOWY BASICS

The human eye and the viewer attached to it are gullible. Visually, the eye and mind together will believe almost anything that you show them. The mind has been thought to believe that anything that has depth creates shadows. Now, shadows are subtle devices that require proper handling to make them do their job correctly. I like to use this analogy to explain the presence of shadows. As a younger man (after the U.S. Civil War), I played a string bass in jazz combos. The purpose of the bass was to accentuate (not dominate) the music. A shadow is much like a bass player, whose absence is noticed but whose presence shouldn't attract attention. In short, if a casual viewer notices your shadow, you did something wrong.

STEP

1

This first image was created using a combination of techniques from the 3-D and the metallic effects chapters. It looks pretty unappealing sitting out there all alone.

FORUM

STEP

2

In the next illustration, one of the drop shadow presets from PHOTO-PAINT 8 has been selected. It is a standard flat (as opposed to a perspective) shadow. Does the shadow do its job? No, it doesn't. Why? Shadows get lighter and more diffused as they move away from whatever is casting the shadow. While an argument could be made that there was a giant carbon-arc spotlight in the lower-right illuminating the text, in essence the shadow has already failed. Shadows and shading are like jokes. If you have to explain them, they don't work.

FORUM

The illustration here uses the same shadow shown previously, except the opacity of the shadow has been reduced from 100 percent to 50 percent. This softens the shadow, and now it makes the eye believe that it might be a real shadow after all. For the distance that the letters are from the shadow, I must either bring the shadow in closer or make it more diffused. It is in the area of diffusion (called feathering) that we experience the primary limitation of the Drop Shadow command. In the next image, I have applied a Gaussian blur to the shadow at a radius setting of 5.0.

The shadow is now barely noticeable and, more important, it is doing its job. It should make the eye and the mind of the viewer believe that the text we created has depth. Yet one thing is still missing. Have you figured it out? What is missing is the first thing we should always look for when creating a shadow. Look at the letters—they have a whitened edge in the upper and right sides. The apparent light source is therefore somewhere in the upper-right corner of the image and our shadow should be on the opposite side, or the lower-left.

The finished shadow is shown with a marble fill background just so we can see the shadow is falling on something.

THE MECHANICS OF SHADOWS IN PHOTO-PAINT

When PHOTO-PAINT creates a shadow with the Drop Shadow command, it groups the new shadow object with the object that was used to create the original shadow. To work with a shadow by itself, you must first ungroup it from the original object. After selecting the grouped objects with the Object Picker tool, you can select the Ungroup button in the Property Bar (if it is visible—I swear, it is one of the shyest buttons I have ever known), choose Ungroup from the Object menu, or press CTRL+U. Once it is ungrouped from the original object, you can control its softness (pass the Charmin, please) two ways. You can change how transparent it is with the Opacity slider at the bottom of the Objects Docker window (Objects Roll-Up in PHOTO-PAINT 7). Or, you can determine the softness of the shadow with the Gaussian blur filter. The only restriction with using Gaussian blur is that once the blur has been applied, your only option is to Undo it. On the other hand, you can change the opacity setting as many times as you want.

PUTTING A PERSPECTIVE ON SHADOWS

The addition of the Perspective feature of the Drop Shadow command in PHOTO-PAINT 8 is neat. I personally find the controls a little difficult to manage, but hey, that's just me.

S T E P

1

In this first illustration, I applied the default setting for the Perspective (Top-Right). Pretty ugly stuff. Never fear, in the next illustration I took advantage of the controls built into the Drop Shadow Perspective feature and modified them to create the shadow shown.

2 First, we know from reading the previous section about shadows that it should never be at 100 percent opacity, so I changed it to 50 percent. Next, the Feather value (softness) is set to zero (they haven't read this book yet), and so I changed it to 12. Earlier I said that the feathering of the Drop Shadow was the weak point in the Flat shadows; the same is true of the Perspective. Now that I have badmouthed their feather, I must praise the Fade control. You see, as the rope appears to be getting farther from the surface, the shadow should be getting lighter. That is what the Fade control determines. After creating the perspective drop shadow in the image shown, I ungrouped it and gave it a Gaussian blur at a radius setting of 4. Now that's perspective.

Variations on a Theme

VARIATIONS ON A THEME USING PHOTO-PAINT 7

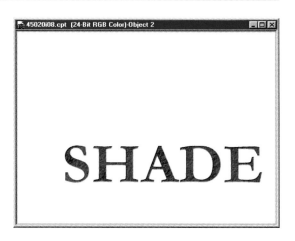

This time the variation is not something different but rather doing the same thing on a program that doesn't offer the luxury of an automatic perspective. So how do you make a perspective shadow in PHOTO-PAINT 7? It is really quite simple. Just follow the instructions outlined next. First, duplicate the object that you want to use to create a shadow. In my illustration, I have placed the word "SHADE" on a 4 × 3 image and filled it with Above the Earth Texture Fill from Samples 7. Select the bottom (original) object and make the top object invisible. Change the Objects Roll-Up to Single mode, and from the Edit Fill dialog box make the object Black. A quick way to do it is select Paint color (if it's black). The object is now officially a shadow.

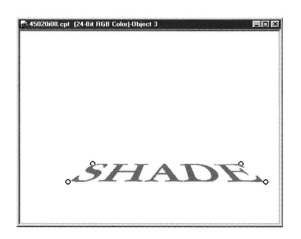

Next, change the Opacity slider in the Objects Roll-Up to 50 percent. Click on the Shadow until the Transform handles (the tiny circles in the corners) appear. Click and drag the top-right handle down and to the left until the shadow looks like the one shown. When you are satisfied with it, double-click the shadow to apply the transformation.

To give it the Fade, select the Object Transparency tool. Click on the bottom and drag up to the top of the shadow. Control the transparency gradient properties in the Tool Settings roll-up until the top is faded. To finish it up, change the Opacity back to 100 percent (to emphasize the fade), and in Layer mode of PHOTO-PAINT 7 apply a Gaussian blur at a Radius of 4, as shown.

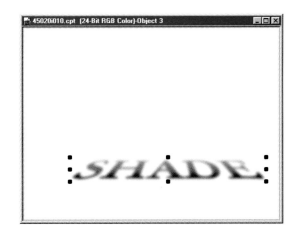

Finally, make the top object visible, as shown in the middle image. To show off the shadow, I applied a marble tile bitmap fill and then used my favorite filter in Kai Power Tools 3.0 (Planar tiling) to make the background, which I then applied a Vignette filter (using white), as shown in the bottom image.

Well, I hope you enjoyed and learned something from our shadowy topic. There is a lot more to learn about shading and highlights, but that's another story and another book.

The Shadow Knows
IN COREL**DRAW**

VERY EASY SOFT SHADOWS

I've thrown caution to the wind, and modified a Japanese symbol (#92), shown in Figure 16-1, even though I haven't a clue what it means. My hunch is that it says "DRAW Is Easier," but what do I know? To create a soft gray shadow on a white background, follow these steps.

STEP

1

Copy the original symbol to the clipboard (CTRL+C) and fill the symbol on the page 40% Black.

Figure 16-1: A Japanese character from the Symbols Library

STEP

2

Create a duplicate (+ key), apply a white fill, send it to the back, and move it down and left, as shown in Figure 16-2. (I've added the red outline so you'll be able to see the white version.)

Figure 16-2: The symbol is filled 30% Black, and a White duplicate is made, offset, and sent to the back

3

Select the white and gray symbols and apply a 20-Step Blend (CTRL+B). Paste the original symbol on top. Figure 16-3 shows the results. Now, that wasn't hard, was it?

Figure 16-3: The 30% Black symbol is Blended with the White creating a soft gray shadow; the original symbol (in Red) is pasted on top

ALMOST-EASY SOFT SHADOWS

Sometimes the shape you're creating a soft shadow for is more complex. While a simple yellow circle does not fit the more complex category, the technique applies.

1

Copy the original shape to the clipboard. Fill the shape on the page with the beginning shadow color, which in this case is 40% Black.

2

Apply a Contour to Outside (in the Effects menu, select Contour), Steps 15, Offset .01 inch (this number will vary, depending upon the size of the circle), and make the Fill Color White, as shown in Figure 16-4. (The Contour steps are displayed in blue outline in the rectangle to the right.)

Figure 16-4: A 15-Step Contour effect is applied to gray circle, creating a soft shadow

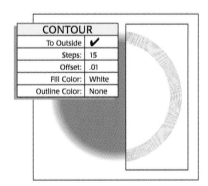

CONTOUR	
To Outside	✔
Steps:	15
Offset:	.01
Fill Color:	White
Outline Color:	None

STEP

3

Paste the original shape on top, as shown in Figure 16-5.

Figure 16-5: A copy of the original circle is placed on top

STEP

4

To make the shadow even smoother, create a white rectangle about 1/4 inch all around and send it behind the Contour group, select all but the yellow circle, and Convert to Bitmap (in the Bitmaps menu, select Convert to Bitmap). Select the bitmap shadow and apply a Gaussian Blur (in the Bitmaps menu, select Blur) with a Radius of 15. (In DRAW 8 set the Radius to 5). Figure 16-6 shows that it's not hard at all.

N O T E

DRAW 8 can "inflate" a bitmap, causing it to expand to the width of the applied Bitmap Effect, in this case a Gaussian Blur, so in DRAW 8 there is no need for the White rectangle.

Figure 16-6: The Contoured shadow is converted to bitmap and a Gaussian blur applied

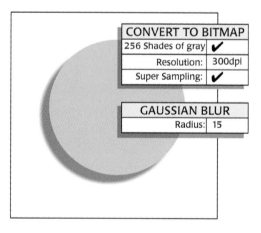

CONVERT TO BITMAP	
256 Shades of gray	✔
Resolution:	300dpi
Super Sampling:	✔

GAUSSIAN BLUR	
Radius:	15

EASY SOFT SHADOWS

If you need to apply a soft shadow to an object, such as this seahorse symbol (Animals 1, #93) on a colored background, follow these steps.

Place the seahorse symbol over a Turquoise-filled square background as shown in Figure 16-7.

Figure 16-7: A seahorse symbol is placed over a colored square

Copy the seahorse to the Clipboard (CTRL+C). Apply a Sea Green fill to the seahorse.

Apply a 10-Step Contour to the seahorse using Turquoise (the background color) as the Contour Fill Color.

STEP

4

Paste a Copy of the seahorse from the Clipboard and position it as shown in Figure 16-8.

Figure 16-8: A Contour is created using the square's color for the Contour fill color

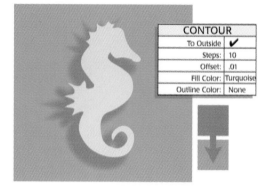

ANOTHER METHOD

You can use a Blend to produce a colored soft shadow that is similar to the Contour method by following these steps.

STEP

1

Place a seahorse symbol over a Turquoise-filled square background as we did in the previous Contour exercise. Place a Copy in the Clipboard.

STEP

2

Make a duplicate of the seahorse and position it to the left and down about 1/4 inch in each direction as shown in Figure 16-9.

Figure 16-9: Two duplicate seahorses, one filled a darker color, one filled the background color

3

Fill the bottom seahorse the same color as the background color (Turquoise) and the upper sea horse Sea Green.

4

Apply a 50-Step Blend. This produces a similar shadow to the Contour but not as desirable because of the feathering produced by the Blend.

Paste a copy of the seahorse on top as shown in Figure 16-10.

Figure 16-10: A 50-Step Blend produces a soft shadow over which a lighter copy is placed

NOT VERY HARD SOFT SHADOWS

If you need to apply a soft shadow to a bitmap, the process is a tad less easy, but certainly not in the rocket science category. Follow these steps.

Draw a square and apply a bitmap background. I've used a 2-Color Bitmap Pattern Fill with Ice Blue dots over a Turquoise background.

Apply a Sea Green fill to a seahorse symbol and a place it over a white rectangle. Select the seahorse and the white rectangle and Convert to Bitmap as shown in Figure 16-11. (The white rectangle is not necessary in DRAW 8).

Select the bitmap and apply a Gaussian Blur with a radius of 25 (for DRAW 8, use a radius of 5).

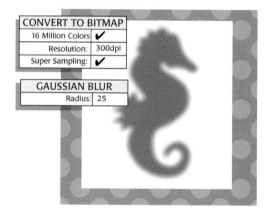

Figure 16-11: A seahorse symbol is placed over a white background and both are Converted to Bitmap

Place the bitmap over the top of the polka-dotted background.

4 Select the bitmap and apply an Interactive Transparency (Uniform, Subtract, 30%). The white disappears, leaving a richly colored shadow, as shown in Figure 16-12. You can use black instead of the dark blue-green color I've used, but the shadow color will not be as rich.

Figure 16-12: Transparency is applied to the bitmap

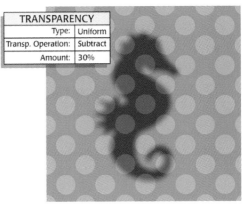

5 Paste a copy of the original seahorse over the blurred, transparent bitmap. Apply a wavy 2-color Bitmap fill and add an eyeball. Figure 16-13 shows the final effect.

Figure 16-13: A copy of the seahorse is placed on top and given a wavy 2-Color Pattern Fill

TIP

You can use the Transparent Background option to remove the white background when Converting To Bitmap. If you chose this option, your background color needs to be set to none, not white. If you're using Accurate Color Correction or Simulate Printer Colors for your display, select the Use Color Profile option when you Export an image in a bitmap file format.

Variations on a Theme

Here are some additional soft shadow techniques. I've included a peek at DRAW 8's Interactive Drop Shadow Tool for users still using DRAW 7. While I was in DRAW 8, I used the new Interactive Distortion Tool to create a jagged edge to cast a more realistic shadow on a grass surface. There are a couple of additional examples but rather than tell you about it, let's just do it.

NO BULL SOFT SHADOWS

I filled a square with a Bitmap photographic wood fill (Wood04.cpt) from the Tiles folder on CD-ROM #2. I placed a cow skull symbol, #61 from the Animals 1 library on the Symbols roll-up, in the center and added a pair of glowing red eyes, which look back at the viewer. I copied the skull and background to the clipboard. I filled the skull black, applied a Contour, filled the square white, and converted both elements to bitmap. I pasted the original image and sent the wood bitmap beneath the bitmap shadow. I then applied Transparency to the shadow bitmap. I placed the orange skull on top and applied a Stucco Texture Fill from the Samples Texture Fill library. I altered the colors of the Stucco fill to Walnut and Light Orange, producing a credible-looking rusty surface. I added "BUM STEER" set in Bertram BT and copied the fill from the skull. I made a duplicate of the type, filled it walnut, applied an Interactive Transparency, and used it as a hard drop shadow for the type. The results are shown here.

NO-BRAINER

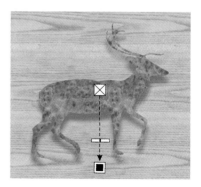

The easiest way to create a soft drop shadow is to use DRAW 8's new Interactive Drop Shadow tool , as you can see here. I filled a stag symbol with a bird's-eye maple Bitmap Pattern fill, centered it over a wood grain-filled square, selected the stag, and dragged in the direction I wanted the shadow to fall. The directional arrow can be interactively dragged to determine the direction of the shadow. The slim white rectangle can be dragged up and down the directional path to adjust the softness of the shadow. The process is so simple I don't even know why we're bothering with this chapter.

To create a more realistic soft shadow for the red ball, I created an ellipse and applied a Black to 50% Black Linear Fountain Fill. I used DRAW 8's Interactive Distortion Zipper Effect to produce a spiked edge, which will cast a more convincing shadow on the grass surface. I converted the spiked-edged shadow to Bitmap, applied a radius 3 Gaussian Blur, then applied a Uniform Transparency, Subtract, amount 50.

WE HAVE IGNITION

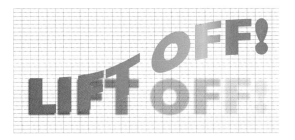

Here, I applied a Double Arc Envelope to the red type and dragged the left side up to create the impression of the type lifting off the blue grid. I left a duplicate of the type on the grid with no envelope. I Converted the Text To Curves and then broke the type apart (CTRL+K). I Combined the letters for "LIFT" and applied a Linear Fountain Fill beginning with Black and ending with 60% Black. I applied a 50% Black fill to the O, a 45% Black fill to the F, a 40% Black Fill to the second F and a 35% Black Fill to the exclamation point. I individually selected the letters and converted them to Bitmap. I applied increasing amounts of Gaussian Blur to the letters. Finally I selected all the bitmap letters, grouped them, and applied a Uniform Transparency, Multiply, amount 50%. The effect is the shadow becoming lighter and less sharp the farther it is from the type which, by the way, is what actually happens in real life.

WITHOUT A SHADOW OF DOUBT

You can see by how short this chapter is that soft-edged drop shadows are a snap to create in DRAW 7. DRAW 8 has an automatic drop shadow generator, but given how easy and flexible the techniques presented in this chapter are to apply, I can't see why you would need to use it. It is pretty impressive, however, and once you've used it you'll probably get lazy and complacent and forget all these cool techniques.

To review, we've discovered how easy it is to create soft-edged drop shadows using simple Blends and Contours. Adding an additional step and converting the blend or contour to bitmap softens the shadow even more. Adding a Gaussian blur to the bitmap shadow softens it considerably. Finally, adding transparency to the bitmap shadow is icing on the cake and enables the soft-edged shadow to be placed upon any vector or bitmap object. This technique can be used for creating buttons and other Web page graphics. Soft drop shadows can be used under initial capital letters as drop caps in paragraph text. And let's not forget how a soft drop shadow can make logos pop off business cards, letterheads, and envelopes.

TIP

To re-create the Zipper effect in DRAW 7, use the Polygon Star tool to create a 32-point star. Convert the star To Curves, and use the Shape Tool to make the points more random.

BACK to BACK

Creating embossed effects has been one of my favorite computer tricks for almost as long as I've used a computer to create images. It's just an illusion, and our brain makes the illusion work. In our world, light generally originates above us, the primary source being the sun or an overhead light. Shadows almost always fall beneath objects. So, when we see an object with a lighter edge on top and/or a darker edge on the bottom, our brain interprets this to mean the object is raised or embossed because the light from above is making the top facing surface lighter or the edge farthest away from the light source darker. Conversely, when we reverse this by placing the lighter edge on the bottom and the darker edge on top, our brains interpret this as the object being recessed or debossed because the light is reflecting off the bottom edge while the top edge is in shadow. So to create an embossed effect, we just provide visual cues (sort of a cerebral nudge-wink) and let the brain do the rest.

This might be one area where I'm willing to concede that PAINT has an ever-so-slight advantage. And young Huss will be in filter heaven. But we DRAW users are clever and resourceful, no? We can always find ways to achieve stunning effects even if occasionally we have to work at it. In my half of the chapter, I'll show you techniques for creating very credible embossed and debossed effects without ever leaving the comfort of DRAW. And whereas the PAINT users will know how to use the BOSS filter, we'll not only know how to create embossed and debossed effects, we'll know how and why the illusion works.

Embossed & Debossed Images

IN COREL **PHOTO-PAINT**

MILES OF TILES WITH THE BOSS AND COMPANY

Recently, I was able to go back into PHOTO-PAINT and experiment with effects that I hadn't had time to explore. To my surprise, I found a wealth of effects possible, with filters that made their first appearance in PHOTO-PAINT 5, Plus and a relatively unused mask mode (XOR).

When I lived in the Far East, I was fascinated by the detailed ceramic and terra-cotta tiles that had been made there for centuries. In this first part of this chapter, we will learn to use XOR masks to create a very intricately patterned tile similar to those I used to stare at and sketch. These tiles can be tiled (no pun intended) or can be used for Web pages or as the starting point for other projects. In addition, you are going to learn some of the great things that can be done with a filter called The Boss.

The Boss has been a part of PHOTO-PAINT since the release of PHOTO-PAINT 5 Plus. While The Boss may seem like an odd name, you must understand that it was originally designed by the folks at Alien Skin software to be a "super embossing" filter in their Black Box series of filters. The problem with any filter, be it in Photoshop or PHOTO-PAINT, is the tendency of users to let the name confine their thinking. You will learn that this is one of the most powerful filters in PHOTO-PAINT.

NOTE

This chapter uses PHOTO-PAINT 7 and 8.

MAKING A PATTERN (NOT SIMPLICITY)

This tile begins with the creation of a pattern. We could use anything symmetrical as the basis for the pattern, but we are going to learn how to create one using grids and the XOR mask mode. I specifically created this mask to be used with the Tile filter later in the exercise.

STEP

1

Create a new file that is 5 × 5 inches, 96 dpi, using 24-bit color. If you later want to use this as part of a Web page, you can convert it to 256 colors (8 bit) after completing the project. From the Tools menu, select Grid and Ruler Setup. Select Grid settings area and change to Frequency. Change the Horizontal and Vertical values to 4.0 per inch. Also check Show Grid and Snap to Grid. Click OK. From the Toolbox, select the Circle Mask tool from the Mask tool flyout. From the Mask menu, choose Mode and select XOR.

STEP

2

Beginning at the intersection of the grid 1 square down and 1 square right in the upper-left corner, click the mouse button first and then press and hold CTRL to drag a circle 4 squares wide. Click the Mask Overlay button to see the resulting circle mask more clearly. Beginning at the center of the first circle mask, click the mouse and then press and hold CTRL, click and drag down and to the right another circle that is 4 squares wide. And from the center of that circle, click and drag a circle that is 5 squares wide. Repeat these steps on each of the four corners until it looks like the one shown.

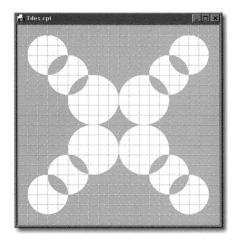

STEP

3

Beginning at the intersection of the grid at a point that is 5 squares down and 5 squares to the right of the upper-left corner, click and drag a circle 10 squares wide. Beginning at the intersection of the grid at a point that is 8 squares down and 8 squares to the right of the upper-left corner, click and drag a circle 4 squares wide. The result is shown.

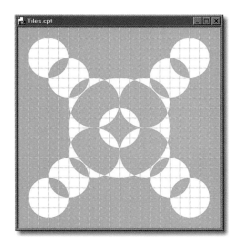

In the next two steps we are going to create a flower using overlapping circles. Click at the center of the circle in the upper-left corner and, while pressing and holding CTRL, drag a circle up and to the left, creating a circle 2 squares wide. Repeat this for the remaining three quadrants of the circle. Create a circle that is 2 squares wide that covers the center of the circle. The result, indicated by the black circle, is shown.

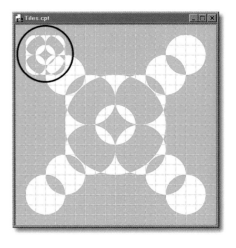

Repeat step 4 on the remaining seven circles in the image. The result, shown here, shows what the resulting image should look like. Note that on some circles, there is one quadrant that will already be occupied by a circle mask that was applied to an adjacent circle. Don't overlap those quadrants.

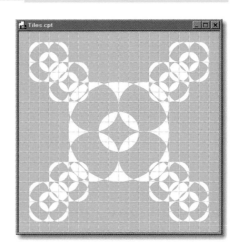

Beginning at the intersection of the grid at a point 2 squares down and 8 squares to the right of the upper-left corner, create a circle 4 squares wide. Repeat this on the remaining three sides until it looks like the image shown. Take heart, we are almost done.

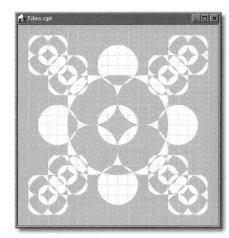

STEP

7

Repeat the technique in step 6 to create the flowers out of the four circles we just made. The result is shown.

STEP

8

Click on the center of the upper-left flower and drag a circle that is 14 squares wide to the center of the lower-right flower. At the point that is 7 down and 7 to the right of the upper-left corner, drag a 6-square-wide circle. For the last touch, change to the Square Mask tool and drag a 2-square-wide square in the center. The final mask is shown. At this point, I recommend saving the mask to disk. From the Mask menu, choose Save and then select To Disk. Save the file as Flower Mask.CPT.

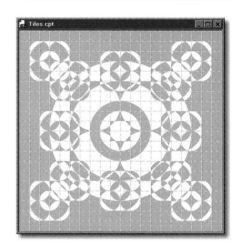

SELECTING THE RIGHT MATERIAL FOR YOUR TILE

You've done all of the hard work (making the pattern), now the rest of the project is the fun part. First, we need to choose the material we are going to use for the tile to be made of. We will use a light marble, although a dark polished wood also looks very good.

STEP

1

If you closed the previous image, load the mask FLOWER MASK.CPT. Then from the Mask menu, select Save and choose Save as channel. When prompted, name the channel Flowers. Delete the Mask by clicking the Delete Mask button on the Toolbar. From the Edit menu, choose Fill. In the Edit Fill and Transparency dialog box, click the Bitmap fill button and click Edit, opening the Bitmap Fill dialog box. Click the Load button and locate the Tiles folder on the DRAW or PHOTO-PAINT CD. In Tiles, locate the file \TILES\MARBLE\LARGE\MARBL06l.CPT. Select it and click the Open button and then click OK to close the Bitmap fill and click OK again to apply the fill. Now we have a solid square of marble and a mask hiding in the wings (or channel, as the case may be).

STEP

2

From the Mask menu, choose Load and then select Flowers. This loads the channel as a mask. From the Image menu, choose Adjust and select Gamma. In the dialog box, select a value of .4 and click OK. This darkens the unprotected areas to enhance the effect of The Boss filter. From the Effects menu, choose 3D Effects (Fancy in PHOTO-PAINT 7) and select The Boss. Change the settings of the dialog box to Width 6, Smoothness 50, Height 70, Drop off Flat, Brightness 90, Sharpness 50, Direction 135, and Angle 45. Click OK. The resulting image is shown.

STEP

3

Now this tile is great, but I think it gets a lot better. Invert the Mask and apply The Boss filter again (CTRL+F). Now it really has a ceramic tile look.

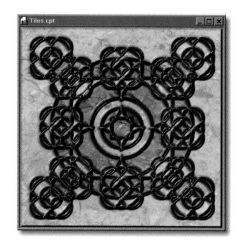

MAKING A WOOD TILE

This part of the chapter is a variation of the first part. We will spend more time on the embossing and less time on the construction of the pattern. First, we need to make a background image.

STEP

1

Create a new image that is 5 × 5 inches, 24-bit color at 72 dpi resolution. From the Edit menu, choose Fill. In the Edit Fill and Transparency dialog box, click the Bitmap fill button and then click Edit. When the Bitmap Fill dialog box opens, click the Load button. From the Import dialog box, locate the file on the Corel CD called \TILES\WOOD\LARGE\WOOD21L.CPT. Click the Open button and then click OK. The entire image should be filled with the wood fill.

STEP

2

Click on the Text tool in the Toolbox. Change the font to Zapf Dingbats BT at a size of 300 (no kidding). Click inside of the image and type the letter a. Select the Object Picker in the Toolbox (making the text into an object). Select Align from the Objects menu and align the object To the Center of Document. The result is shown.

3

If using PHOTO-PAINT 7, enable Preserve Image. Select Convert to Mask. This action makes a mask out of the object. Because Preserve Image is enabled, the object remains. From the Objects Docker window, delete the object; in PHOTO-PAINT 7, open the Objects Roll-Up (CTRL+F7) and delete the object—we don't need it anymore. From the Image menu, select Adjust and choose Gamma. Change the Gamma to .85 and then invert the mask.

From the Effects menu, choose 3D Effects (Fancy in PHOTO-PAINT 7) and select The Boss. When the dialog box opens, change the following parameters: Width 10, Smoothness 50, Height 80, Drop off Gaussian, Brightness 65, Sharpness 25, Direction 135, and Angle 45. Click OK. The result is shown. Now we are going to create some slick tiling around the edge.

4

From the Mask menu, choose Select All to mask the entire image and then reduce the mask by selecting Shape from the Mask menu and choosing Reduce. When the dialog box opens, enter a width of 28 pixels. Invert the Mask again. From the Effects menu, choose 2D Effects and select Tile. Change the Number of Tiles to 12 on both the Horizontal and the Vertical settings. Click OK. PHOTO-PAINT uses the entire image as a source, but it can only apply the resulting tile in the masked area. The result is shown. The reason why the original mask size is so critical is if the mask doesn't match the size of the tiles, then only part of the images will be in the tiles. The way to determine the correct size is to experiment.

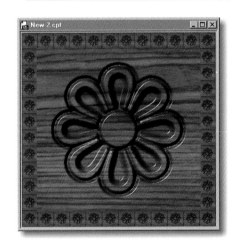

STEP

5

Open The Boss filter again and change the Sharpness value to 0 and click OK. The resulting tile is shown.

STEP

6

From this point, there are several ways to go. You can leave the mask in place and select the Tile filter, setting it to 2 on both horizontal and vertical. The mask causes a unique pattern to develop, as shown. Removing the mask and applying the same Tile filter produces the next pattern shown.

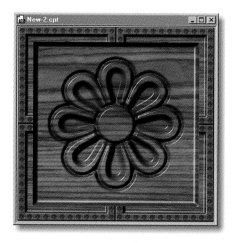

TILING CONSIDERATIONS

When you want to make a tiled border, you are going to need to experiment a little with each image. It is the combination of two values that determines how the border will appear. The values are the size of the masked area (created by the Reduce command) and the number of tiles selected. You should select a border size that seems appropriate. If you make the border width too small, your tiled edge pattern may be unrecognizable. After you pick the size of the border, you then open the Tile dialog box, click the lock icon next to the Preview button (this causes the preview to be updated every time you make a change to the tile values), and start changing the number of tiles. I always start with 12. An easy way to change the numbers is to click in the value box and use the up and down arrow keys to change the values. You will notice as you move up and down that the pattern will shift around inside of the border as the size of the tile changes. If you cannot get the tile to fit in the tiled area without cutting part of it off, you need to note if the border is too small or too large, cancel the Tile filter, and change the size of the mask border. Generally, you won't have to do this more than once.

MAKING A GOLD INSET

Using the same techniques we used to make the wood tile, this allows you to create what appears to be a material that is inset into the background.

Repeat step 1 of the previous exercise ("Making a Wood Tile"). For step 2, instead of typing the letter a, press and hold ALT and type **0170** on the numeric keypad. After creating a mask, delete the object, and from the Edit menu select Fill. From the Edit Fill and Transparency dialog box, click the Fountain Fill button and then the Edit button. From the Fountain Fill dialog box, choose the Cylinder-Gold 01 preset. Change Angle to 45 and Steps to 999. Click OK to close the dialog box and click OK again to apply it. The image will look like the one shown.

S T E P

1 This next step gives the gold fill a brushed metal look. From the Effects menu, select Noise and pick Add Noise. When the dialog box opens, enable Gaussian noise and change the Level setting to 5 and the Density to 80. Click OK. From the Effects menu, select Blur and choose Motion blur. The Direction should be at 135 and the Distance (PHOTO-PAINT 8) or Speed (PHOTO-PAINT 7) set to 15. Click OK. From the Effects menu, select Sharpen. Choose Directional Sharpen and a value of 100 percent. Click OK.

S T E P

2 Invert the Mask. From the Effects menu, choose Fancy and select The Boss. When the dialog box opens, change the following parameters: Width 18, Smoothness 30, Height 30, Drop off Gaussian, Brightness 65, Sharpness 20, Direction 135, and Angle 45. Click OK. The result is shown.

STEP

3

Use the same technique described in step 4 of the previous exercise: From the Mask menu, choose Select All to mask the entire image and then reduce the mask by selecting Shape from the Mask menu and choosing Reduce. When the dialog box opens, enter a width of 28 pixels. Invert the Mask again. From the Effects menu, choose 2D Effects and select Tile. Change the Number of Tiles to 12 on both the Horizontal and the Vertical settings. Click OK. Except this time use a Mask Reduce value of 25 and a Tile value of 11. The resulting image is shown. If portions of the tile are cut off, Undo (CTRL+Z) the Tile filter action and adjust the Tile value until it comes out without the edges cut off, as shown.

Variations on a Theme

MILES AND MILES OF TILES

There are so many variations to these procedures that it is almost scary. Here are just a few additional techniques and ideas.

The images shown are examples of what happens when you apply the Planar Tile filter from the popular KPT 3.0 collection to the tiles we made in this chapter.

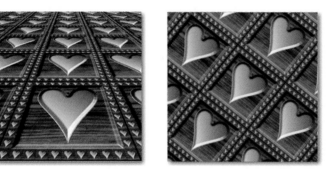

MORE EMBOSSED TILES

The image of four different tiles placed side-by-side gives you an idea of the embossing patterns that can be created with the technique using XOR masks and grids and the embossing ability of The Boss filter.

ADDING ORNAMENTS

One more item to consider is adding ornaments to the tiles. This image shown contains an embossed Zaph Dingbat character and a simple red sphere. The sphere is made by using the Ellipse Shape tool to make a circle almost the size of the tile with a Radial fill of Red wash (set to Render as Object). The red circle is resized to the desired size.

THE ORIENT EXPRESS

Here is a great variation of the tile with which we began this exercise. The image shown was created with a pattern similar to the one we used in the exercise, but at the final step, the mask was not inverted and The Boss filter was not reapplied. Instead, the Tile filter was applied at a setting of 12, which caused the tiled portion to be applied outside of the inset area.

PORTAL TO ANOTHER WORLD

What else can you do with a tile? Of course, you can really go off the deep end, as I did in making the image called The Portal, shown here. The tile had the Video Feedback filter (KPT 3.0SE filters in the Effects menu of PHOTO-PAINT 7 only) applied to create the multiple arches and the tile pathway that leads down the center. I used the third-party plug-in filter KPS Planar Tile, previously mentioned, for the pathway. In a separate image, I used a Freehand mask to isolate the part that is now the pathway under the lamp, made it an object, and dragged it into the image. Next, I applied the Lighting Effect filter with several lights pointing straight up. It affected the background but left the pathway untouched. The lamp is a floating object and the light at the end of the tunnel is the Lens Flare filter.

LAST BUT NOT LEAST

It seemed fitting to end the section with the embossed tile that started it. This variation is the simplest one of all. I just applied the Tile filter to it. Since it is symmetrical, each time the filter is applied, the new image creates a new pattern.

Does this mean we have exhausted The Boss? We haven't even scratched the surface. There seems to be no limit to what can be achieved using different combinations of the Tile and The Boss filters. Happy embossing and tiling.

Embossed & Debossed Images

IN COREL**DRAW**

HOP THIS WAY

I invited my good friend Pierre Lapin, who lives in a warren in the Animals 2 Symbols library (#53), to assist me in performing a little embossing magic. First we'll ask Monsieur Lapin to rise to the occasion. Three things give Pierre his embossed appearance, shown in Figure 17-1: the lighter (highlight) edge on the top, the darker (shadow) edge on the bottom, and the slightly lighter color of Pierre himself compared to the background color. Here is the process in step (or hop) form.

Figure 17-1: Three different colored versions of the rabbit create an embossed, or raised, look

STEP

1

Draw a 2 1/4-inch square with a Gold fill.

STEP

2

Add a rabbit symbol from the Animals 2 Symbols library with the same Gold fill applied.

3

Make two duplicates. Position one duplicate up and left about one or two points and apply a Pale Yellow fill.

4

Position the other duplicate down and to the right about one or two points and apply a Walnut (dark brown) fill.

5

Bring the original rabbit to the top.

Figure 17-2: Reversing the order of the images creates a debossed, or recessed, look

If we reverse these effects, as seen in Figure 17-2— that is, make Pierre a tad darker than his background, put the shadow edge on top, and place the highlight edge on the bottom—voila! Pierre appears to be debossed, or then again, he might just be feeling recessive. Here are the required hops for creating a recessed rabbit.

FEELING RECESSIVE

1

Draw a 2 1/4-inch square with a Gold fill.

2

Add a rabbit symbol from the Animals 2 Symbols library with the same Gold fill applied.

STEP

3

Make two duplicates. Position one duplicate up and left about one or two points and apply a Walnut (dark brown) fill.

STEP

4

Position the other duplicate down and to the right about one or two points and apply a Pale Yellow fill.

STEP

5

Bring the original to the top.

We know these things automatically. How? Because of what are known as visual cues. I'll explain. We expect the source of light to be overhead, right? And shadows generally lie underneath the object casting them. We know that because I explained it in the opening paragraphs of this chapter. So, when the highlight edge is on top and the shadow is on the bottom, then the visual cue is: this object is embossed. On the other hand, when the highlight is on the bottom edge and the shadow is on top, the visual cue is: this object is debossed. We can reinforce the visual cue by making the embossed object slightly lighter than the background and the debossed object slightly darker.

RX FOR EASY, SMOOTH EMBOSSED IMAGES

The previous technique works effectively for small images or images with highlight and shadow edges that are relatively slight. Nurse Symbol (a.k.a. #119) has been granted a temporary leave of absence from the Signs Symbol library, where she is on call 24 hours a day. She will demonstrate the smooth emboss method shown in Figure 17-3.

Figure 17-3: Converting the three shapes to bitmap and applying a Gaussian Blur makes the effect more realistic

CONVERT TO BITMAP	
16 million colors	✔
Resolution:	300dpi
Super Sampling:	✔

GAUSSIAN BLUR	
Radius:	10

S T E P

1

Draw a 2 1/4-inch circle and apply an Ice Blue fill.

S T E P

2

Center a 2-inch Ice Blue–filled Nurse Symbol, make two duplicates (multiple personalities?) and position them, as you did with the rabbit in the previous section.

S T E P

3

Use the Fill Color Dialog (inside the fill tool) to lighten and darken the Ice Blue fill.

STEP

4   Modify the fill for the main nurse making it slightly lighter. Modify the highlight and shadow versions of the nurse to make one lighter and the other darker shades of Ice Blue. (In DRAW 8 simply click and hold down the cursor over the Ice Blue swatch on the on-screen palette and a pop-up menu containing 48 shades and values will appear for you to select from.)

STEP

5   Select the three nurses and convert the image to bitmap (in the Bitmaps menu, select Convert to Bitmap).

STEP

6   Apply a Gaussian Blur (in the Bitmaps menu, select Blur), with a radius between 3 and 10. (In DRAW 8 use a setting of .5 to 1). The Gaussian Blur softens the three shapes, making the emboss appear smoother and more realistic. Note the magnified example in the inset on the left side of Figure 17-3.

MORE MENTALLY TAXING, DOUBLE-DIPPING EMBOSSES

Young Huss and his PHOTO-PAINT pals definitely have the advantage on this next double-emboss, but that doesn't mean we DRAW devotees can't do it just as fancy. It just requires a little concentration and a few more steps.

S T E P

1

Create a rectangle 1 1/4 inch by 2 inches and fill it 30 percent Black.

S T E P

2

Create a dollar sign, (I've used Benguit BK, 120 points) place a duplicate down at about a 45-degree angle, and create a 3-Step Blend for a grand total of five objects, shown in Figure 17-4. (I've colored the images for easier reference.)

Figure 17-4: Two dollar signs are used to create a 3-Step Blend

S T E P

3

Separate the Blend (in the Arrange menu, select Separate) and Ungroup the elements.

S T E P

4

Move the blue dollar sign up and left about 1 point in each direction.

STEP

5

Move the red dollar sign down and right about 1 point in each direction, as shown in Figure 17-5.

Figure 17-5: The first and last dollar signs are moved closer to the middle

STEP

6

Bring the middle dollar sign (yellow) to the front (SHIFT+PAGEUP).

STEP

7

Select the red and blue symbols and the background, and send all three to the back (SHIFT+PAGEDOWN), as I've done in Figure 17-6.

Figure 17-6: The red, blue dollar signs and background are sent to the back, the yellow dollar sign is brought to the front

OK, now this is where you have to concentrate (at least I do; maybe you're quicker than I am).

STEP

8

Fill the yellow symbol 20% Black. Fill the highlight edge (the next one up from the center symbol) 10 percent Black. Fill the red symbol 80 percent Black.

STEP

9

Fill the symbol just under the center symbol 80 percent Black, and fill the blue symbol 10 percent Black, as I've painstakingly done in Figure 17-7.

Figure 17-7: The dollar signs are filled with shades of gray producing an embossed, debossed effect

Pretty cool effect, don't you agree? And we did it without fancy filters, tricky layers, channels, or other such wuss stuff. Now, for the icing on the cake.

STEP

10

Convert the whole enchilada to bitmap, grayscale, super sampling, the works!

STEP

11

Apply a Radius 5 Gaussian Blur (use Radius 1 for DRAW 8). Looks terrific, but wait.

STEP

12

From the Bitmaps menu, select Add Noise, Gaussian, and set the Level and Density to 30 (Figure 17-8). Just like money in the bank!

Figure 17-8: The dollars signs are Converted to Bitmap, Gaussian-Blurred, and Noise is added

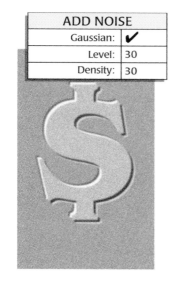

ADD NOISE	
Gaussian:	✔
Level:	30
Density:	30

A HEARTY EMBOSS

I can hear some of the PAINT pundits out there pooh-poohing my last effort, saying, that's all nicey-nice, Mr. Smarty Pants, but I bet DRAW can't do an emboss effect on a pattern, can it? Well, it just so happens it can, so nyah, nana, nah, nah! We'll accomplish this using DRAW's Trim effect.

STEP

1

Draw a 2-inch square and center a Red-filled 1 3/4-inch Zapf Dingbat heart symbol (#167 in the Zapf Dingbats Symbol library).

STEP

2

Duplicate the heart symbol twice, offsetting one White-filled duplicate up and left and the other, a Black-filled duplicate, down and right about two points in each direction.

Bring the original heart symbol to the top as shown in Figure 17-9.

Figure 17-9: A Red Zapf Dingbat heart symbol and two duplicates are positioned over a square

We'll use the center symbol as a cookie cutter to trim out a freestanding highlight and shadow edge. Open the Trim roll-up (in the Arrange menu, select Trim). Select the center heart, (Red) click in the Other Objects box, then click on the Trim button. An oversized arrow cursor appears—use it to click on the white heart as shown in Figure 17-10.

Figure 17-10: The Trim menu with the Other Object(s) option checked

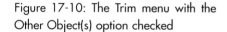

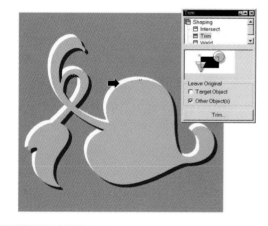

This leaves the cookie cutter but removes the portion of the white heart symbol directly underneath. In Figure 17-11, I have deleted the cookie cutter, so you can see the remaining white edge and the whole of the as yet untrimmed Black duplicate.

Figure 17-11: The Red heart symbol (the cookie cutter) has been temporarily removed to show the effect of the Trim operation on the White heart symbol

STEP

6

Uncheck Other Objects on the Trim roll-up, and with the Red heart selected, click the Trim cursor on the black heart. When Other Object is not selected, the cookie cutter object politely deletes itself after it has performed its open heart surgery, as shown in Figure 17-12.

Figure 17-12: The Black and White remaining edges after the Trim operation create an embossed look

STEP

7

Apply a marbleized paper Bitmap fill (MIDLAGEM.CPT) from the Tiles\Paper folder on CD-ROM #2 to the background square (select the Bitmap option in the Pattern Fill dialog box).

STEP

8

Change the White highlight edge to Peach, and apply the Lens roll-up settings shown in Figure 17-13.

Figure 17-13: The White edge is changed to Peach and a Color Add Lens applied

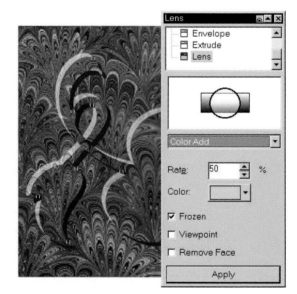

Select the shadow edge, apply a Ruby Red fill and a Color Limit (subtractive color) Lens, with a rate of 75 percent, as shown in Figure 17-14.

Figure 17-14: The shadow edge is changed to Ruby Red and a Color Limit Lens applied

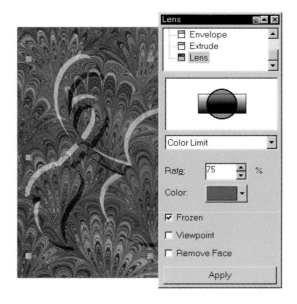

I've used colors instead of white and black to create a richer, more natural-looking highlight and shadow. Figure 17-15 shows the finished example. Heartening indeed.

Figure 17-15: The final image gives the impression of an embossed heart shape on marbleized paper

Variations on a Theme

I 've covered some of my basic embossing and debossing techniques. In this section I'll provide additional examples, plus cover more involved techniques using DRAW's Extrude, Bevel function.

Here's a really easy way to create a textured emboss effect using Texture Fills. I centered a Baskerville Bold italic ampersand over a square and applied a modified Recycled Paper Texture Fill (Styles Library). I changed the paper color to white and the fibers to Pale Yellow and Ghost Green. I made two duplicates of the ampersand and spaced them diagonally about 1 point apart. I filled the duplicates with the same texture fill. Now here's the trick. I used the Brightness settings to make the background slightly darker (-5 percent), the highlight lighter (+15 percent) and the shadow darker (-20 percent).

I used the same technique to create the double emboss effect covered earlier in this chapter. The dollar sign is Goudy Old Style XBlk. The double emboss uses shades of gray and has been converted to a grayscale bitmap. I made a duplicate rectangle, applied a Bitmap Pattern Fill (CRZYLACM.CPT) from the Tiles-Paper folder on CD-ROM 3, and centered the rectangle over the gray double emboss. I applied an Interactive Transparency to the paper, Subtractive, 50 percent. I added the text in Goudy Modern MT.

D RAW's Extrude, Bevel function can create some very slick emboss effects. It should be noted that these effects are very complex and if your computer is wanting for power or RAM memory, you may want to keep the fills simple. I centered a circular symbol (from the Military Symbols library) over a square. The square is filled with a Bitmap paper fill from the Tiles-Paper folder (PAPER01M.CPT), the military symbol is filled with a green marble bitmap fill (MARBL22M.CPT) from the Tiles-marble folder. I applied an Extrude, Bevel effect to the square and the symbol individually using the Use Bevel, and Show Bevel Only options. I used Extrude Lighting to add the highlights and shadow edges. Because of the complexity of the extrude and lighting effects, this file took about ten minutes on my Pentium 200 to export to TIFF file format at 266dpi.

Here, I used the Polygon Tool to draw a five-sided pentagon and applied one of DRAW 8's new Bitmap fills. The fill is one of the default fills that appear when you open the list of fills and has a handsome rough hand-quarried look that contrasts well with the elegance of the 150 point Perpetua Bold V. I used the Extrude-Bevel and Lighting functions to add the bevel to the pentagon. The next part gets tricky. I placed a copy of the V in the Clipboard. I selected the V and applied a Contour effect, to Outside, 1-Step, amount .07 inches shown here in red outline. I Separated the Contour and deleted the inside shape. I filled the larger V with the same stone fill as the pentagon, then applied an Extrude-Bevel with the amount set to .07 inches which is the same amount as the Contour but in the opposite direction. The inside of the Extrude is now the original size of the Perpetua V. Clever? I applied Extrude Lighting effects placing three light sources towards the bottom so that the letter appears recessed or chiseled. I Pasted a copy of the V, applied a gold-type fountain fill, and positioned it over the Extruded V. Not content to stop while I was ahead, I made a duplicate V, applied the stone fill, then applied an Interactive Transparency, Difference, amount 65 percent to add depth and texture to the Gold letter.

HERE'S LOOKING AT YOU

The wonderful turquoise fill used here is another new Bitmap fill in DRAW 8. It was in the Tiles-Design folder of all places! The odd symbol that looks like a pair of glasses is from the Bookshelf Symbols 1 Symbols library. I used the Trim technique covered in the decorative heart example to make two edges. I filled the whole symbol white and applied an Interactive Transparency, Lightness, 50 percent. I filled the highlight edge 60 percent Black (I know this sounds odd, but it works) and applied Interactive Transparency, Add, 0 percent. I filled the shadow edge Dark Green and applied Interactive Transparency, Subtract, 30 percent. I used the same gold fill for the golden eyeballs but changed the Fill Type to Radial.

EMBOSS-DEBOSS DEBRIEFING

I would point out how well this technique works for Web graphics and logos if I hadn't mentioned the fact in every other chapter. So, I'll have to be a little more imaginative. The double emboss that we used on the dollar sign can be used to create the look of hand-tooled lettering on leather. The embossed heart on the elegant marbleized paper would make a swell cover graphic for a brochure or advertisement. And, of course, for fear of being repetitious, I won't remind you how ducky this technique is for creating 3-D buttons for the Internet and other multimedia pursuits. There, I've said it.

If you were paying close attention, you would know by now that embossed effects have a highlight and shadow edge that can be pretty easily created by merely stacking three items and offsetting them slightly. Making the raised object slightly lighter than the background color or pattern helps reinforce the visual cue that the surface is raised. Conversely, making the object slightly darker than the background color gives the visual cue that the object is recessed. You may all rise and be dismissed.

INDEX

COREL
MAGAZINE

GET THE WHOLE PICTURE FOR HALF PRICE!
WE'LL MEET YOU 1/2 WAY

We want you to get a FULL ANNUAL SUBSCRIPTION TO *COREL MAGAZINE* FOR 1/2 PRICE! That's right, a full year's worth of the most exciting and dynamic computer graphics magazine for the design professional and business graphics user today—all for a mere $19.98*U.S.!

This is no half-hearted offer. No indeed. Written by CorelDraw users for CorelDraw users, each colorful issue of *Corel Magazine* helps you get the very most out of your software and hardware.

Read *Corel Magazine*, and if you like it even half as much as we think you will, we'll meet you half-way—take us up on our offer. Just fill out the attached card and fax it back for faster service. We're certain you'll appreciate getting the whole picture at half the price!

(*First time subscribers only!)

Fax To: 512-219-3156 • P.O. Box 202380 • Austin, Tx 78720
WWW.CORELMAG.COM

○ **YES! I WANT THE WHOLE PICTURE FOR 1/2 PRICE!** Sign me up for my full annual subscription to *Corel Magazine*. By responding to this special one-time offer, I'll pay only $19.98 U.S. and save 50% off the regular sub-scription rate of $39.95 U.S. (Offer Expires January 31, 1999)

Fax: 512-219-3156

○ **PLEASE BILL ME $19.98 U.S.**

○ **PAYMENT ENCLOSED**
(Offer restricted to U.S. only)

NAME:

TITLE:

COMPANY

ADDRESS

CITY   STATE

POSTAL CODE/ZIP

COUNTRY

PHONE   FAX

E-MAIL ADDRESS

1. **Do you use CorelDraw?**
A. Yes   B. No
If yes, which version do you use?
A. V3   B. V4   C. V5
D. V6   E. V7
F. Other_____
On which platform?
A. Windows
B. Mac
C.Other_____

2. **Primary use of CorelDraw (circle all that apply:)**
A. Multimedia
B. Publishing
C. Technical Documentation
D. Advertising
E. Training
F. Medical Imaging
G. Packaging
H. Artistic Design
I. Signs/Silkscreening/Stenciling
J. Other_____

3. **Do you specify, authorize, or purchase computer graphics products or services?**
A. Yes   B. No
If yes, circle all that apply:
A. Workstations
B. PCs
C. Monitors/boards
D. Input devices/scanners
E. Printers/output devices
F. Hard disks/CD-ROM/tape drives
G. Other_____

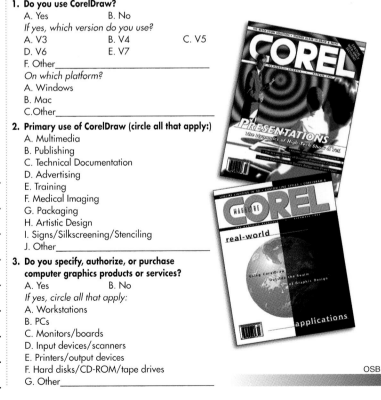

OSB